W9-CKD-307

*Professionalization, Partnership,
and Power*

SUNY Series

FRONTIERS IN EDUCATION

Philip G. Altbach, Editor

The Frontiers in Education Series draws upon a range of disciplines and approaches in the analysis of contemporary educational issues and concerns. Books in the series help to reinterpret established fields of scholarship in education by encouraging the latest synthesis and research. A special focus highlights educational policy issues from a multidisciplinary perspective. The series is published in cooperation with the School of Education, Boston College.

Class, Race, and Gender in American Education—Lois Weis (ed.)

Excellence and Equality: A Qualitatively Different Perspective on Gifted and Talented Education—David M. Fetterman

Change and Effectiveness in Schools: A Cultural Perspective—Gretchen B. Rossman, H. Dickson Corbett, and William A. Firestone

The Curriculum: Problems, Politics, and Possibilities—Landon E. Beyer and Michael W. Apple (eds.)

The Character of American Higher Education and Intercollegiate Sport—Donald Chu

Crisis in Teaching: Perspectives on Current Reforms—Lois Weis, Philip G. Altbach, Gail P. Kelly, Hugh G. Petrie, and Sheila Slaughter (eds.)

The High Status Track: Studies of Elite Schools and Stratification—Paul William Kingston and Lionel S. Lewis (eds.)

The Economics of American Universities: Management, Operations, and Fiscal Environment—Stephen A. Hoenack and Eileen L. Collins (eds.)

The Higher Learning and High Technology: Dynamics of Higher Education and Policy Formation—Sheila Slaughter

Dropouts from Schools: Issues, Dilemmas and Solutions—Lois Weis, Eleanor Farrar, and Hugh G. Petrie (eds.)

Religious Fundamentalism and American Education: The Battle for the Public Schools—Eugene F. Provenzo, Jr.

Going to School: The African-American Experience—Kofi Lomotey (ed.)

Curriculum Differentiation: Interpretive Studies in U.S. Secondary Schools—Reba Page and Linda Valli (eds.)

The Racial Crisis in American Higher Education—Philip G. Altbach and Kofi Lomotey (eds.)

The Great Transformation in Higher Education, 1960–1980—Clark Kerr

College in Black and White: African-American Students in Predominantly White and in Historically Black Public Universities—Walter R. Allen, Edgar G. Epps, and Nesha Z. Haniff (eds.)

Textbooks in American Society: Politics, Policy, and Pedagogy—Philip G. Altbach, Gail P. Kelly, Hugh G. Petrie, and Lois Weis (eds.)

Critical Perspectives on Early Childhood Education—Lois Weis, Philip G. Altbach, Gail P. Kelly, and Hugh G. Petrie (eds.)

Black Resistance in High School: Forging a Separatist Culture—R. Patrick Solomon

Emergent Issues in Education: Comparative Perspectives—Robert F. Arnove, Philip G. Altbach, and Gail P. Kelly (eds.)

Creating Community on College Campuses—Irving J. Spitzberg and Virginia V. Thorndike

Teacher Education Policy: Narratives, Stories, and Cases—Hendrick D. Gideonse (ed.)

Beyond Silenced Voices: Class, Race, and Gender in United States Schools—Lois Weis and Michelle Fine (eds.)

Troubled Times for American Higher Education: The 1990s and Beyond—Clark Kerr

Higher Education Cannot Escape History: Issues for the Twenty-First Century—Clark Kerr

The Cold War and Academic Governance: The Lattimore Case at Johns Hopkins—Lionel S. Lewis

Multiculturalism and Education: Diversity and Its Impact on Schools and Society—Thomas J. LaBelle and Christopher R. Ward

Professionalization, Partnership, and Power

Building Professional Development Schools

Edited by
Hugh G. Petrie

State University of New York Press

Published by
State University of New York Press, Albany

© 1995 State University of New York

All rights reserved

Printed in the United States of America

No part of this book may be used or reproduced
in any manner whatsoever without written permission.
No part of this book may be stored in a retrieval system
or transmitted in any form or by any means including
electronic, electrostatic, magnetic tape, mechanical,
photocopying, recording, or otherwise without the prior
permission in writing of the publisher.

For information, address State University of New York Press,
State University Plaza, Albany, N.Y., 12246

Production by Cathleen Collins
Marketing by Fran Keneston

Library of Congress Cataloging in Publication Data

Professionalization, partnership, and power : building professional
    development schools / Hugh G. Petrie, editor.
        p.   cm. — (SUNY series, frontiers in education)
    Includes bibliographical references and index.
    ISBN 0–7914–2605–X. — ISBN 0–7914–2606–8 (pbk.)
    1. Laboratory schools—United States—Case studies. 2. Teachers—
Training of—United States—Case studies. 3. Teachers—In-service
training—United States—Case studies. 4. College-school
cooperation—United States—Case studies. I. Petrie, Hugh G.
II. Series.
LB2154.A3P77   1995
371.1′46—dc20   94–39617
                                                                          CIP

10 9 8 7 6 5 4 3 2 1

*To Carol
who is one of those inventing
professional development schools*

Contents

Acknowledgments

I first began to think seriously about the idea of professional development schools nearly a decade ago, during my early work with the Holmes Group, that association of research universities devoted to the systemic reform of teaching and teacher education. I am deeply indebted to my colleagues in that early reform effort, especially Judy Lanier, Frank Murray, Harry Judge, Gary Sykes, Chuck Case, and Kathy Devaney. They and many others have kept alive the commitment to the steady work of educational reform.

I also want to thank Phil Altbach, Mwalimu Shujaa, and Lois Weis, my co-editors at *Educational Policy*. Several years ago, we became convinced that some real experiments with implementing the ideas of professional development schools were beginning to emerge. We announced a call for a special issue of *Educational Policy* devoted to professional development schools. We were delighted with the response. Indeed, we received so many good manuscripts that the idea for this book was born.

I also want to thank my graduate assistant, Pat Maloney. Her editorial, administrative, and organizational skills are simply amazing. Her persistence has kept the other authors and me going. I want to mention as well my editor, Lois Patton, who has become over the years a real colleague for us at the State University of New York at Buffalo.

However, it is all the men and women across the country who have been working on professional development schools whom I would like to specially acknowledge here. They are the real stars of this still unfolding drama. It is their daily commitment to inventing this new kind of organization that deserves special recognition and thanks. Without their efforts, this book would never have been written. It is also these folks who are even now writing the sequel. All of us committed to educational reform owe them a real debt of gratitude.

HUGH G. PETRIE, Editor

Introduction: Perspectives on Professional Development Schools

In March 1993, the journal, *Educational Policy*, published a special issue on Professional Development Schools. Only six of the many papers submitted could be published at that time. However, an additional seven papers explored other aspects of this emerging innovation and were also worthy of publication. Given the widespread interest in professional development schools, I believed that the early results of this most important reform deserved a wider audience. Subsequently, I commissioned four new papers that, along with the 13 submitted to *Educational Policy*, constitute this book.

The general concept of professional development schools, regularly established and governed schools that, jointly with higher education, assume special responsibilities for inquiry and the professional preparation of educators, is rapidly becoming a staple recommendation of educational policy. These new kinds of institutions are believed by many to be one of the major features of a reformed system for the preparation of educators, continuing professional development, and research into teaching, learning, and schooling. Although professional development schools are only beginning to obtain a foothold in the educational landscape, the problems and promises of their implementation already have major policy interest.

Despite this general interest in the idea, there are still a large number of different perspectives on just what constitutes a professional development school. First, in *Tomorrow's Schools*, and more recently in *Tomorrow's Schools of Education*, the Holmes Group called for the establishment of Professional Development Schools in close conjunction with research universities. John Goodlad, in *Teachers for Our Nation's Schools*, proposed university-based Centers for Pedagogy that would have close connections to real schools. The Pittsburgh school system has been nationally recognized for a number of years for its continuing professional development program in Schenley High School. The American Federation of Teachers has instituted a program of Professional Practice Schools. The National Education

Association sponsors a Mastery in Learning pilot program. Title Five of the Higher Education Act, reauthorized in 1993, calls for the establishment of professional development academies. Goals 2000, the signature education legislation of the Clinton administration, the reauthorization of the Office of Educational Research and Improvement, and the reauthorization of the Elementary and Secondary Education Act, all call for one or another kind of new emphasis on professional development.

Given these various approaches to the concept of professional development schools and the fragmentary results of the early experiments with them, it is not surprising that this volume does not speak with a single voice. No "one best conception" of professional development schools emerges in these pages, if, indeed, one ever could be developed. The book is intended primarily to bring early results of a wide variety of attempts to experiment with the general concept of a professional development school to the attention of the field. Such early results, along with the sometimes critical and always insightful analyses of the trail-blazers in this area, should help to refine the next generation of efforts. We are still in the early stages of the reform and there will necessarily be different theoretical justifications, policy analyses and emphases.

Thus, in this section John Goodlad explores the long history of school-university partnerships and what his own group, the National Network for Educational Renewal, has come to call "partner schools." These schools, intended to create a symbiosis with higher education, were designed with Goodlad's postulates in mind. They have already been in operation long enough for Goodlad to derive a number of lessons concerning school-university partnerships. These lessons of culture clash, power and resources, and shared leadership and professionalism are echoed by other writers throughout the volume.

Frank Murray, Chair of the Board of the Holmes Group, follows with design principles and criteria for professional development schools derived from the Holmes Group agenda. Murray emphasizes the interconnectedness of these criteria and the problems that ensue when the reforms are implemented piecemeal. The reader will also note that, consonant with the research universities of which it is comprised, professional development schools as conceived by the Holmes Group emphasize research and inquiry, and the preparation of advanced professionals as well as beginning teachers.

Absent from these perspectives, however, is one that emphasizes a predominant role for the professional practitioner in the schools. This kind of approach to professional development schools might be exemplified by the teacher centers in New York or the Schenley Professional Development Center in Pittsburgh or the professional development activities in Jefferson County in Kentucky or the initiatives contained in recent federal legislation such as Goals 2000 and the reauthorization of the Office of Educational

Research and Improvement and the Elementary and Secondary Education Act. Such a perspective tends to cast higher education in a much more junior role, providing some research-based knowledge, but clearly subservient to initiatives from the field.

It is unfortunate that we do not have any independent perspectives from the field in this volume. However, the major lesson of the book is that the two cultures of higher education and the schools do not always consort easily in implementing this new reform. And, of course, one of the features of the culture of higher education is that professors do write, while that feature is still largely absent from the culture of school practitioners. Consequently, the voices of practitioners in this volume are almost always mediated through and with the voices of those in higher education. Perhaps as the general idea of professional development schools continues to develop, we will hear more and more from practitioners who express their own unique perspectives on this reform. In this volume, however, the focus is on partnerships between the schools and higher education.

The selections in this volume, then, emphasize that professional development schools are works in progress. However, despite the multiple perspectives exemplified in this volume and the fragmentary nature of the results thus far, several themes do emerge. First and foremost is the theme of culture clashes between higher education, and how it sees professional development schools, and the field, and how it sees professional development schools. These clashes are central. When they are dealt with well, they are a key to successful experiments. When they are dealt with badly, they are often the major reason for the failure of the experiment. The clashes range from the different kinds of organizations represented by the schools and the academy through the different day to day interests and objectives of the individual participants to fundamental questions of power. Whose innovation is a professional development school, anyway? Part II of the book is devoted to these culture clashes.

Although there are inevitable culture clashes, when the differing ways of approaching the world are rubbed up against each other in professional development schools, these clashes sometimes result in culture changes in both organizations. These culture changes are often still at the margins, but they do hint at how schools and colleges and universities might begin to look very different as the participants engage each other around the themes of inquiry, joint preparation of education professionals, and continuing professional development in which practitioners have more responsibilities for pre-service education and professors are more closely connected to ongoing professional development in the schools. A new vision of the professionalization of education begins to emerge from these initial sketches of culture change that are explored in Part III.

Early discussions of professional development schools tended to focus rather narrowly on teacher education and collaboration between individual schools and individual institutions of higher education. As the reform has taken root, the concept has broadened to include the preparation of a whole range of educational professionals. Furthermore, the problems of establishing a professional development school in different kinds of contexts have become more apparent, while, at the same time, the potential of the idea as a policy initiative has attracted the attention of state and federal policymakers. A variety of ways of extending the concept of a professional development school are discussed in Part IV.

Although initially very persuasive as a reform strategy, professional development schools have drawn a number of critics as well. Are they just another innovation that sounds good in theory but that cannot be implemented? Is the view of professionalism and partnership implicit in the idea of professional development schools one that simply provides technical, hyper-rationalized solutions to our educational problems, leaving the fundamentally unequal power relationships unchanged? What about the equity agenda in educational reform? Will professional development schools help or hinder the efforts of minorities and women to obtain more and better educational opportunities? These questions are raised in a penetrating way in Part V.

Finally, it has become increasingly apparent that the applied social science style of scholarship that is so typical of traditional educational research is by no means the only, or even the most important, style of inquiry for professional development schools. Theoreticians tend to look for general laws. Practitioners, however, are interested in what they ought to do in particular cases. Unfortunately, behavioral research has not yielded general laws with anything even approaching the specificity required by practitioners to make their individual, context-bound decisions. In Part VI a new paradigm of behavioral research is sketched that gives promise of better matching the tools of inquiry to the demands of the field.

A professional development school is a new kind of organization, its outlines only beginning to emerge from the early experiments. Despite the problems detailed in these chapters, it is, nevertheless, one of the educational reforms that gives most promise of bringing about major systemic changes in the whole educational system, as research, development, implementation, and the preparation of future practitioners are all conceived as linked and integrated activities in a professional development school.

Part I

Perspectives on Professional Development Schools

JOHN I. GOODLAD

Chapter One

School-University Partnerships and Partner Schools

The current wave of interest in professional development schools appears to have risen out of proposals to join universities and schools in order to improve pre-service teacher education (Goodlad, 1984; Holmes Group, 1986). Alternative designations, such as "teaching" or "clinical" schools, suggest a kinship of professional development schools and the "teaching" hospitals in medical education. Although some of the accompanying language invokes the laboratory school lineage, few of today's advocates argue the connection; indeed, when they do, the effort seeks more to deny than to affirm kinship.

Within a very short span of years, the words "professional development school" (PDS) have been attached to a wide range of concepts and practices. Most commonly, they are used to convey the idea of a school that participates quite actively in the pre-service teacher education program of a college or university. But, in both concept and practice, this participation ranges from taking on a cadre of student teachers isolated from one another in classrooms (like cars scattered about in a parking lot) to a symbiotic partnership in which school and university personnel share the decisions of operating both the school and the entire length and breadth of the teacher education program.

Original version was first published in *Educational Policy 7* (1), March 1993, © 1993, Corwin Press, Inc. Reprinted by permission of Corwin Press, a Sage Publications Company.

Sometimes, however, the focus is on in-service teacher education, with the school occasionally named a professional development center rather than a PDS. Or, the PDS is a center of inquiry in which individuals from both sets of institutions study—presumably to improve—teaching, learning, and perhaps teacher education. Occasionally, the PDS is envisioned as a laboratory school in a school district rather than on a university campus in which individuals from both join for purposes of designing exemplary educational practices.

This chapter focuses on the pre-service teacher education role of professional development schools in the context of school-university partnerships. Several colleagues and I began more than a dozen years ago to promote both the concept and the creation of school-university partnerships as a strategy for school improvement. We had in mind from the beginning that the bumping together of university and school cultures would have a positive effect on both institutions. At the core of this symbiosis was the concept of partner schools; schools in which school-based and university-based individuals come together for the simultaneous renewal of both schooling and the education of educators. The partner school was our conception of a professional development school.

The balance of this chapter addresses the genesis and nature of our conception, progress to date with the developmental effort, and some of the major problems and issues confronted and yet to be confronted. I begin by describing the current status of a teacher education improvement initiative that assumes the necessity of simultaneously renewing the preparation programs of teachers and a collaborating group of schools in which these future educators learn to be stewards of schools—moral standards, if you will.

At the time of writing, 14 teacher preparation settings are joined in the National Network for Educational Renewal (NNER) for purposes of simultaneously renewing schools and the education of educators. They are committed to putting in place sets of conditions embedded in 19 postulates developed in a comprehensive inquiry conducted through the Center for Educational Renewal at the University of Washington (Goodlad, 1990). "Postulates" are defined as essential presuppositions or premises in a train of reasoning. They are norms, not goals or objectives. Just as Abraham Flexner (1910) defined the academic, laboratory, and clinical conditions essential to robust programs in medical education, the 19 postulates define conditions of commitment, support, student selection and guidance, curriculum, and laboratory facilities essential to healthy programs in teacher education.

For example, Postulates 6 and 15, taken together, presuppose for teacher education the selection of no more students than can be accommodated in the available array of laboratory settings, which are to include "exemplary schools for internships and residencies" (Goodlad, 1990, pp. 57, 61). The elaboration of Postulate 9 describes cohort groups of students (e.g., the class of 1996) coming through the program together and then breaking into smaller cohort groups interning together in partner schools. The net effect of Postulates 6, 9, and 15 is to presuppose for the conduct of teacher education conditions differing markedly from those described in the center's research reports.

The 14 settings now constituting the NNER are committed to the daunting challenge of securing these conditions for teacher education during a short span of years. Instead of future teachers entering their programs when they wish, taking prescribed courses in any order, progressing with little or no peer socialization, and then going individually to work with individual cooperating teachers in individual classrooms, they will proceed quite differently. They will be fully informed at the outset regarding expectations, screened carefully in batches at specified times, grouped so as to ensure both formal and informal socialization into teaching, and placed in partner schools in teams or cohorts. Their internships are to be in the whole of the school and its immediate context, not just in classrooms. The partner schools receiving them, in turn, will be engaged seriously in a renewal process in which school and university personnel are joined. The rhetoric of simultaneously renewing schools and the education of educators is to be translated into reality.

So say the expectations and the commitments, among other things. But every step of the doing is difficult and demanding.

GENESIS

Out of what context did the National Network for Educational Renewal, the overall initiative to which its members are committed, and especially the required partner schools arise? The genesis dates back at least to the 1960s and particularly to the school reform movement that received a robust boost from the Elementary and Secondary Education Act of 1965.

Even though the highly influential James B. Conant had released his book on the reform of teacher education in 1963 (Conant, 1963), there was scarcely a hint in the school reform movement subsequently that teacher education played a role. Surprisingly, there appeared to be no general surprise in this neglect. Improvement of the two together had not been part of previous educational reform eras, either in rhetoric or deed (Su, 1986). This was not to be until the second half of the 1980s.

The educational reform era of the 1960s is sometimes referred to as one of bad ideas. There are better explanations for its demise. First, there was a context of a United States of America losing confidence in itself. The Vietnam war contributed harshly. The "faith index" regarding how our people viewed representatives of the most respected occupations and professions dropped sharply. A troubled people is not a venturesome one; change is threatening. Second, energy that might have gone to innovation shifted to evaluation. That is where significant federal dollars were spent in the late 1960s and early 1970s. Third, post hoc inquiry suggested a flawed federal change strategy (House, 1974).

But, in retrospect, a powerful fourth factor brings us to the degree to which the schooling enterprise lacks mechanisms for change. In most states, teachers are employed 180 days a year to teach school. In the final analysis, the bold organizational, curricular, and instructional changes proposed for schools in the 1960s were to be carried out by teachers, just as is expected today. But teachers were (and are) expected to keep the present regularities clomping along simultaneously. This is like asking Boeing Aircraft employees to build the 777 while working full-time on the 727, 737, 747, and 767. The new model would never come off the assembly line.

But even if we were insightful and fiscally generous enough either to employ teachers an additional month or two each year, or to hire additional cadres to develop tomorrow's schools, teachers would require much different and much more preparation to bring it off.

By the second half of the 1960s, rhetorical school reform was in high gear, but the gap between rhetoric and reality closed very little. Many school faculties managed to cope with innovations from the outside by folding them innocuously into the ongoing culture of their schools (Sarason, 1971, 1982). Many of the changes proposed, such as nongrading, team teaching, and curricular revision, addressed whole schools, not merely classrooms. Several colleagues and I set out to better understand the phenomena of school change (commonly referred to nowadays as "restructuring") by creating the League of Cooperating Schools, comprising 18 schools in 18 districts. We discovered early on that none of these schools, selected to ensure considerable diversity with respect to size, locale, student population, and more, was characterized by a process of renewal. There were not in place the processes and structures through which teachers were engaged in continuously inquiring into and thoughtfully effecting changes. Indeed, we found practice ranging from no whole or partial faculty decision making to periodic meetings directed almost exclusively to ad hoc announcements and current problems or crises. In a few instances, principals were terrified over our expectation that they would meet regularly with teachers for purposes of discussion, decision making, action, and evaluation (DDAE) regarding the changes they said they desired to make. Thanks to financial support from the Kettering Foundation and several other philanthropic agencies, we were able to mount a substantial in-service program for teachers and principals and to note over the six years of close association with these schools both the development of renewing processes and rather significant departures from some of the traditional norms of schooling (Bentzen & Associates, 1974; Goodlad, 1975). It is fair to say that we started virtually from scratch with principals and teachers whose lexicon of preparation simply did not include "collegiality," "renewal," or "stewardship of schools." In a subsequent nationwide study of more than twice as many schools, we found a considerable range in the existence of collegial processes designed to take care of the daily business of schooling but little variation around a low-level norm in regard to renewing ongoing instructional and curricular practices (Goodlad, 1984).

The federal and state initiatives of the 1960s and 1980s directed to the redesign or restructuring of schools provide ample evidence of the inherent difficulties. No doubt, frustration on the part of policymakers contributed to their joining grassroots reformers in language and concepts regarding site-based management, with accompanying exhortation regarding the need to "empower" principals and teachers to effect change. There is a cruel edge to such admonitions, given the regularities of conducting the schooling enterprise referred to earlier, the powerful modeling of these regularities of schooling experienced by future teachers while they are students, and the narrow limitations of their preparation programs. Teacher education programs simply have not been directed to the conduct of schooling (Sarason, Davidson, & Blatt, 1962, 1986), let alone the mission and ideals of school stewardship (Goodlad, 1990).

The parental, political, and bureaucratic influences and controls now impinging on schools may be so powerful and intractable that empowered, well-prepared teachers with additional weeks of time for renewal may not be sufficient to effect the called-for restructuring. Nonetheless, the surge of interest in coupling universities and schools for purposes of more effectively preparing teachers is timely and necessary, if not sufficient (Carnegie Forum on Education and the Economy, 1986; Goodlad, 1986/1987; Holmes Group, 1986). Of particular promise is the concept of a school where personnel from both sets of institutions join in renewal and the socialization of teachers-to-be in the process. This is the concept of the partner school to which the 14 member settings of the National Network for Educational Renewal are committed.

SYMBIOTIC SCHOOL-UNIVERSITY PARTNERSHIPS

Symbiosis, in the nonparasitic interpretation of the word, means the intimate living together of two dissimilar organisms in a mutually beneficial relationship. For the five decades since World War II, the relationship between schools and universities has not been symbiotic. There has been a good deal of interaction, but it has been almost exclusively interindividual, not interinstitutional. Teachers needed advanced degrees; they were obtained in university classes. But praxis in regard to school-keeping, on one hand, and teacher-educating, on the other, was rarely shared. University professors needed students and teachers for their research, in institutions increasingly demanding it. But little of it was communicated directly back to the sites, and the forms and means of writing it up and publishing in refereed journals made the results almost inaccessible to practitioners (Johnson, 1989). With individuals as the unit of selection in both teaching and research, the changing conditions and circumstances of schooling were scarcely noticed in the universities.

Perhaps, then, we should not be surprised that professors of education were virtually absent from the scene during the events surrounding and in the immediate aftermath of the publication of A *Nation at Risk*, as Sizer (1984) pointed out. Perhaps we should not be surprised today, when the notion of school-university collaboration is virtually de rigueur, to find that there is little in the form of past experience or funded knowledge to guide individuals on both sides of the street in the demands involved. Clark's (1986) exhaustive review of the literature extending back over several decades revealed interinstitutional symbiosis to be almost a nonevent. Su's (1990) more recent review, involving direct communication with supposed school-university partnerships, revealed only a few beyond those of the National Network for Educational Renewal to be more than projects involving a clutch of professors and teachers. Even when these projects had their beginnings in what might be called an interinstitutional context, some became rather quickly the exclusive domain of these participants—very much in the pattern of past projects initiated by individual professors.

Given these findings, the concept of universities and schools joining symbiotically in the simultaneous renewal of partner schools and the education of future teachers in them presents daunting challenges. Nonetheless, it is possible to squeeze out of them a potentially useful implication: innocence regarding what to do and how to do it is widely shared on both sides. Symbiosis implies satisfaction of the needs of both partners. Up to now, in relations involving school and university personnel, the former have been virtually subservient. At best, when universities have occasionally sought to work with schools, their stance commonly has been one of noblesse oblige.

Several colleagues and I have been involved in and witness to efforts to develop symbiotic school-university partnerships for over 12 years in more than a dozen settings. Some of the underlying concepts began to take shape in our minds as we worked with the League of Cooperating Schools in the late 1960s and early 1970s. No money went to the schools, although they could have made very good use of such. What they benefited from was technical support in the form of direct consultation, research findings, carefully selected readings, conferences around key topics and themes, and more. What they may have benefited from most was our moral support. As one teacher passionately put it, "It was so helpful to know that some people beyond ourselves knew what we were doing and cared." What my colleagues and I gained was an incredible opportunity to inquire into the complex circumstances of determined principals and teachers—often rejected as "ratebusters on funny farms" by their colleagues in other schools—endeavoring day by day to change the conditions of their schools.

Missing was the involvement of a university seeking to engage future teachers in school renewal as part of their pre-service education. Our staff was not in any way responsible for or involved in teacher education. No doubt, the absence of this important component contributed to our much later decision to study contemporary teacher education so as to understand it better.

Perhaps more important, the absence of pre-service teacher education in this enterprise, together with the obvious omission of preparation for school stewardship in the education of the teachers with whom we worked, impressed on us the need for joining the renewal of schools and the education of educators. Beginning in the late 1970s, we began to strive toward this end. Our first effort, the Southern California Partnership, marked up notable successes on the school side, but mostly failures on the university side (Heckman, 1988). The second, resulting in the Brigham Young University Public School Partnership, has been largely a success story from its founding in 1984 (Williams, 1988). The dozen with which we have since been involved represent rigorous collaborations that vary quite widely in the degree to which symbiosis has embraced the renewal of schools simultaneously engaged in the renewal of educator preparation (Clark, Heckman, Wilson, & Soder, 1991).

What problems have we encountered and what have we learned? Sirotnik's (1991) summary and analysis addresses many of the problems and issues identified a few years earlier by several pioneers in the experiential arena of school-university partnerships (Sirotnik & Goodlad, 1988):

Lesson 1: Dealing with Cultural Clash

School systems and universities are not cut from the same cultural cloth. The norms, roles, and expectations of educators in each of these educational realms could not be more different, for example, the regimen of time and space in the schools versus the relative freedom of these precious commodities in the university setting; an ethic of inquiry in the university versus an ethic of action and meeting immediate needs in the schools; a merit system with promotion and tenure in the university versus an egalitarian work ethic in the school. . . . These two cultures are quite different, and it is hard to fit them together in productive, long-term, useful ways.

Lesson 2: Dealing with Schools of Education

[Of the two sides of the partnership fence] the university side, usually the school (college or department) of education, is the more intractable. . . . The primary culprit is a misguided reward system that is an outgrowth of misplaced values, status deprivation, and identity crisis.

Lesson 3: Sustaining Leadership and Commitment

One of the more consistent and enduring findings in the research on complex organizations has to do with the importance of leadership at the top and the ability to clearly, authentically, and consistently communicate mission, vision, a sense of what the organization can and must be about. This appears to be essential to maintaining school-university partnerships of the type I have been describing. University presidents and deans, school superintendents, executive directors—these leaders need to be visible and clearly supportive of the partnership concept and effort.

Lesson 4: Providing Adequate Resources

Much leadership is symbolic. But symbols, ceremony, and celebration will not go far unless they are backed up by resources. . . .

Lesson 5: Modeling Authentic Collaboration

An ethic of collaboration and collaborative inquiry and action, more than anything else, characterizes (or ought to characterize) the processes that go on in a school-university partnership. What it means to collaborate needs to be modeled every step of the way. Since building partnerships is mostly a two-steps-forward/one-step-backward kind of activity, inappropriate, unilateral decisions can destroy the process.

Lesson 6: Living with Goal-Free Planning, Action, and Evaluation

Often, in fact, it is precisely as a result of activity that we become clearer about what we are doing and why we are doing it. Consequently, the world of human activity in and between educational organizations does not lend itself well to concrete, sequential models of planning and evaluation.

The subtitle of this lesson is "living with ambiguity," and our mentor is the organizational theorist, March. For March, ambiguity is not a dirty word. Not only does he tolerate it, he embraces it. Closure is a dirty word. Rarely is it ever achieved. In fact, if it is achieved, it is a good sign that either the issues are trivial or people are jumping to conclusions too quickly.

Lesson 7: Avoiding the Quick-Fix Syndrome

The "quick-fix" syndrome and its kissing cousin, the "let's get something up on the scoreboard" syndrome, are extremely hazardous to the health of school-university partnerships, especially early in their formative stages. . . . There often is a perceived press to get something up on the scoreboard so that various publics believe something actually is going on. Yet, if it is a serious partnership effort, a lot is going on: structures are being built, lines of communication are being established, working relationships and collaborative processes are being nurtured, and some activities are being explored by pockets of work groups here and there. Unfortunately, structures and processes do not happen overnight, and they cannot be hung on the evaluative hooks the public has grown accustomed to for education and schooling—standardized test score averages, for example.

Lesson 8: Winning the Process/Substance Debate

The debate apparently revolves around this question: What work is of most value—making things happen or the happening of things? The only way to win this debate is to render it a nonissue; it is, indeed, a false dichotomy to be put alongside a number of other classic problematical dualities (qualitative-quantitative; theory-practice; talk-action; etc.). There is great substance in process and great process in substance. Developing new ways for educators to communicate with one another and engage in work to solve problems of common concern is highly substantive. Developing and evaluating new programs (e.g., for the education of educators) demands much attention to process.

Lesson 9: Avoiding Over- and Understructuring

Organizing and governance structures are important for developing and sustaining school-university partnerships, but they take different forms depending upon local contexts. The Puget Sound Educational Consortium is highly structured. The Southern Maine Partnership is organized very informally. Both of these partnerships appear to be working well. But watch out for both over- and understructuring; either may interfere with the work most important to partnership efforts. Ultimately, the crucial points of coordination are at the levels where real work is taking place, with the rest of the coordination and structure being in place to *support* that work.

Lesson 10: Translating Leadership as Empowerment and Shared Responsibility

The partnership ethic must be enculturated at all individual and organizational levels. The power to lead cannot reside in just one or several charismatic figures. The more leadership is spread around, the better off the partnership will be.

This should not be seen as contradictory to Lesson 3 and the importance of leadership at the top, of communicating and sustaining vision and mission, and of backing it all up with resources. Power, however, is not a finite concept. The more it is shared, the more there seems to be. And with power comes responsibility; responsible leadership entails creating the opportunities for responsible leadership in others. A viable, school-university partnership cannot depend on the presence or absence of one or several human beings. Certainly, being an "idea champion" is important for leadership, but charisma is not the foundation of partnership. (Sirotnik, 1991)

The creation and refinement of partner schools is a special case of school-university collaboration and symbiosis, involving essentially the problems and issues identified in Sirotnik's analysis. To this special case we now turn.

TOWARD PARTNER SCHOOLS

As stated earlier, 14 settings embracing universities and schools are committed to putting in place the conditions for teacher education embedded in 19 postulates. These postulates include the selection and development of partner schools in which future teachers will receive a significant part of their preparation. Six of these have been involved in school-university partnerships for several years; indeed, they have been part of the laboratory of more than a dozen such from which Sirotnik's 10 lessons were derived. The others have not been so involved.

All of the first group of six have been exposed quite extensively to the rhetoric of simultaneously renewing schools and the education of educators and encouraged to develop partner schools for this purpose. Under the partnership umbrella, school and university personnel engage together in an array of joint programs and projects, including the redesign of preparation programs for school principals, improving curricula in mathematics and the sciences, bringing computers into the educational delivery system, expanding teachers' instructional repertoire, conducting principals' academies, and the like. Several have made steady progress toward the development of partner schools. The University of Washington, for example, has been working with four middle schools in four of its partner school districts in the Puget Sound Educational Consortium with a view to these becoming teacher education sites. Brigham Young University, at last report, has about two dozen partner schools in the BYU–Public School Partnership, mostly at the elementary level. Joint efforts at the secondary level have resulted in "emphasis" programs— exemplary curricular and instructional practices in several of the standard teaching fields.

Figure 1.1 depicts the agenda to date of the six settings described above. The additional commitment they now share with the others is depicted in Figure 1.2. The broad agenda of the first six continues, but it is sharpened considerably by the goal of effecting renewal in schools shared educationally by school districts and a university.

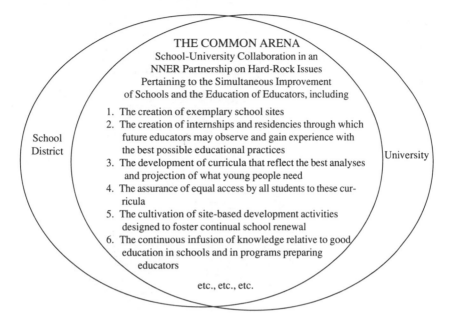

THE COMMON ARENA
School-University Collaboration in an
NNER Partnership on Hard-Rock Issues
Pertaining to the Simultaneous Improvement
of Schools and the Education of Educators, including

1. The creation of exemplary school sites
2. The creation of internships and residencies through which future educators may observe and gain experience with the best possible educational practices
3. The development of curricula that reflect the best analyses and projection of what young people need
4. The assurance of equal access by all students to these curricula
5. The cultivation of site-based development activities designed to foster continual school renewal
6. The continuous infusion of knowledge relative to good education in schools and in programs preparing educators

etc., etc., etc.

School District

University

Fig. 1.1. An agenda of hard-rock issues addressed to the simultaneous renewal of schools and the education of educators.

In my judgment, there is no way for the eight settings where school-university partnerships do not yet exist to avoid the problems analyzed by Sirotnik in deriving lessons from experiences with this kind of collaboration. Indeed, even though the university settings have been members of the National Network for Educational Renewal for less than a year (at date of writing), most are in negotiation with districts for purposes of beginning the partner school collaboration to which they are committed. Before them lie the many problems and forging of agreements for which neither side has had much previous experience. On the plus side, however, is a groundswell of current support for the idea of professional development schools, a reasonably focused agenda, top-level commitment from designated leaders of the several institutions, and association with companion settings through the National Network for Educational Renewal. The Center for Educational Renewal, in turn, draws on the varied experiences described earlier in providing technical and moral support, increasingly encouraging NNER members to draw on one another as each gains some success.

CONCLUDING COMMENTS

Little has been said previously about the role of university departments in the arts and sciences. The implicit assumption running through what pre-

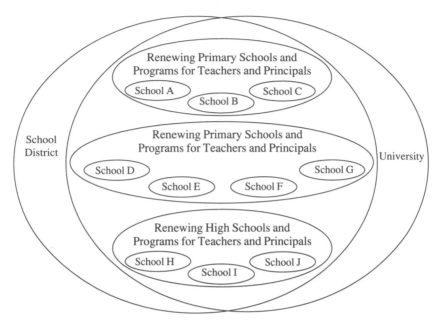

Fig. 1.2. Site-based school renewal and the simultaneous education of educators.

cedes is that the university side of the partnership involves these as well as schools, colleges, and departments of education (SCDEs). But the reality of practice is only beginning to reflect this assumption. Teacher education and SCDEs are not the same thing. Indeed, the several top-ranked schools of education in the United States prepare only a few teachers or none at all (Clifford & Guthrie, 1988; Goodlad, 1990; Judge, 1982). Although professors in the arts and sciences provide a very large part of the knowledge that teachers need, they have been largely passive, alienated, or disengaged in the campus conduct of teacher education. The 14 settings of the NNER committed to the renewal of teacher education are on a level field with respect to readiness for and progress in the three-way faculty collaboration—teachers in partner schools, professors of education, and professors in the arts and sciences—stipulated in several of the 19 postulates. Although the school-university partnerships in six of the 14 settings have engaged in activities involving professors other than in education, engagement of the arts and sciences has been modest. Now, however, those six confront the same challenge faced by the others and bring to it, overall, about the same amount of experience. Consequently, the demands of this three-way collaboration have risen to a prominent place on the agenda. A conference representing all three sets of actors held in early February 1992 showed no lack of readiness on the part of delegates from the arts and sciences to address the renewal agenda.

Another topic omitted on preceding pages pertains to staffing and financing both partner schools and the rest of an exemplary teacher education program. The history of teacher education is one of neglect and low status (Herbst, 1989). Theobald's (1991) probe into financing revealed low dollar input into teacher education in relation to the generation of courses when this enterprise was compared to other programs in a college of education. Substantial involvement in teacher education by tenure-line professors by itself will make teacher education more costly.

In addition to the added costs involved in securing equity for teacher education on college and university campuses, there are the costs of embracing partner schools as a necessary condition. Teachers are accustomed to having more and more functions thrust on them. But it is unreasonable and unrealistic to assume that several or all of the teachers in a partner school are to take on the tasks of renewing their schools and teacher education without some adjustments in their present schedules and commitments. It is also folly to assume that professors' involvement in partner schools is something simply to be added to present assignments and, perhaps, left out in the process of determining merit salary increases and promotions. Although there are creative ways to involve interns in conducting the business of partner schools, it is reasonable, nonetheless, to assume that an elementary school faculty of 35 teachers should be increased by at least three to enable that school to function effectively as a partner school (Theobald, 1990). Also, a great deal of attention must be given to the matter of credit for all participants in the reward structure of their respective institutions.

In assuming that developing the necessary number of partner schools involves most or all of the complexities of creating and refining school-university partnerships—and I am convinced that one must make this assumption—it becomes apparent that a commitment to such schools must be taken very seriously. The recent sudden surge of papers in journals and reports at conferences of professional development schools in vigorous and even advanced functioning raises in my mind an image of something less than or certainly different from what I have endeavored to convey. I worry that at least some of these reports are the product of what Sirotnik (1991) warned against in his Lesson 7—the drive to get something on the scoreboard. Surely, these reported success stories are not a repetition of the glowing reports of nonevents that characterized the school reform movement of the 1960s. But if a good many of them are, then we will experience once again the failure generated from an appearance of early success (in a 1992 untitled, unpublished work, Soder refers to this phenomenon with the words "nothing fails like success").

The goal of school and university personnel joining in all aspects of designing and renewing the teacher education enterprise, with renewing partner or professional development schools as part of the whole, is critically important. But it will be attained neither easily nor quickly. Gehrke (1991) warned against the "trophy mentality"—what counts is "having" a professional development school: "'Having one' is good for public relations purposes and institutional reputation" (p. 44).

It is important for those engaged in what I have endeavored to describe to celebrate their periodic successes. But, for years to come, the concept of teachers and professors engaged in renewing each of 10 or 20 or 30 partner schools and together welcoming into them from the nearby university cohort groups of fledgling teachers will continue to be more a vision than a reality. We must not be put off by believing that we cannot attain it or by thinking that we are already there.

REFERENCES

Bentzen, M. M., & Associates. (1974). *Changing schools: The magic feather principle.* New York: McGraw-Hill.

Carnegie Forum on Education and the Economy. (1986). *A nation prepared: Teachers for the 21st Century.* Washington, DC: Author.

Clark, R. W. (1986). School/university relations: partnerships and networks (Occasional Paper No. 2, Center for Educational Renewal). Seattle: University of Washington, College of Education.

Clark, R. W., Heckman, P., Willson, C., & Soder, R. (1991). *Summary reports of site visits: National Network for Educational Renewal school-university partnerships 1989–1990* (Tech. Rep. No. 12, Center for Educational Renewal). Seattle: University of Washington, College of Education.

Clifford, J. C., & Guthrie, J. W. (1988). *Ed school.* Chicago: University of Chicago Press.

Conant, J. B. (1963). *The education of American teachers.* New York: McGraw-Hill.

Flexner, A. (1910). *Medical education in the United States and Canada.* New York: Carnegie Foundation for the Advancement of Teaching.

Gehrke, N. (1991). Simultaneous improvement of schooling and the education of teachers: Creating a collaborative consciousness. *Metropolitan universities, 2,* 44.

Goodlad, J. I. (1975). *The dynamics of educational change.* New York: McGraw-Hill.

Goodlad, J. I. (1984). *A place called school.* New York: McGraw-Hill.

Goodlad, J. I. (1987). Linking schools and universities: Symbiotic partnerships (Occasional Paper No. 1 rev. Center for Educational Renewal). Seattle: University of Washington, College of Education. (Original work published 1986)

Goodlad, J. I. (1990). *Teachers for our nation's schools.* San Francisco: Jossey-Bass.

Heckman, P. E. (1988). The Southern California Partnership: A retrospective analysis. In K. A. Sirotnik & J. I. Goodlad (Eds.), *School-university partnerships in action* (pp. 106–123). New York: Teachers College Press.

Herbst, J. (1989). *And sadly teach.* Madison: University of Wisconsin Press.

Holmes Group. (1986). *Tomorrow's teachers: A report of the Holmes Group.* East Lansing, MI: Author.

House, E. (1974). *The politics of educational innovation.* Berkeley, CA: McCutchan.

Johnson, W. R. (1989). Teachers and teacher training in the twentieth century. In D. Warren (Ed.), *American teachers: Histories of a profession at work* (pp. 237–256). New York: Macmillan.

Judge, H. (1982). *American graduate schools of education.* New York: Ford Foundation.

Sarason, S. B. (1982). *The culture of school and the problem of change.* Newton, MA: Allyn & Bacon. (Original work published 1971)

Sarason, S. B., Davidson, K. S., & Blatt, B. (1986). *The preparation of teachers: An unstudied problem in education.* Cambridge, MA: Brookline Books. (Original work published 1962)

Sirotnik, K. A. (1991). Making school-university partnerships work. *Metropolitan universities, 2,* 19–23.

Sirotnik, K. A., & Goodlad, J. I. (Eds.), (1988). *School-university partnerships in action.* New York: Teachers College Press.

Sizer, T. R. (1984). *High school reform and the reform of teacher education* (Ninth annual De Garmo Lecture). Minneapolis: University of Minnesota Press.

Su, Z. (1986). *Teacher education reform in the United States, 1890–1986.* (Occasional Paper No. 3, Center for Educational Renewal). Seattle: University of Washington, College of Education.

Su, Z. (1990). School-university partnerships: Ideas and experiments, 1986–1990 (Occasional Paper No. 12, Center for Educational Renewal). Seattle: University of Washington, College of Education.

Theobald, N. D. (1990). The financing and governance of professional development or partner schools (Occasional Paper No. 10, Center for Educational Renewal). Seattle: University of Washington, College of Education.

Theobald, N. D. (1991). Allocating resources to renew teacher education (Occasional Paper No. 14, Center for Educational Renewal). Seattle: University of Washington, College of Education.

Williams, D. D. (1988). The Brigham Young University–public school partnership. In K. A. Sirotnik & J. I. Goodlad (Eds.), *School-university partnerships in action.* (pp. 124–147). New York: Teachers College Press.

FRANK B. MURRAY

Chapter Two

Design Principles and Criteria for Professional Development Schools

A number of individuals and organizations . . . advocate a new kind of school that is dedicated to the improvement of educational outcomes for students through research and development and the improvement of teaching and teacher preparation. These schools have been called *Professional Development Schools* by the Holmes Group, *Professional Practice Schools* by the American Federation of Teachers, *Mastery Learning Sites* by the National Education Association. These schools are regular K–12 public schools that have formed an enduring partnership with a university capable of mounting a powerful research and development agenda . . . to improve the quality of teaching and teacher education, improve the quality and effectiveness of educational research, and produce higher levels of learning among students, particularly among students most at risk of failure.[1]

In 1990, the Holmes Group made the case for the establishment of an entity they called the professional development school, or the PDS (Holmes Group, 1990). The PDS is a regular public school that serves teacher education the way the teaching hospital serves medical education, and the way the agri-cultural extension service serves the agricultural community. The PDS is the place where *all* the elements of educational reform might come together—the community, the school board, the teacher, the pupil, the principal, the social

---

Original version was first published in *Educational Policy 7* (1), March 1993, © 1993, Corwin Press, Inc. Reprinted by permission of Corwin Press, a Sage Publications Company.

service agencies, the district, the university school of education, and the university academic disciplines.

Although the PDS has some of the attributes of laboratory and demonstration schools, the PDS is neither in the traditional senses. The great university-based laboratory schools, on the whole, failed to bring in some key reform ingredients, such as a diverse student body, an empowered teaching force, a democratic school organization, and the constraints and benefits of membership in a public school district (Nystrand, 1991).

The PDS is more than a site that university-based educational researchers can arrange in accordance with the demands of their research paradigms and designs. Nor is the PDS simply a demonstration school, important as they are, because its purpose is not to demonstrate the utility of a pedagogical or curricular innovation that does not, or could not, exist elsewhere. Apart from the PDS design itself, the Holmes Group and others are not advocating a particular pedagogical model or curriculum scope and sequence.

To understand what the PDS is, it is necessary to understand the problem in American teacher education it was designed to solve, namely the paradoxical problem of the student teaching and clinical experience components of the teacher education program at a research university. The paradox is that while teachers universally praise their student teaching experience as the most valuable part of their teacher education program, university faculty often find it the most distant and intellectually regressive aspect of the program because many student teachers quickly conform to the traditional and prevailing practices of their supervising teacher (Murray, 1986b).

Until recently, student teachers rarely have had the opportunity to put into practice a novel, cutting-edge, or counter-intuitive teaching technique. Student teachers are no exception to the rule of "regression under stress," and under the stress of teaching on their own, often for the first time, they invariably fall back on a set of novice teaching behaviors they possessed long before they entered teacher training. Like many teachers, parents, and children, they teach exclusively by telling and showing the correct behavior or answer. The gap between current schooling practices, and sites in which ambitious and modern teaching can be practiced, is the fundamental problem the PDS is designed to solve.

In *Tomorrow's Teachers* (1986) and *Tomorrow's Schools* (1990), the Holmes Group, like many other reform-minded groups, made it clear that reform, even the modest reform of the student-teaching course, would not succeed if it were done piecemeal, one classroom at a time (Murray, 1986a). A systemic approach that coordinated the reform of all segments of schooling, not just individual teachers with their individual students, was needed. Thus, the PDS was designed to speak to all aspects of the reform agenda, which is the primary reason the PDS must be a whole school that is part of a regular school district and subject to all the pressures of real schools in real communities.

First and foremost, the PDS must be a modern school. It must have the features of a good school as those have emerged by consensus over the last decade from the scholarly and reform literature, most notably from the work of the Coalition of Essential Schools and the Re:Learning Project, the Effective Schools movement, the Child Development Project, Levin's Accelerated Schools Project, and Comer's School Development Program.

The goal of the PDS can be seen clearly through the case of Maurice,[2] a pupil in the Holmes Middle School in Flint, Michigan. We learn that were Maurice granted three wishes, he would wish for a safe place to live—no street violence, murders, and drugs. He likes his teachers and school and believes that school learning is important only because some part of it (like knowing the highest mountain in Kenya) could be a pivotal topic in a job interview; otherwise, he can see no connection between schooling and anything else he cares about. When he is pressed he claims to like mathematics, but he can barely retrieve the word, *algebra*, the subject he is studying, and he can think of no use for it at all.

Here we have Maurice, a bright and savvy child, and here we have algebra, one of the glories of the human mind, an exquisite and powerful method for determining the unknown from the known, and a prerequisite for the kind of knowledge upon which the modern world is based. The fundamental and overriding problem of the PDS, and all schools, is how to connect Maurice with school subjects like algebra—how to create the conditions in which Maurice will actually understand algebra, or any other school subject, and apply its power to the problems he encounters in Flint, Michigan.

Six design principles define the PDS, and if the school were designed with these in mind, Maurice's school would be a place where the likelihood that he would understand algebra would be significantly increased.

PRINCIPLE ONE: UNDERSTANDING AS THE GOAL OF THE SCHOOL

The primary and overriding goal of the school is to have all its pupils understand, not just learn, their lessons. The school must accept nothing less than the goal of Maurice, not just learning algebra and passing school tests on what he has learned, but understanding algebra and thinking algebraically. Understanding represents a qualitative change in what is merely learned; it is an "all or none" event, in other words. It is one thing to have learned that the shortest distance between two points is, in fact, a straight line, but it is quite another to understand that it must be a straight line, and if it were not, many other things we know to be true, could not be true. To understand the necessity, not just the truth, of the line being the shortest pathway, is to understand the subject in a qualitatively different manner.

A further implication of the principle is that whatever the situation or problem, whether encountered in the school or outside, Maurice should have the confidence to attack the problem intellectually.

The principle entails several features that are described below.

Standards and rubrics

The school's faculty must clarify their standards for the degree to which each pupil has understood each subject studied in the school. The standards, implicitly applied in the teacher's daily evaluation of each pupil's work, should contain criteria by which all can know whether a student's work meets the standard, is well below it, or is well above it. The scoring rubric, by which the student's accomplishments and progress are noted, is at the heart of the matter and is dependent upon the teacher's theory (naive or sophisticated) in two domains—(1) a theory of children's and adolescents' cognitive development and understanding, and (2) a theory of the complexity and sophistication of the subject matter. If a child, who had pluralized *mouse* as *mice*, for example, suddenly pluralizes it as *mouses*, a naive teacher might score the event as an unfortunate regression that requires remediation, whereas a professional teacher will see the "error" as temporary and a sign of cognitive advancement. If a child arrives at the correct answer to a multiplication problem through serial addition, should that response be scored as superior or inferior to the response of a child who arrives at an incorrect answer through multiplication? Do college students who correctly calculate the mean, median, and mode operate at scoreably different standards of sophistication if their reasoning is based on a calculation algorithm, a mechanical model of balance, an algebraic deduction, or a special case in the calculus? Upon what theory and by what means would the instructor determine whether some solutions are more sophisticated, elegant, significant, and so forth than other solutions?

Big ideas

Because students require more time to understand material than to learn material, the curriculum must be restricted to matters that are truly indispensable to a life of the mind and the life of the nation. Because these matters are important, the teacher must make *complete* provisions for each pupil's understanding and mastery of them.

This feature is sometimes called the "less is more principle" in the sense that, while Maurice will be exposed to less information, he will master what is taught so that he ends up having more. Maurice, in other words, will understand what he has learned, and, if he does, he will have accomplished what few teachers and adults have accomplished.

Dialectical instruction

The aforementioned goals are intertwined and cannot be accomplished unless the mode of instruction is personal and responsive to Maurice's needs and requirements. To accomplish these goals, a high premium must be placed upon self-scheduling and self-pacing in which Maurice determines, whenever possible, the school tasks to be completed, the rate at which they will be completed, and the degree of teacher assistance that will be solicited.

Understanding cannot be produced by the teacher's art alone, by didactic telling, or by showing and coaching, although the pupil may learn and remember what the teacher said and may imitate what the teacher did. Maurice's understanding of algebra is dependent upon dialectic—upon *his* active investigation and experimentation, guided, when necessary, by his teacher's skillful questioning and conversation. Maurice cannot be given algebra or the idea of necessity by his teacher; rather Maurice must invent necessity or algebra and its coherent solutions. Unlike "solutions" that are learned, the dialectical outcomes are personal and extraordinarily resistant to forgetting.

Active pupils

Pupils will not understand their lessons if the teacher's role is merely to deliver information, however important information is in high-level thinking. While dialectic requires the pupil to do something overtly—to speak, respond, and question—there are other features of teaching for understanding that require the pupil to be active because nothing will be understood if the pupil is not active.

Modern views of intelligence and cognition, for example, are clear that knowing is negotiated, distributed, situated, constructed, developmental, and affective—all features of knowing that entail action and alter traditional schooling.

Negotiation

The teacher does not in fact have the power, regardless of how well the school is managed, to transfer knowledge to the pupil, and this means that Maurice's intellectual cooperation is a precondition of his inventing what he knows and understands. Maurice's teacher must begin the lesson with what Maurice brings to the lesson; they must negotiate what is important and privileged and to what aspects of Maurice's prior understanding the lesson will be linked and assimilated.

Distribution

Because the range of things to be known and understood exceeds the cognitive capacities of our minds, knowing must be distributed across technological devices, books, lists, and, increasingly, other people with whom we must cooperate and interact. The amount of mental space available for active processing is severely limited (perhaps to as few as seven simultaneous events), and consequently complex thought is critically dependent upon other devices for assisting the mind in its handling the other factors embedded in complex problems.

In particular, the use of computer technology in the classroom not only shifts instruction from the teacher to the student but shifts the student's activity from learning to understanding (Sheingold, 1991). The Geometric Supposer, a computer program that encourages students to "do geometry," is one example. Its use irrevocably changes the predetermined sequential nature of the school curriculum, the authority for knowledge, and generally forces instruction into a modern format (e.g., Scardamalia & Bereiter, 1991).

Situation

In the last several years the cognitive science literature has demonstrated repeatedly that understanding is also dependent upon, and critically shaped by, its context or its place—by the situation in which it takes place. It proves very difficult to document aspects of thought that transcend particular circumstances and generalize as widely as traditional school pedagogy and curricula assume. It seems to be the case that understanding is dependent upon, and critically shaped by, its context or its place and by specialized knowledge.

Constructed

Several lines of theory suggest that what we understand is best seen as an invention or construction, provisionally and personally erected to permit sense to be made of a particular set of physical, social, and historical factors. The mind is increasingly seen as a "top down" expectancy-driven and meaning-seeking system. The mind appears to make sense of what it finds through a recurring process of global apprehension, followed by increasing differentiation and a subsequent synthesis of the differentiated parts into more comprehensive and coherent constructions.

Developmental

These mental constructions also seem to be qualitatively different from each other over time and are based upon different mechanisms and logic. It is not simply that the older pupil has more information than the younger one, which of course he does, but rather that the older pupil reasons in a new and novel manner that is not available to the younger pupil. The pupil's understanding, in other words, cannot be reduced or decomposed into the intellectual possessions of his younger self. His new understanding emerges from his prior understanding the way "wetness" emerges from the combination of two gases, oxygen and hydrogen. The later constructions cannot be predicted from any features of the child's prior understanding just as wetness could not be predicted from any feature of a gas.

Affective

Cognition and intellectual functioning are increasingly seen as integrated with the other features of the mind. The systematic and ancient links between knowing, emotion, and motivation must be respected in pedagogy as knowing is surely in the primary service of pervasive and powerful noncognitive factors.

Valid Assessment

Finally, the commonly used school tests often indicate that the pupil has mastered a subject when it is perfectly plain that in another setting the pupil has very little grasp of it. The important things that Maurice has mastered should be apparent in works he can exhibit and in things he can make, compose, and design. It should be evident in the real and personally significant problems he can solve, in the stories he can tell and write, and so forth. The demonstration of recently acquired knowledge through artificial school tasks, tasks that are unlikely to occur elsewhere in life, are not as valid as real-world tasks that reveal what the pupil truly knows and can do.

Recently, this criterion of understanding has been called *authentic assessment* in the sense that the pupil's performance unambiguously indicates that the pupil has understood the true or authentic concept, skill, or disposition.

PRINCIPLE TWO: CREATING A LEARNING COMMUNITY

None of the other goals will be forthcoming unless the school itself is, in all aspects of its operation, a model of the community values—decency, honesty, integrity, democracy, altruism—that it hopes to have its pupils acquire. More than outcomes in their own right, these values are inherent in, and inseparable from, the negotiated dialectical process that yields understanding.

The tone of the school should make it clear that school is a place where serious and important work takes place, a place where professional people practice their profession, and so forth. The importance of the work conducted in the school is reinforced and enabled by the involvement of other important people in the community, especially parents and other supporters of the pupils. who, along with the teachers, make it clear that they also are learners whose own understanding is enhanced by the interactions with all members of the school community.

All the features of Principle One, in other words, apply to this principle, and in fact to all the remaining design principles—and vice versa.

PRINCIPLE THREE: GOALS OF THE SCHOOL APPLY TO ALL PUPILS

The limits of Maurice's, or any pupil's, potential achievement in a subject area simply cannot be predicted in the behavioral sciences with a confidence that would permit the school to have standards for some pupils that were lower than the standards for other pupils. Based upon our current knowledge of cognitive science, there would be no justification in concluding that Maurice was capable of understanding only some of the algebraic manipulations that need to be taught. The fact that some children, like Maurice, are harder to teach than others does not warrant the school's holding hard-to-teach children to lower standards of learning and understanding.

The entitlement to understand the curriculum, which is embedded in design Principle One, is similar—from a policy perspective—to the American "entitlement" to drive a car. The nation is committed to having a very wide spectrum of natural driving talent accommodated on the highways through training, elaborate and expensive engineering devices in automotive and traffic safety designs, insurance policies, and constant societal intervention and vigilance. Far from an empirical question, the issue of each and every student's understanding, like automobile driving, is a matter of commitment to the kind of inclusive society upon which a democratic republic depends.

PRINCIPLE FOUR: CAREER LONG LEARNING AND DEVELOPMENT)

The Professional Teacher

Teaching makes a claim to being one of the learned professions to the degree teachers can demonstrate that they can do important things that few other college educated persons can do. Only then will they be afforded the autonomy, compensation, and prestige of the other professions. Teachers, in collaboration with their colleagues, should know enough to be fully responsive to all the demands of the classroom, calling in expert help only in rare instances when a problem exceeds their level of training and skill.

An inevitable consequence of the foregoing features of the PDS is that teachers must continually learn and understand their work differently and more powerfully. Dialectic, being inherently unpredictable in its course, minimizes the teacher's dependence on the routine and the tested. It requires the teacher, novice and expert alike, to continually invent and discover, to be a cognitive apprentice and learn and understand teaching in the same way Maurice comes to understand algebra.

The professional teacher, especially in the PDS, stands in sharp contrast to the traditional professional who seemingly holds all the knowledge and all the power in the relationship with the client and who, by that fact, is entitled to decide, alone or in consultation with other professionals, what is best for the client. The consequences of the traditional professional role are that knowledge is mystified and made inaccessible, social distance between the professional and client is increased, and there is no reciprocity of effort as it is the professional and not the client who works on the problem.

As these consequences of traditional professionalism clearly would work against Maurice's understanding, it is no surprise that teachers must have another view of professional work—work in which, by necessity, the client's ability and talent is a determining factor in the outcome of the professional's work. Teaching is the prototypical case for a view of the professional as a catalyst who creates the conditions in which the client achieves understanding, health, justice, salvation—all outcomes of the learned professional's work.

PRINCIPLE FIVE: THE PDS RESEARCH MISSION

The Holmes Group insists that the PDS engage in inquiry that contributes to the scholarly literature. This mission, perhaps the most novel and distinctive of the PDS criteria, carries the school beyond the level of inquiry and reflection that is inherent in dialectical teaching for understanding.

Status enhancement

Engaging in educational research, even as a member of a research team, may increase the teacher's self-esteem and status, increase the teacher's literacy, place the teacher on the cutting edge, and prompt the invention of research-based innovations. Each of these is a worthy outcome of a teacher's participation in a research program, but none is sufficient reason for bringing the research program to the PDS itself because there are more direct ways of raising self-esteem, status, increasing literacy, and so on.

Research is conducted to solve practical and theoretical problems so that knowledge can be more complete and coherent. The test the PDS must meet is whether educational research is improved by this new collaboration between university researchers and classroom teachers.

Weakness in traditional educational research

Until the last two decades, scholarship in education relied heavily upon findings from other disciplines, particularly the behavioral sciences. The transfer of those findings, collected in nonschool settings, to issues of educational practice has been generally unsatisfying. Within the last 20 years, however, the powerful methodologies of the behavioral sciences have been turned on classrooms themselves, not just on distant laboratory simulations of instructional settings, with the result that life in classrooms has been studied in such a way that fairly convincing and counterintuitive conclusions about schooling are now possible. How does the PDS improve upon this trend?

Researchers in the behavioral sciences, as was noted above, are identifying factors and mechanisms that appear to operate uniquely in particular historical periods and contexts. In earlier research paradigms, these contextual and cohort-specific factors were controlled experimentally or statistically, because they were viewed as uninteresting noise or as factors whose investigation had to be postponed until better research techniques became available.

The pervasive character of these situated factors, however, has meant that consideration of these troublesome factors can no longer be postponed or ignored. Substantial effects can be attributed now to factors that appear to be features of a particular context, social or cultural group, gender, generational cohort, geographic location, historical time period, and so forth (Murray, 1991).

The Particular Case

PDS inquiry is about understanding the particular case, while traditional university-based inquiry seeks more universal explanations and contributions to general theory. PDS research is about a particular student and his or her understanding of a particular idea. At the moment, the powerful mechanisms embodied in the surviving large-scale theories (e.g., Piaget, Vygotsky, Skinner, Kohlberg, etc.) provide helpful, but incomplete, accounts of the rich case study documentation of classroom life.

The situation is not unlike Piaget's rejection of traditional behavioral science methods in his pioneering investigations of the young pupil's thinking about basic school subjects in favor of extensive dialectical interviews of individual children. The logic of PDS research is in the tradition of the early Genevan work, and, surprisingly, it is also in the Skinnerian tradition of single subject demonstrations of the powerful local and contingent factors that determine the events at hand.

PDS research is directed at local action and the particular child. It is about matters that apparently are not penetrated easily by traditional experimental designs that employ controls for chance and other seemingly irrelevant factors.

Theoretical Contributions

While the outcome of PDS research is inherently particular, its findings must be accommodated in the end by large-scale theories. It is not widely appreciated that cooperative research projects, between developmental psychologists and teachers, have advanced the field at a theoretical level. Throughout the 1960s and early 1970s, for example, researchers all over the world confirmed the young child's inability take the point of view of another (egocentrism). In fact, curriculum and instructional designs routinely accepted the immutability of the young child's limited competence (Cox, 1980).

When teachers and mothers entered graduate programs in substantial numbers in the 1970s and researched these issues, they, based on their unique familiarity with children, devised experiments that showed that young children were able to take the point of view of others. Young children, for example, were found to reduce the complexity of their speech when they spoke with even younger children, and they would select different toys for a younger child than they would select for a peer (Cox, 1980).

These inquiries led to a reevaluation of the child's cognitive competence that in turn supported the invention of pedagogical techniques, like cooperative learning and reciprocal teaching, that now presuppose the young pupil's competence to take the point of view of another pupil (Murray, 1992). It would not be hard to document other cases where the unique perspectives of school teachers and specialists have shaped the prevailing academic learning and developmental theories (Fosnot, 1989).

PRINCIPLE SIX: INVENTING A NEW INSTITUTION

School Organization and Finance

Obviously, the school must be organized and financed in a manner that allows the foregoing principles to be salient features of the school. Like all other professionals, the teacher would need time for reflection, planning, and consultation (Stigler & Stevenson, 1991). The increase in the proportion of personalized and dialectical instruction means, of course, that teachers will need time to work with all pupils on an individual basis during the school day and to evaluate the pupil's exhibitions of his or her understanding of the curriculum. In time, as increasing professional competence warrants it, and as the teacher's need to rely upon support staff outside the classroom is reduced, class enrollments could be brought in line with the overall funded teacher-student or unit count ratios.

None of the goals of the school can be accomplished unless the teacher has the time to know Maurice well. Every goal is compromised when there is insufficient time for a genuine interaction between the teacher and each pupil.

Integrated Support Services

A coordinated plan of operation, following the principle of distributed intelligence, is essential if the mission of each teacher and each of the separate state agencies that have responsibility for the welfare of children is to be achieved. The school is a sensible central point for the delivery of services that will increase the likelihood that pupils will understand their lessons. A team approach is required in which representatives of each children's service agency coordinate efforts on the child's behalf so that each member of the team is fully aware of the other's activities.

Decision Making in the PDS

The implementation of the PDS rests upon the PDS staff's ability to be thoughtful about the design principles and to make decisions in light of them. Good decisions could be said to have three connected components that, if attended to, should increase the likelihood that the decision will be correct, effective, and wise.

1. Is the decision informed? Is it grounded in the pertinent academic literature and a sound reading of the local context?
2. Is the decision rational and coherent? Is there a clear rationale for the decision, a rationale that often must go beyond the scholarly literature on the subject?
3. Is the decision realistic? Is there a feasible plan for the implementation of the decision?

Adherence to the six PDS design principles rests with the school's awareness of the what others have thought and written, a clear-headed analysis of the local context, a reasoned formulation of a decision that shows how it flows from the literature and the analysis, and a strategy for implementing the decision that shows how it will bring about the results the decision was meant to accomplish.

Like the six design principles and the criteria that define each, the answers to these three questions presumably influence each other. The answers are not linked in a linear, causal chain in which the former determine the latter. Rather the causal chain between them is reciprocal and interactive. The discussions among the faculty of the school that are needed to formulate a good plan of implementation, for example, can be expected to shape the answers to the other questions—the decision itself may change and evolve differently and the literature that was truly relevant to the decision may be seen differently.

The answers to the three questions are dependent upon the PDS staff's capacity for local inquiry, which is why the PDS research mission distinguishes the PDS from other school reform strategies and why the PDS reform is so critically dependent upon a deep understanding of the PDS design principles by the faculty and administration of the school.

OBSTACLES TO THE IMPLEMENTATION OF
PROFESSIONAL DEVELOPMENT SCHOOLS

The emergent literature on Professional Development Schools indicates that efforts to create these schools have proceeded to the point at which individual schools and universities have agreed to declare that a PDS has been initiated, but not to the point where there have been documented improvements in student or teacher learning and understanding as a result of the PDS innovation (Abdul-Haqq, 1992; Winitzky, Stoddart, & O'Keefe, 1992). The literature also draws attention to several practical obstacles to PDS reform—increased costs (e.g., $48 million for 18–24 PDSs in Michigan), teacher and faculty workload issues (equity, tempo, rewards, autonomy, cultural sensitivity), time constraints inherent in collective bargaining provisions, state in-service regulations, the university reward structure, equity and access for non-PDS schools, top-down versus bottom-up initiation strategies, and so forth (Nystrand, 1991; Rushcamp & Roehler, 1992).

In the few instances when adequate provisions for these practical matters have been made, successful outcomes are not assured, however, because the obstacles to PDS reform are often deeper; the parties to the reform, even when they adopt a new technique, often do not understand the reform slogans or goals of the reform in a way that allows them to profit from the adoption of an innovation (Brown, 1991). Hampel (1992), for example, documented a four-year, statewide effort in Delaware by 15 schools to take on the attributes of the PDS and found that while some school practices changed (e.g., an increase in team approaches to instruction), the changes were fragile and not conceptually based. Thus, like school subjects learned, but not understood, the reforms are short-lived and deprived of the flexibility that characterizes knowledge.

The very goals of the PDS need to be applied to the reformers themselves because there is a resistance to press the implications of the reform goals to the point where they make a difference in the reformer's understanding (Farnham-Diggory, 1990). Too often these implications are seen in isolation and only in the negative; as what they are not—exhibitions and authentic assessments are not standardized tests (when, of course, they could be), but it is not clear what they are. "Less is more" means only less will be covered with little sense of the "more" that will result. "All kids can learn" means that special education will be eliminated, but it does not address what will replace it. Hard thinking is needed about the practical implications of these innovations; what they are, why they are necessary, and how they *qualitatlvely* change schooling.

Failure to understand the implications of the "all kids can learn" reform slogan, for example, proved to be a crippling obstacle to one Delaware school's reform aspirations (Hampel, 1992). Should this Delaware school, for example, have implemented fully the research finding, confirmed in hundreds of studies over decades, that student achievement is higher overall when students of different abilities are taught together than when students of differing abilities are taught in separate classrooms? Or is this research flawed because the measures of school success were too modest, or because the most able students were never really challenged, or because the tests of ability were poorly related to the lessons? Or is the research literature largely irrelevant because the issue is about the kind of society we want, not how hard it is to achieve it? Is the issue akin to the nation's goal, mentioned earlier, of having nearly all its citizens drive cars by re-engineering the driving task so that wider bands of the driving-talent spectrum can be accommodated on the roads? The Delaware experience indicates that the implementation of the PDS is critically dependent on the issue of how well the reformers answer the foregoing questions.

Three Tests of Misunderstanding

There are at least three indicators that the reformers have not understood the PDS design principles. One is the failure to see that the principles are interconnected and that none can be implemented without the others. These principles are interrelated and are implications of each other. If any one were truly present, the others would be joined with it, and similarly the denial of any one undermines the others. Less is only more if each student understands; she will not understand if she is not expected to nor if the principles of active cognition are violated and so forth. A second is that the principles are not new, but have clear antecedents in historical practice and theory (Farnham-Diggory, 1990). The third is the failure to see that the principles are developmental and cannot, as a result, be achieved quickly. The PDS design principles entail qualitative or developmental change on the part of the school. Changes of this sort, in contrast to quantitative or learned changes, cannot be accelerated (Murray, 1991); sudden or effortless changes, in fact, are taken by developmental psychologists as a sign that the change was not developmental or fundamental, but rather a change that is temporary, caused by a peripheral mechanism, and not authentic.

Smith (1989) has shown in another Delaware PDS site that even under ideal teacher-coaching conditions—one on one—highly motivated, knowledgeable, and experienced teachers were still unsure and shaky after ten months of practice in their efforts to implement a PDS teaching technique. Even though they had practiced the technique in a variety of settings, had video and stimulated recall analysis of their teaching performance, and had personal feedback of their efforts, they were at risk whenever the lesson took an unusual turn (Smith & Neale, 1990).

In summary, each design principle is derived from the literature, represents a qualitative change in school practice, and can be derived from the other principles. Schools that drive toward understanding (Principle One) cannot set the principle aside for some students (Principle Three), nor can they succeed without a school-wide approach (Principle Two), or without a professional teaching staff (Principle Four) that has a capacity for inquiry (Principle Five) embedded in a new organization and decision-making system (Principle Six). Similarly, Principle Five (inquiry) cannot be implemented independently of Principles Four (community) and Six (new organization) in the service of One (understanding) and Three (same goals for all) by the staff described in Two (professional teachers). Principle Three (same goals for all), to take another example, only makes sense, in terms of Principle One (understanding) and is feasible only if the other principles are in place in the school's design.

Finally, it should be clear that the PDS is connected, not just to the university teacher education program, but to every other stakeholder in the reform of schooling. The PDS is the place where all the elements of educational reform come together—the community, the school board, the teacher, the pupil, the principal, the social service agencies, the district, the university school of education, and the university academic disciplines.

NOTES

1. Higher Education Amendments of 1972. Committee on Education and Labor, United States House of Representatives, February 27, 1992, 102-447.

2. A videotape of Maurice and two other Flint, Michigan, students can be obtained from the Michigan Partnership, Erickson Hall, Michigan State University, East Lansing, MI 48824-1034.

REFERENCES

Abdal-Haqq, I. (1992). Professional development schools: An annotated bibliography of selected ERIC sources. *Journal of Teacher Education, 43*(1), 42–45.

Brown, R. (1991). *Schools of thought: How the politics of literacy shape thinking in the classroom.* San Francisco: Jossey-Bass.

Cox, M. (1980). *Are young children egocentric?* New York: St. Martin's Press.

Farnham-Diggory, S. (1990). *Schooling.* Cambridge, MA: Harvard University Press.

Fosnot, C. (1989). *Enquiring teachers, enquiring learners: A constructivist approach for teaching.* New York: Teachers College Press.

Hampel, R. (1992). *Re:Learning: The third year.* Unpublished manuscript, Newark, DE: University of Delaware.

Holmes Group. (1986). *Tomorrow's teachers*. East Lansing, MI: Author.

Holmes Group. (1990). *Tomorrow's schools: Principles for the design of professional development schools*. East Lansing, MI: Author.

Murray, F. (1986a). Goals for the reform of teacher education: An executive summary of the Holmes Group report, *Phi Delta Kappan*, September, 28–32.

Murray, F. (1986b). Teacher education: Words of caution about popular reforms. *Change*, September/October, 18–21.

Murray, F. (1991). Questions a satisfying developmental theory would answer: The scope of a complete explanation of developmental phenomena. In H. Reese (Ed.), *Advances in child development and behavior* (Vol. 23, pp. 39–47). New York: Academic Press.

Murray, F. (1992). Restructuring and constructivism: The development of American educational reform. In H. Beilin and P. Pufall (Eds.), *Piaget's theory: Prospects an possibilities* (pp. 287–308). Hillsdale, NJ: Lawrence Erlbaum Associates.

Nystrand, R. (1991). Professional development schools: Toward a new relationship for schools and universities (Trends and Issues Paper No. 4). Washington, DC: ERIC Clearinghouse on Teacher Education, 1–25.

Rushcamp, S., & Roehler, L. (1992). Characteristics supporting change in a professional development school. *Journal of Teacher Education, 43*(1), 19–27.

Scardamalia, M., & Bereiter, C. (1991). Higher levels of agency for children in knowledge building: A challenge for the design of new knowledge media. *Journal of the Learning Sciences, 1*, 37–68.

Sheingold, K. (1991, September). Restructuring for learning with technology: The potential for synergy. *Phi Delta Kappan (73)*, 17–27.

Smith, D. (1989). *The role of teacher knowledge in teaching conceptual change science lessons*. Unpublished doctoral dissertation, University of Delaware.

Smith, D., & Neale, D. (1990). The construction of subject matter in primary science teaching. In J. Brophy (Ed.), *Advances in research on teaching subject matter knowledge*. Greenwich, CT: JAI Press.

Stigler, J., & Stevenson, H. (1991). How Asian teachers polish each lesson to perfection, *American Educator, 15*, 12–20.

Winitzky, N., Stoddart, T., & O'Keefe, P. (1992). Great expectations: Emergent professional development schools. *Journal of Teacher Education, 43*(1), 3–18.

Part II

Culture Clashes

In this section, a number of clashes among cultures in attempting to develop a professional development school are described. Trish Stoddart notes particularly the theoretical versus practical approaches to pedagogy typically exemplified by the university and the school. "Constructivism" may be the current reigning theory among scholars of how people learn, yet it is typically presented to skeptical teachers in a didactic way that tends to contradict the very lesson intended to be learned. Nor is it clear, Stoddart argues, that the way in which inquiry should be conducted in professional development schools is to teach teachers how to conduct traditional university research. (This topic is addressed directly in Part VI.) She describes the evolution of a professional development school project that required a difficult negotiation among participants of the differentiated roles they would play. She also notes that perhaps the most difficult culture in the professional development school mix is that of the relatively isolated school of education itself.

James Henderson and Richard Hawthorne continue the descriptions of particular examples of culture clashes with their contribution. They especially note the culture clash over power relationships and call for more power sharing in professional development schools. Whereas Stoddart's work resulted in differentiated roles for teachers and university faculty, Henderson and Hawthorne call for the creation of a community of learners. However, their experience echoes Stoddart's problems in finding a common ground between teachers and university faculty over didactic versus constructivist teaching. Also addressed is the issue of the culture of the school of education with its traditional promotion and tenure guidelines that are seen as often incompatible with the kind of work required in a professional development school.

The culture clash between different conceptions of good teaching is continued in James Collins's chapter. He notes the very different approaches to writing and what are fit subjects for writing taken by teachers and university faculty in the urban professional development site in which he worked. A great deal of effort was required to identify these different perspectives and articulate them so that they might be addressed. He also suggests that somewhat different conceptions of the aims of schooling may be at work in the ways in which university educators listen to, but do not always hear, school educators. Also apparent are the beginning reflections on the culture changes needed in a school of education if we are to move beyond partnerships to true collaboration.

David Labaree extends the theme of culture clashes to a consideration of the reasons school administrators and teachers might cooperate with universities in professional development activities. He notes that the universalistic research approaches of universities are often of little help with the particularistic problems faced by teachers. Even though involvement with university faculty may be welcomed by some teachers as a way of reflecting on their practice, the university's perspective is often more compatible with that of school administrators. The culture of school administrators echoes the power theme insofar as they often want to maintain power over teachers rather than promoting professionalism by sharing power with teachers. The university, too, wants to keep its own prestige and power through its exclusive access to the social authority of science.

Professionalization, partnership, and power—what they mean, who will define them, and how they are to be implemented—are the themes running through the culture clashes described in this section.

TRISH STODDART

Chapter Three

The Professional Development School
BUILDING BRIDGES BETWEEN CULTURES

During the past six years, the Holmes Group has presented a vision of schooling where practicing teachers and university faculty members work together in partnerships to improve the teaching and learning of students and novice teachers (Holmes Group, 1986, 1990). The location for this collaboration is the professional development school, which would provide superior opportunities for teachers and administrators to influence the development of their profession and for university faculty to increase the professional relevance of their work through (1) mutual deliberation on problems with student learning and their possible solutions; (2) shared teaching in the university and schools; (3) collaborative research on the problems of educational practice; and (4) cooperative supervision of prospective teachers and administrators. (Holmes Group, 1986)

The professional development school, as described above, requires significant changes in the roles of school and university faculties and in the relationships between them that would blur the boundaries between teaching, teacher education, and research (Lampert, 1991). The Holmes Group, however, has not provided a clear vision of what these restructured roles should look like nor how they will be developed and supported.

Original was first published in *Educational Policy 7* (1), March 1993, © 1993, Corwin Press, Inc. Reprinted by permission of Corwin Press, a Sage Publications Company.

As Fullan (1982) pointed out, educational change requires not only a good idea but a theory of change by which to guide the process. To date, the Holmes Group has been strong in presenting a vision of teaching and teacher education but weak in describing how this vision will be implemented. The development of school-university partnerships is not a simple process. It requires collaboration between two groups of professionals who come from different cultures, have developed different forms of expertise, and operate under different organizational conditions and reward structures (Goodlad, 1990; Stoddart, 1992; Sykes, 1990; Winitzky, Stoddart, & O'Keefe, 1992). Throughout this century, such collaborative ventures have typically failed (Stallings & Kowalski, 1990). If the professional development school is to avoid the same fate as the laboratory school and the portal school, the Holmes Group must shift from vision to process. In support of this movement, this chapter explores issues of collaboration in professional development schools in the context of the vision, the change process, and the development of organizational structures that support collaborative relationships between school and university faculties. The author draws on data from three projects at the University of Utah to raise issues and discuss obstacles that must be overcome if the Holmes Group goals are to be achieved.

THE VISION: WISDOM OF THEORY VERSUS WISDOM OF PRACTICE

The Holmes Group (1986, 1990) calls for major shifts in the pedagogy practiced in public schools and universities—a move from didactic teacher-directed instruction to conceptually based egalitarian approaches. This vision is based on recent research on cognition, development, and subject-specific pedagogy that has brought about a revolution in ideas about how children learn (see, e.g., Anderson, 1984; Brown, Collins, & Duguid, 1989; Case & Bereiter, 1984; diSessa, 1982; Piaget, 1970; Schocnfeld, 1987). The findings of this research demonstrate the ineffectiveness of traditional didactic approaches to instruction. Many educational researchers advocate the use of constructivist, "hands on" inquiry-oriented instruction designed to promote students' conceptual knowledge by building on prior understandings, active engagement with the subject matter content, and application to real-world situations (Dole & Niederhauser, 1991; Driver, 1983; Hewson & Hewson, 1988; Lampert, 1985, 1988; Smith & Anderson, 1984). These new ideas have been extremely influential in university and policymaking circles. Several recent national reports have argued for a move toward conceptual approaches to teaching and learning that emphasize the social and cognitive construction of knowledge (AAAS, 1989; NCTM, 1989; NCTE, 1988; NSTA, 1989). These views of teaching and learning, however, are not as widely accepted in the public schools. Studies of

U.S. schools indicate that traditional didactic approaches emphasizing the use of lecture, textbook, and drill and practice still predominate (Cohen, 1990; Cuban, 1991; Goodlad, 1984; Porter, 1988; Stodolsky, 1988).

Teachers often resist using constructivist approaches because these methods challenge widespread views of instruction and could potentially disrupt well-worn patterns of practice (Sykes, 1990). The underlying pedagogical assumptions frequently run counter to their training and experience. More than 70 percent of the current teaching force are over 30 years of age and went through teacher education more than 10 years ago (National Center for Education Statistics, 1990). In the 1960s, 1970s, and early 1980s, most teacher education programs emphasized a behavioral, skills-based competency approach to instruction that emphasized the replication of knowledge over transformation (Stoddart, Losk, & Benson, 1985). This philosophy also forms the basis for many of the current student testing and teacher evaluation programs (Popkewitz & Lind, 1989). Popkewitz and Lind (1989) argued that such organizational structures create a standardized approach to practice and discourage teacher innovation. They press teachers to focus on issues of classroom management, control, and covering the curriculum rather than teaching for understanding.

This divergence between the views of pedagogy espoused by university and school faculties has been observed across the country. Goodlad (1990), after studying teacher education programs in 29 universities nationwide, concluded that the vision of teaching propounded by education schools differs significantly from methods used by teachers or mandated by school district administrators or state policymakers. It is particularly apparent to teacher educators who adhere to the constructivist paradigm (Roth, Rosaen, & Lanier, 1988; Stoddart, 1992). While working at the University of Vermont, for example, Raths found that a clash of cultures arose over the education school's belief that teachers should use an "inquiry model" to elicit responses from students and help them think through the curriculum and surrounding schools that favored a "charismatic model" in which teachers supply students with the correct answers (Raths, 1991, p. 23).

In sum, we have a wisdom of theory that has not been widely accepted in practice and a wisdom of practice constructed in an environment that has in many cases discouraged innovation and experimentation. In this situation, as O'Keefe, who serves as a school district–university liaison, pointed out,

> the truth is none of us are experts. . . . [We] have to attend to the lives and realities of teachers. But the truth is what we're doing in schools ain't necessarily the answer any more. We all have to be in the business of reconstructing what might be some of the answers—together. I don't think we have it in the schools. And I don't think you have it on campuses either. It's going to take both of us. (quoted in Holmes Group, 1991a, 19)

The idea that the development of practical theory of pedagogy will require a collaboration of practitioners and university researchers is widely accepted. The unresolved issue for us is how to combine expertise and develop a shared perspective in an equitable and democratic manner. Although it is acknowledged that collaboration requires an assumption of parity between the partners and mutual respect (Clift, Veal, Johnson, & Holland, 1990), it is not so widely recognized that it also requires some coherence in the partners' perspectives. School and university faculty members with deeply held but widely diverging beliefs about teaching, learning, and teacher education will have difficulty developing a good collaborative relationship or a coherent program of teacher education.

Many teachers see theory as of no practical use to them and are often resistant to it. They may view it as being produced by outsiders who claim to be experts at generating valid knowledge about educational practices. Theory for teachers is simply the product of power exercised through the mastery of a specialized body of techniques. It negates their professional culture that defines teaching competence as a matter of intuitive craft knowledge, tacitly acquired through experience (Elliot, 1989). Or, as a teacher at a recent Holmes Group meeting succinctly stated to a group of researchers,

> You guys don't know how to do it. . . . You cannot come into the school as experts. You're going to have to come in offering a service. In coming in you have to realize that you've got big feet. You've got more degrees than we do, you've got an easier life, you earn more money than we do, and you have more prestige than we do. (Holmes Group, 1991a, p. 19)

For an innovation to succeed, those who implement the program must share ownership of the vision. In many cases, there is little agreement in theory or practice between school and university personnel on what is exemplary practice. As the views of the teacher quoted above indicate, there are often misconceptions about role and expertise. For the professional development school (PDS) to succeed there must be a shared vision of pedagogy and mutual respect. We must build a bridge between the two cultures.

THE CHANGE PROCESS: TOP-DOWN
VERSUS BOTTOM-UP APPROACHES TO COLLABORATION

University-school partnerships have typically been characterized by a "top down" relationship whereby the university delivers information to the school (Clift et al., 1990). A large body of research, however, demonstrates that such an approach is ineffective in bringing about instructional change (Elmore, 1987; Guskey, 1986; McLaughlin, 1990). Teachers typically appropriate the innovation into their existing practice. It has increasingly been recognized that change must occur from the "bottom up" in that teachers must take ownership of the new curriculum and instructional practices (Carnegie Forum on Education and the Economy, 1986; Elmore, 1987). One approach has been to involve teachers in action research projects that focus on the concerns of individual teachers and schools (Clift et al., 1990; Elliot, 1989; Stenhouse, 1971; Tikunoff & Ward, 1983). Both top-down and bottom-up approaches were tried in the evolving PDS project at the University of Utah. As will be illustrated in the cases presented here, these categorizations represent an oversimplification of the collaborative process in which neither partner is wholly active or wholly passive.

A series of staff development seminars was delivered to teachers in two PDSs, in which a university faculty member explained the constructivist theory that was the underpinning of the teacher education program—an essentially top-down approach. This theory was presented in the context of elementary school teaching. The university faculty member selected a series of short readings, which provided examples of constructivist curriculum and instructional practice in the domains of elementary mathematics, reading, and science, and showed videotapes of classroom instruction using this approach. The seminars took place at the school site; the PDS cooperating teachers were released from teaching duties to attend and were given continuing education credit.

These seminars were not successful. In a follow-up evaluation, 60 percent of the teachers rated the seminars as "not relevant to my instructional practice. " In one school, the PDS teachers clearly found the seminars oppressive and showed classic signs of resistance, refusing to read the assignment or engage in discussion. In the other school, the PDS teachers were willing to engage in discussion, but most did not agree with constructivism in theory or in practice. One particularly telling incident occurred during the viewing of a videotape showing Maggie Lampert (1985), a nationally renowned mathematics educator, using social constructivist methods to teach graphing ("The Voyage of the Mimi"). A group of about six teachers began to show increasing signs of tension as the videotape progressed. In the subsequent discussion, they explained that they strongly disagreed with Lampert's continual use of questioning to guide students' reasoning and her refusal to give students the answer because it was "inefficient, and "it took too long to get to the point." One teacher summed up the group's feeling when she said, "I wanted to scream! I wanted to jump up there and give them the answer." These teachers felt a strong compulsion to teach didactically. The university faculty member's presentation of constructivist pedagogy did not convince them of the efficacy of this approach.

In this situation, the constructivist teacher educator was not practicing what she preached about learning. In the seminars, she had conducted "show and tell" lessons about constructivism. The information was not made personally relevant to the PDS teacher-learners; they were not allowed to construct their own understanding; and they never took ownership of the knowledge.

Another faculty member developed a bottom-up action research project with a group of elementary PDS teachers. The model adopted was similar to that described by Clift et al. (1990):

> Collaborative action research in its most recent form is characterized by its group orientation, focus on practical problems of individual teachers or schools, emphasis on professional development, and construction of an environment that provides time and support for teachers and university staff to work together. Participants agree to work together on a common goal. Research findings and techniques are often used in seeking solutions, and teachers and researchers sometimes co-author reports of their findings and the process of collaboration (p. 53).

Clift et al. emphasized that the action plans of the school, not the ideas of the university, should guide the research project. The university researcher in this project planned to undertake every step, from framing research questions to data collection and analysis, to writing up the findings in collaboration with the PDS teachers.

This work emerged as a very time-consuming and fragmented process. In the first year, the faculty member met with the PDS teachers weekly to help them develop an understanding of the research process and identify an issue. The group explored several possible research topics, including class size and cooperative grouping. It took the entire academic year to settle on a mutually agreeable topic: class size. The problem arose then whether the group should review the large and somewhat confounding literature on class size and what questions they should answer. During the second year, the project foundered when the group could not clearly define the problem they wanted to study or how to go about it. The dilemma that the university researcher encountered was how closely she should guide the process. She believed that if she imposed her ideas and methodology on the teachers, it would not be a truly collaborative process. She wanted the project to be grounded in the teachers' practice and to address an issue of importance to them. However, without some training in research design and some understanding of the prior research, the PDS teachers found it extremely difficult to develop a research project. The project is now on hold for a year.

The failure of this project raised in the minds of the teacher education faculty the same sorts of questions about efficiency that the PDS teachers had raised about Lampert's constructivist approach to mathematics. These faculty members echoed the question posed by an elementary school teacher at the South Central regional meeting of the Holmes Group:

Why should teachers become researchers in addition to all the extremely important things teachers need to be good at? Is that an efficient way to handle the knowledge base question? (Holmes Group, 1991b, p. 17)

By imposing a university research and publication paradigm on public school teachers, we may lose the main benefit of collaboration—the combination of different forms of expertise and different perspectives. The critical question about such collaborative research and development projects is whether all participants should play the same role or be expected to have the same expertise. It is quite likely, and legitimate, for participants to have different interests.

This perspective is underscored in a recent article that included the reflections of school and university faculty members on their participation in a six-year collaborative action research project (Berkey et al., 1990). The university researcher's reflections focused on scholarly productivity and dissemination. He was concerned that teachers do not have "voice, ownership, and control" in the project because they do not write scholarly papers or present at conferences. In contrast, the teachers and administrator discussed the ways in which the collaborative project changed their personal practice.

What is needed is a collaborative staff development and research paradigm that respects the expertise and meets the needs of both public school teachers and university teacher educators and the development of a knowledge base for teaching and teacher education.

COLLABORATIVE STAFF DEVELOPMENT AND RESEARCH: DIFFERENTIATED ROLES

As a consequence of the experiences described above, a group of public school and university faculty members involved in the University of Utah PDS project began developing a new form of collaborative project designed to respond to differentiated needs and differentiated roles. The functions of research and development were separated. The school and university faculties came together because of a mutual interest and mutual need.

The project was based in a socially and culturally diverse elementary school that was on Chapter 1 probation because of low mathematics scores. School faculty members requested assistance from university faculty members to improve their mathematics curriculum and student achievement. Three faculty members with research programs focusing on developing constructivist approaches to mathematics instruction agreed to move their program to the school. In addition to becoming involved in a new research site, the mathematics educators saw the potential of developing a PDS site where new approaches to mathematics instruction would be modeled for teacher candidates. Two faculty members agreed to conduct staff development activities and coteach with PDS teachers four mornings a week. A third university faculty member, with expertise in teacher learning and development and school change, offered to coordinate research and reflection activities. This individual and three graduate students trained in qualitative methods observed the coteaching activities and interviewed and videotaped university faculty members and teachers. Data also were collected on student achievement and attitudes toward mathematics. The coteaching university and school faculty members did not have to spend time collecting data but had access to the data and were involved in the analysis.

The public school teachers used the interviews and videotapes as an opportunity to reflect on their own practice and student responses to the new instruction. The university faculty members originally saw the interviews and observations primarily as data sources for publication. Circumstances, however, soon pushed them to use the data to reflect on their own teaching practice. The purpose of the project, therefore, met multiple needs of school and university faculties: (a) to significantly improve the teaching and learning of mathematics in the school, (b) to help teachers critically analyze and reflect on their practice, (c) to contribute to the knowledge base on mathematics instruction, staff development, and school restructuring, and (d) to develop a PDS site where teacher candidates could observe and be coached by teachers with expertise in constructivist approaches to mathematics instruction.

An extremely important aspect of the project was the locus in the classroom and the in-depth analysis from multiple perspectives of the university and school coteachers and research team. The group had the potential to collaboratively develop a practical pedagogy informed by theory, research, and practice. It could also develop a PDS where curriculum and instruction reflected a consensus view of good practice. In reality, it was not that simple. Coteaching was extremely stressful for both the school and university faculties. Both groups of faculty members, used to working in isolation and with a marked degree of autonomy, were unclear about their relative roles. For example, in one classroom, discipline became a bone of contention. Both the teacher and the university faculty member thought that students were out of control in the coteaching situation. Both assumed the other should take responsibility for it. According to Bill (all names fictitious), the university coteacher, David, the classroom teacher, "had no discipline system." According to David,

> I told him [the university coteacher] that they were a lively group. And he said, "No problem." And I interpreted that to mean he would handle that. So I kind of just sat back initially and felt like I didn't want to usurp his authority by saying that is not appropriate behavior. Correcting the kids. I felt like he should do it. And I don't know that he was really waiting on me to do that either, but

between us we ignored a lot of behavior. Students saw me ignoring behavior that I typically would not ignore, so that just escalated the system.

In another situation, university coteacher, Wendy, became concerned that school coteacher, Carol, was not participating in the teaching. Carol frequently sat at her desk during the coteaching session and did clerical work or stood at the back of the room. Debriefing sessions with her revealed that, like David, she was unclear on her role. Furthermore, she was never sure beforehand where the university coteacher would go with the lesson: "She's an intuitive teacher. She might change midstream, depending on what's happening with the kids or a particular answer." As the discussion progressed, it became clear that the teacher was uncomfortable with the fact that the students were picking up the new method quicker than she was:

> I see these kids being faster with what she's doing than I am. When they explain it to me I can see that they're correct and can understand what they're doing. But they're quicker than I am . . . I'm a little uncomfortable. Because if they say "Mrs. Smith, is this right?" I don't know. Hopefully, I can figure it out by the time they finish explaining. But it makes me feel a little uncomfortable.

The coteaching process made both classroom teachers feel inadequate. David said, "I feel I'm letting the kids down. I'm somehow inadequate as a teacher because I couldn't do it the way they wanted me to right off the bat." Both David and Carol felt usurped by the university coteacher.

Difficulties in personal interactions between school and university faculties in collaborative research projects are not unusual. Berkey et al. (1990) describe a stage in their project that they refer to as the "screaming period." During this period, teachers felt the university researchers were criticizing their practice and that there was little mutual understanding. One teacher commented, "It was as if we were talking at each other but not hearing each other."

The Utah project went through a similar process. The tensions between the university and school coteachers escalated to the point where the classroom teachers wanted to withdraw from the project. The university participant, a researcher who was involved in a series of debriefing meetings with the school and university coteachers, began to be drawn into the role of mediator. She arranged a meeting of the group to raise issues and clear the air. A turning point came when she pointed out to the university faculty members that they were not practicing what they preached. Although they believed that learners constructed understanding through personal experience and should take ownership of the knowledge, they expected teachers to learn the new method through observation, "sort of like osmosis," Bill remarked. The situation was also once again top-down, with the university faculty members acting as experts who took over the classroom and the school faculty members as novices. In this situation, the university faculty were forced to reexamine their own practices.

The university group realized that it needed to give teachers the opportunity to experience the new instructional approaches as learners, that they should act more like teacher educators than expert classroom teachers modeling practice.

The school faculty also wanted the university faculty to act more like teacher educators. School faculty members made it clear that they did not want the university faculty to "take over their classrooms." They were eager to learn about the new approaches to mathematics instruction and be supported in their classrooms, but they wanted to maintain control. They pushed the university faculty to differentiate their expertise and function more as teacher educators than classroom teachers. A new structure was developed so that school faculty members were given time to personally work through each lesson before it was taught to students. Roles and rules were negotiated by the coteachers before each session, and after the lesson they sat down and discussed it. Through this new structure, a dialogue about the pedagogy began to develop, and each partner began to accommodate to the other's perspective. The school coteachers pointed out to the university coteachers that because they did not formally evaluate the students "they were not sure where things were going," so while "students were doing more difficult problems, they could not see their progress," and this made them anxious. The university coteachers pointed out to the teachers the importance of "letting kids figure things out for themselves" and deemphasizing the idea of "one right answer."

Throughout the whole process, the coteachers were held together by their interest in figuring out how to help students learn mathematics more effectively. As students began to respond positively to the new pedagogy, to demonstrate they could "think like mathematicians," enthusiasm for the project grew in both groups. The findings of this project underscore the results of prior research that demonstrated that teachers are motivated to engage in staff development and school change activities because they want to become better teachers (Guskey, 1986), and for the vast majority of teachers, becoming better teachers means enhancing the learning outcomes of their students (McLaughlin, 1990). It is important to emphasize that this was true of *both* school and university participants.

Inch by inch, a new pedagogy is beginning to evolve. Systematic documentation, through videotapes, interviews, and participant-observation, provides data for both theoretical and applied analysis. It is likely that in this situation the majority of writing and publication will be done by the university faculty. Four teachers, however, are interested in participating in the development and dissemination of a model of school change based on this experience. Several others would like to coteach with teachers in other schools to disseminate the pedagogy. What is beginning to emerge is not a dichotomy in expertise between the two groups but a difference in figure and ground. The university faculty members, who came in with a primary emphasis on theory and research, were forced to look closely at themselves as teachers and to examine the difficulties of translating theory into practice. They began to emerge more strongly as scholar-practitioners. The teachers, who initially focused on raising the mathematics achievement scores, began to think about what it means to know mathematics and the differences between the replication and transformation of knowledge. They began to examine the possibility that they could become practitioner-scholars. All of their views of themselves as professionals changed.

A STRUCTURE FOR COLLABORATION

In the Utah project, it has become increasingly apparent that collaboration in PDSs takes a great deal of time, emotional and intellectual energy, and commitment. School teachers and teacher education faculty members are already engaged in professions that are cognitively demanding and labor intensive. Jackson (1986) has described the complexity of classrooms and the intensity of student-teacher interactions. The RATE studies have documented the heavy load of teacher education faculty members in teaching, field supervision, and research (Ducharme & McManus-Kluender, 1990). The burden of the implementation of the Holmes Group agenda, however, typically falls on the shoulders of teachers and a small number of teacher education faculty members.

Teachers, used to working in relative isolation, must open up their classrooms to university faculty members and teacher candidates, who often have ideas very different from themselves. Teachers must spend time in meetings providing input and support to the teacher education program, sit on admissions committees, and so on. They are asked to become involved in research projects. All of this is in addition to their regular load. In the University of Utah program, PDS teachers are given release time by student teachers and the provision of district staff development days to participate in collaborative projects. They are also given continuing education credit for their work. In addition, the administrations of the college of education and three cooperating school districts have funded collaborative appointments. Two experienced elementary school teachers work full-time with the teacher education program as clinical professors. At each PDS school site, a teacher facilitator is released full-time to work with teacher candidates and cooperating teachers by the provision of two interns. The provision of time for teachers to be involved in PDS development is a clear recognition of the enormous human resources that this enterprise requires.

Little, however, has changed for the teacher education faculty. The time it spends in PDS development is in addition to its regular teaching load. The tenure and promotion system still rewards research and publication in scholarly journals over applied research and service. There is little support for the PDS enterprise outside the teacher education group. This situation points to a key weakness in the Holmes Group agenda—the lack of support from within the graduate schools of education themselves.

GRADUATE SCHOOLS OF EDUCATION: THE THIRD CULTURE

The graduate school of education is, in fact, a third culture that must also be negotiated with in the PDS enterprise. Over the past 30 years, a dichotomy has developed between the research and professional education functions in many of the education schools of the major research universities that make up the Holmes Group (Borrowman, 1956; Clifford & Guthrie, 1988; Judge, 1982; Lanier & Little, 1986; Powell, 1976). This frequently results in a two-tier system of researchers and clinicians that severs research from practice and erodes the effectiveness of professional education (Clifford & Guthrie, 1988). For the PDS to succeed, the cultural divide within the graduate schools must be bridged. This will not, however, be a simple process because divisions between research and practice are often institutionalized in colleges' hiring, merit, and promotion procedures and in the allocation of resources.

Divisions within graduate schools of education evolved from the belief that the presence of vocational training programs debased the quality of higher education (Borrowman, 1956; Clifford & Guthrie, 1988; Judge, 1982; Lanier & Little, 1986; Powell, 1976). As a consequence, faculty in departments of education sought to distance themselves from professional education and identify more closely with the academic orientation of arts and sciences departments. Increasingly, tenured faculty members were recruited from academic disciplines other than education, with no experience and limited interest in professional practice (Clifford & Guthrie, 1988). It was argued that education itself is not a discipline and can only be studied from the perspective of another field (Eisner, 1984; Zusman, 1985). The result was the creation of a mini-university within the larger university, with departments of education employing individuals with doctorates in psychology, sociology, political science, economics, anthropology, statistics, mathematics, physics, computer programming, history, philosophy, and so on.

As Lawson (1990) pointed out, such individuals are professional scholars of education, not educators. They owe their allegiance to the disciplines in which they were trained:

> Their work orientations and their research styles are borrowed from parent disciplines in colleges of arts and sciences. Their identities and orientations reflect

their education, and their national professional associations include the name of the parent discipline. (p. 61)

Many of these scholars have little interest in and limited expertise to offer to the PDS program. In my department, which has 10 foundations faculty members and 11 teacher education faculty members, only the teacher education faculty members work with the PDS and with student teachers in the field. This leads to substantial inequity in professional time commitments, although all faculty members are evaluated on the basis of the same criteria.

Within the graduate schools of education, "professional scholars" constitute a powerful group because of their perceived prestige and because their work orientations are congruent with those of faculty members in the colleges of arts and sciences. Under the influence of this group, merit, promotion, and tenure policies have increasingly come to value basic research in the disciplines over applied educational research (Clifford & Guthrie, 1988; Howey & Zimpher, 1989; Schwebel, 1989; Wisniewski & Ducharme, 1989). For instance, in my institution, articles published in journals devoted to foundations disciplines such as history, philosophy, and psychology are more highly rated in faculty evaluation than are articles published in teacher education journals.

Over time, such recruitment and reward systems establish a "colleague climate" that institutionalizes indifference or even hostility toward teacher education (Finkelstein, 1984). Over the past year, foundations faculty members in my department have successfully voted down proposals to give teacher education faculty members course credit for field supervision of teacher candidates and work in the PDS and a proposal to establish a doctoral emphasis area in teacher education, their justification being that allocation of resources to these areas would weaken the Ph.D. program in educational foundations.

Clearly, many of the biggest obstacles to the development of collaborative school-university partnerships in professional development schools lie within the graduate schools of education themselves. Teacher education faculty members, faced with diffused roles and increasingly heavy work loads, confront structural constraints rather than support for working with schools.

The Holmes Group (1986) recognized the difficulty of developing PDSs within the system that now exists. It was argued that not only would schools need to be reorganized but so too would the reward systems of the universities. The group, however, has made little progress toward that goal. Lampert (1991), in discussing how she works as public school teacher, researcher, teacher educator, mentor of graduate students, and policy analyst in her restructured role at Michigan State, pointed out that even the prototypical Holmes Group institution has not figured out how to evaluate and support such work:

> Although I am fortunate to work in an institution that values experimentation with regard to the relationship between the university and the schools, the

norms for evaluating such experimentation have yet to emerge and be formalized. The problem this causes for individuals who do not fall into the traditional pattern are subtle but real. (p. 672)

Without the development of substantial supports, she argued, "it will be difficult to find people who can work productively in the boundary-blurring roles that institutional restructuring creates" (p. 672).

CONCLUSION

The professional development school represents a brave new vision for educational research and development—a place where university researchers and seasoned practitioners can work together in the development of a practical theory of pedagogy. As this chapter points out, however, the dissonance between the cultures of schools and universities and between groups of faculty members within graduate schools of education creates tensions in the collaborative process. Some might argue that graduate schools of education have so distanced themselves from teacher education and applied research that they have no legitimate role to play in these enterprises. This indeed may be the case. If they do not become involved, however, the gap between theory and practice might not be bridged. Putnam, Lampert, and Peterson (1990) pointed to the weak articulation between theory and practice in their discussion of the constructivist instructional approaches advocated by the Holmes Group and many other policymakers. As Sykes (1990) pointed out,

> Such constructivist views contribute compelling accounts of learning but as yet few widely recognized models of teaching. Researchers are beginning to develop and test instructional practices based on constructivist principles, but vanguard ideas about learning produce as many puzzles and dilemmas for teaching as they do clear guidance. (p. 244)

Researchers must join with teachers to test these practices in the real world of school. The collaborative school-university mathematics research and development project described above pushed both researchers and teachers to examine the exigencies of implementing a constructivist curriculum on a daily basis in real classrooms. In the course of this project, the collaborative group of scholar-practitioners are constructing their own knowledge about student and teacher learning, teacher education, school change, and applied research methods. They are developing theory in practice.

The cases described in this chapter point to the complexity of developing a PDS. Establishing effective school-university partnerships will require radical restructuring of roles and reward structures. Too often, as university researchers, teacher educators, and teachers, we seek to change others. If the

Holmes Group agenda is to succeed we need to reform ourselves—examine the flaws and inconsistencies in our organizational structures, theories, and practices. One of the most important consequences of the PDS process described in this chapter was that university faculty members were pushed to examine their own pedagogy. In their turn, public school teachers came to recognize that the university faculty not only did research on teaching but also knew how to teach. The challenge is great, for we must not only change our views of each other but must also change our views of ourselves.

To do that, we must create a new institution, and this may be the greatest challenge. One of the ironies of the Holmes Group is that whereas the biggest obstacles to reform may lie within the colleges of education themselves, the group has spent the past six years looking outward toward the colleges of arts and sciences and the public schools. It is time now for the reformers to reform themselves. As leaders of the Holmes Group, deans of graduate schools of education must confront the difficult dilemmas of resource allocation and reward structures within their own institutions.

The burden of the Holmes Group agenda is falling on the teacher educators, often the most overworked and politically weakest group in the graduate school of education. An increasing number of these faculty members are nontenured women (Ducharme & McManus-Kluender, 1990). These individuals, and the PDS, will not survive if they are not given support, resources, and voice.

REFERENCES

American Association for the Advancement of Science (AAAS). (1989). *Science for all Americans.* Washington, DC: Author.

Anderson, R. C. (1984). Some reflections on the acquisition of knowledge. *Educational Researcher, 13*(9), 5–10.

Berkey, R., Curtis, T., Minnick, F., Zietlow, K., Campbell, D., & Kirschner, B. (1990). Collaborating for reflective practice: Voices of teachers, administrators and researchers. *Education and Urban Society, 22*(2), 204–232.

Borrowman, M. L. (1956). *The liberal and technical in teacher education.* New York: Teachers College Press.

Brown, J. S., Collins, A., & Duguid, O. (1989). Situated cognition and the culture of learning. *Educational Researcher, 18*(1), 32–42.

Carnegie Forum on Education and the Economy, Task Force on Teaching as a Profession. (1986). *A nation prepared: Teachers for the 21st century.* New York: Author.

Case, R., & Bereiter, C. (1984). From behaviorism to cognitive behaviorism to cognitive development: Steps in the evolution of instructional design. *Instructional Science, 13*, 141–158.

Clifford, G. J., & Guthrie, J. W. (1988). *Ed school: A brief for professional education.* Chicago: University of Chicago Press.

Clift, R., Veal, M. L., Johnson, J., & Holland, P. (1990). Restructuring teacher education through collaborative action research. *Journal of Teacher Education. 41*(2), 52–62.

Cohen, D. K. (1990). Teaching practice: Plus ça change . . . In P. Jackson (Ed.), *Contributing to educational change: Perspectives on research and practice.* Berkeley, CA: McCutchan.

Cuban, L. (1991). Reforming again, again and again. *Educational Researcher, 19*(1), 3–13.

diSessa, A. (1982). Unlearning Aristotelian physics: A study of knowledge-based learning. *Cognitive Science*, 6, 37–75.

Dole, J. A., & Niederhauser, D. S. (1991, April). The use of reading in conceptual change science. Paper presented at the annual meeting of the American Educational Research Association, Chicago.

Driver, R. (1983). *The pupil as scientist?* Milton Keynes, UK: Open University Press.

Ducharme, E. R., & McManus-Kluender, M. (1990). The RATE study: The faculty. *Journal of Teacher Education, 41*(4), 45–49.

Eisner, E. W. (1984). Can educational research inform practice? *Phi Delta Kappan, 66*, 447–452.

Elliot, J. (1989, December). *Studying the school curriculum through insider research: Some dilemmas.* Paper presented at the International Conference on School-Based Innovations: Looking Forward to the 1990s, Hong Kong.

Elmore, R. F. (1987). Reform and the culture of authority in the schools. *Educational Administration Quarterly, 23*(4), 60–78.

Finkelstein, M. J. (1984). *The American academic profession.* Columbus: Ohio State University Press.

Fullan, M. (1982). *The meaning of educational change.* New York: Teachers College Press.

Goodlad, J. I. (1984). *A place called school.* New York: McGraw-Hill.

Goodlad, J. I. (1990). *Teachers for our nation's schools.* San Francisco: Jossey-Bass.

Guskey, T. R. (1986). Staff development and the process of teacher change. *Educational Researcher, 15*(5), 5–12.

Hewson, P. W., & Hewson, M. (1988). An appropriate conception of teaching science: A view from studies of science learning. *Journal of Research in Science Teaching, 72*(5), 597–614.

Holmes Group. (1986). *Tomorrow's Teachers.* East Lansing, Ml: Author.

Holmes Group. (1990). *Tomorrow's schools: Principles for the design of professional development schools.* East Lansing, MI: Author.

Holmes Group. (199la). Far West regional meeting. *Holmes Group Forum.* East Lansing, Ml: Author.

Holmes Group. (1991b). South West regional meeting. *Holmes Group Forum.* East Lansing, MI: Author.

Howey, K. R., & Zimpher, N. L. (1989). *Profiles of preservice teacher education programs.* Albany: State University of New York Press.

Jackson, P. (1986). *The practice of teaching.* New York: Teachers College Press.

Judge, H. (1982). *American graduate schools of education: A view from abroad.* New York: Ford Foundation.

Lampert, M. (1985). Mathematics learning in context: The voyage of the Mimi. *Journal of Mathematical Behavior, 4,* 157–167.

Lampert, M. (1988). Connecting mathematical teaching and learning. In E. Fennema, T. Carpenter, & S. Lemon (Eds.), *Integrating research on teaching and learning mathematics.* Madison: University of Wisconsin, Wisconsin Center for Education Research.

Lampert, M. (1991). Looking at restructuring from within a restructured role. *Phi Delta Kappan, 72*(9), 670–674.

Lanier, J. E., & Little, J. W. (1986). Research on teacher education. In M. E. Wittrock (Ed.), *Handbook of research on teaching* (3rd ed.). New York: Macmillan.

Lawson, H. A. (1990). Constraints on the professional service of education faculty. *Journal of Teacher Education, 41*(4), 57–70.

McLaughlin, M. W. (1990). The Rand change agent study revisited: Macro perspectives and microrealities. *Educational Researcher, 19*(9), 11–16.

National Center for Education Statistics. (1990). *Selected characteristics of public and private school teachers: 1987–88.* Washington, DC: U.S. Department of Education.

National Council of Teachers of English (NCTE) (1988). *Report card on basal readers.* Urbana, IL: Author.

National Council of Teachers of Mathematics, Commission on Standards for School Mathematics. (1989). *Curriculum and evaluation standards for school mathematics.* Reston, VA: Author.

National Science Teachers Association (NSTA). (1989). Essential changes in secondary science: *Scope, sequence and coordination.* Washington, DC: Author.

Piaget, J. (1970). Piaget's theory. In P. Mussen (Ed.), *Carmichael's manual of child psychology* (Vol. 1). New York: Wiley.

Popkewitz, T. S., & Lind, K. (1989). Teacher incentives as reforms: Teachers' work and the changing control mechanism in education. *Teachers College Record, 90*(4), 575–594.

Porter, A. (1988). A curriculum out of balance: The case of elementary school mathematics. *Educational Researcher, 18*(5), 9–15.

Powell, A. G. (1976). *The uncertain profession: Harvard and the search for educational authority.* Cambridge, MA: Harvard University Press.

Putnam, R. T., Lampert, M., & Peterson, P. L. (1990). Alternative perspectives on knowing mathematics in elementary schools. *Review of Research in Education, 16*, 57–150.

Raths, J. (1991). Quoted in Field-based teacher education. (1991, March 13). *Education Week*, p. 23.

Roth, K., Rosaen, C. L., & Lanier, P. E. (1988). *Mentor teacher project program assessment report.* East Lansing: Michigan State University Press.

Schoenfeld, A. H. (1987). Cognitive science and mathematics education: An overview. In A. H. Schoenfeld (Ed.), *Cognitive science and mathematics education.* Hillsdale, NJ: Lawrence Erlbaum.

Schwebel, M. (1989). The new priorities and education faculty. In R. Wisniewski & E. R. Ducharme (Eds.), *The professors of teaching: An inquiry.* Albany: State University of New York Press.

Smith, E. L., & Anderson, C. W. (1984). Teaching science. In V. Richardson-Koehler (Ed.), *Educators handbook: A research perspective.* New York: Longman.

Stallings, J. A., & Kowalski, T. (1990). Research on professional development schools. In W. R. Houston (Ed.), *Handbook of research on teacher education.* New York: Macmillan.

Stenhouse, L. (1971). The humanities curriculum project: The rationale. *Theory into Practice, 10*, 154–162.

Stoddart, T. (1992). Commentary: Fostering coherence between constructivism on campus and conventional practice in schools. *Holmes Group Forum, 6*(2), 26–28.

Stoddart, T., Losk, D. J., & Benson, C. S. (1985). *Some reflections on the honorable profession of teaching* (Research rep. No. 85–1). Berkeley, CA: Institute of Governmental Studies.

Stodolsky, S. S. (1988). *The subject matters: Classroom activity in math and social studies.* Chicago: University of Chicago Press.

Sykes, G. (1990). Organizing policy into practice: Reactions to the cases. *Educational Evaluation and Policy Analysis, 12*(3), 243–247.

Tikunoff, W. J., & Ward, B. A. (1983). Collaborative research on teaching. *Elementary School Journal, 83*(4), 454–468.

Winitzky, N., Stoddart, T., & O'Keefe, P. (1992). Great expectations: Emergent professional development schools. *Journal of Teacher Education, 43*(1), 3–18.

Wisniewski, R., & Ducharme, E. R. (1989). Why study the education professorate? In R. Wisniewski & E. R. Ducharme (Eds.), *The professors of teaching: An inquiry*. Albany: State University of New York Press.

Zusman, A. (1985, March). Doctoral study in graduate schools of education: Conflict between research ethos and professional mission. Paper presented at the annual meeting of the Association for the Study of Higher Education, Chicago.

JAMES G. HENDERSON
and RICHARD D. HAWTHORNE

Chapter Four

The Dialectics of Creating
Professional Development Schools

REFLECTIONS ON WORK IN PROGRESS

In 1990, the Holmes Group called for the creation of Professional Development Schools (PDSs) to serve as catalysts in the reform of teaching, teacher development, and schools (Holmes Group, 1990). The mandate was clear; teacher education faculty must become active participants with their school-based colleagues in the facilitation of more meaningful learning for all students. The PDS initiative seemed to be a natural coalescence and extension of several educational change activities: supporting site-based, co-constructivist inquiry on teaching and teacher development; forming partnerships between school and university faculties; envisioning schools as the center of educational change; and fostering teacher and community empowerment.

At Kent State University, a cadre of teacher educators enthusiastically embraced this policy mandate. Given previous positive experiences with colleagues in school settings, our commitment to collaborative approaches to teacher development, and our willingness to confront the complex problems of teaching and schooling, we welcomed the opportunity to pursue the Holmes agenda for reform. The focus of our PDS work is on the formation of school-university professional communities to engage in critical problem solving for the purpose of vastly improving the quality of life and learning in schools and colleges of education. As Eisner (1992) noted, our particular focus is part of an important trend in educational research:

> Much recent research in the United States has focused on the quality and process of schooling. . . . As a result of this work a number of salient features of schools, many of which are quite common, across a variety of schools, have been identified: structural fragmentation, teacher isolation, didactic teaching, treaties between teachers and students, the particular ways in which effective teachers and school administrators relate to students, the emphasis on extrinsic rewards, and the like (pp. 619–620).

Though far more messy and disjointed than the description above captures, our efforts in qualitative change can be represented as several overlapping iterative phases: (a) establishing authentic collaboration for change, (b) socially constructing a moral leadership orientation, (c) practicing dialectical problem solving and critically refining a collective normative position, (d) engaging in an integrated cultural and pedagogical praxis tailored to each PDS site, and (e) undertaking College of Education reform. Following a description of each of these phases, we conclude by presenting a set of recommendations for critical PDS problem solving and reform activities.

ESTABLISHING AUTHENTIC COLLABORATION

Our PDS sites reflect a wide range of partnerships with area schools. One is a long-standing urban teacher education program for early childhood and elementary education students in which the initial teacher preparation program is based in five elementary schools and extends over four semesters. Cohorts of students take blocks of courses that have fully integrated field experience components that are supervised by classroom teachers. These same classroom teachers work directly with university faculty in the design, implementation, and evaluation of the program. Another site is a rural county coalition that supports teacher education students' early fieldwork, provides student teaching supervision, supports professional development activities co-designed by teachers, sustains a principals' academy, and houses a large, Federally-funded mathematics teacher development project jointly led by school and university faculty. This multidimensional site is also providing leadership in the development of an intellectually rich and pedagogically sound rural teacher education program directed toward able and talented area students.

A third site is a comprehensive high school where two teacher education professors, one in English, the other in science, work closely with their classroom counterparts in the development and enactment of experiences that will enhance the respective teacher education students' understanding of academic content, pedagogical content knowledge, students, and community. The English teacher education professor and an English classroom teacher have undertaken and continue to conduct a series of studies related to the teaching of writing and the teaching of prospective teachers about the teaching of writing. They exchange roles on a regular basis and team teach with each other in their respective classrooms. Several other sites with similar, yet contextually unique, collaborative projects came together to form our current 12 PDS sites.

Stimulated by regional and national Holmes Group meetings, university faculty from the relatively independent programs and projects began sharing the joys and frustrations that necessarily accompany such reform efforts. Informal airplane, hallway, and office discussions between two or three turned into regular sessions of sharing and support for eight to 12 teacher educators.

At the college-site sessions, and at many of the school sites, conversations moved from what we should be doing to what we were actually doing and what those practices meant. Narratives about practice were perceived as more pertinent than were abstract discussions about what should be done. On several occasions, colleagues very bluntly stated that we should not turn to the theoretical aspects of our reform efforts without first describing and analyzing what we were doing, why we were doing it, and what it all meant. In short, they wanted to return to the honest exchanges about their experiences, the problem solving they revealed, and the interpretative discussions that animated the initial, informal sessions. As teacher education faculty, we have found that when we talk in-depth about our individual PDS contexts and practices, we create and sustain a climate of trust, regard, support, and shared meaning making in our particular college context. We have also found that this is very difficult to do. The importance of authentic collaboration was dramatically reinforced at several different retreats, some held by specific PDS sites, others involving all sites. On one such occasion, the cross-site steering committee, in response to a request by several site leadership teams, planned a retreat for the purpose of training on proposal writing and designing actual proposals to address specific needs at each site. Deliberations were animated and inclusive, fostering consensus-building and joint problem solving and revealing reciprocal appreciation for the talents, insight, and professional commitments of one another. Once again, the focus was on the realities of the context of practice and students. The deliberations were authentic in large part because the problems under consideration were real and the exchanges were genuine. No power-over games, no theory-over-practice hegemony, and no simplistic technical answers to complex pedagogical problems were engaged. These virtues and skills developed over several years of disjointed and uncertain efforts to create collaborative problem solving.

CONSTRUCTING A MORAL LEADERSHIP ORIENTATION

Due in part to the progressively authentic dialogue representing our emerging maturity in collaborative work, discussions began to elucidate the commonplaces, values, assumptions, and perspectives embedded in our experiences. We recognized that our work was grounded in an unstated but powerful ethical orientation—a moral commitment that was non-negotiable and defined our sense of professional integrity. We rejected the tradition of individualistic liberalism that can be traced back to Hobbes, Locke, and the framers of the American Constitution. As Barber (1984) documented, this form of liberalism is highly distrustful of shared civic activity. Embedded within it is the inevitability of social and political competition: "Autonomous individuals occupying private and separate spaces are the players in the game of liberal politics; conflict is their characteristic mode of interaction" (Barber, 1984, p.4). Because all values are relative to self-interested individuals or social groups, win-lose conflicts are inevitable.

We did not uncritically accept this self-centered, conflict-ridden *mythos*, though we certainly recognized that our basic beliefs and attitudes have been influenced by this sense of "negative freedom" (Greene, 1988) and its social policy implications. We agreed with Barber (1984) that:

> Autonomy is not the condition of democracy, democracy is the condition of autonomy. Without participating in the common life that defines them and in the decision-making that shapes their social habitat, women and men cannot become individuals. Freedom, justice, equality, and autonomy are all products of common thinking and common living; democracy creates them. (p. xv)

As our work evolved, we increasingly became committed to a "strong" sense of participatory democracy (Barber, 1984). In current educational vernacular, our democratic commitment led us to embrace a co-constructivist orientation. We found that meanings in policy and practice contexts must be continuously negotiated by all participants. We understood that we could not practice leadership justified by bureaucratic, psychological, or technocratic sources of authority (Sergiovanni, 1990). We chose to ground our PDS practice on the civic and professional virtues of participative democracy, pedagogical praxis, and collegiality. These were the shared beliefs and commitments that provided the moral authority for our work (Sergiovanni, 1992, pp. 204–206).

DIALECTICAL PROBLEM-SOLVING AND REFLECTION

Our moral leadership orientation required, and continues to require, us to confront four dialectical predicaments that manifest themselves in unique ways at each of our PDS sites. These predicaments can be stated as four questions: (1) How do educational organizations shift from a power-over to a shared power relationship? (2) How do we transform individualistic practices into community-grounded practices? (3) How do we encourage co-constructivist teaching over narrow technical teaching? (4) How do we evaluate our work on the basis of long-term qualitative impact rather than reductionistic achievement measures? These four dialectics frame the transitional status of our problem solving and critical reflections. We are literally midstream between our socialization into one culture and our efforts to move toward the foggy shore of another.

To further complicate this dialectical problem solving, our moral leadership orientation did not automatically provide the critical scaffolding we needed to guide our daily work. We needed to look within as colleagues co-constructing a sense of the common good in our own reform practices. We formed our critical scaffolding through sharing and analyzing stories and other artifacts from our PDS work. Through examination of our language, the ways we were framing problems, the problems we chose to engage and not engage, and our embedded values and assumptions, we established a practice-oriented "coda" that remains open to continuous refinement. An elaboration of the four dialectical predicaments describes the problematics from which our critical coda emerged.

Predicament One: From Power-Over Management to
Democratic Power Sharing

While expressed differently in each of the various PDS sites, the central concern has been that of power sharing. The distribution of power within most schools and colleges of education is that typically found in bureaucratically structured organizations. Policy boards (including unions) and administrators control hiring, personnel evaluation, and the distribution of rewards; make teaching assignments; allocate funds for and plan professional development activities for teachers/professors; and control the allocation of time for curriculum and professional development work.

Collaboration implicitly means that power—the ability to allocate resources toward the attainment of selected ends—will be shared. Collaboration also suggests that framing the foci and criteria for evaluation will be deliberated and decided by all parties.

The evolution from power-over to shared power is a journey that tests the resolve of one's commitment to democratic values. The desire to retreat to the comfort of familiar bureaucratic structures and norms to obtain a sense of security or closure is ever-present and compelling. For many, the uncertainty and messiness of democratic processes evoke a strong sense of personal vulnerability. For others, there is insufficient assurance that power sharing will in fact lead to better teaching and learning.

In more than one PDS site, the dominance of power-over relationships is so ingrained that neither principals nor teachers even consider the possibility of sharing power to address the problematics of their work. Yet at one site, the principal has scheduled times for several cooperating teachers and interns to meet on a regular basis to address concerns or matters of professional interest. In a very incremental way, teachers in several schools are beginning to consider curriculum and professional development needs of their own.

At one of the initial PDS sites (now a major PDS site affiliated with a neighboring university), the faculty addressed the power-sharing issue by forming a faculty senate. While faculty senates are not particularly novel today, this one served as a prototype for others five years ago. Key to its success has been the repeated enhancement of group communication skills, faculty-initiated workshops for learning conflict resolution strategies, and a variety of self-assessment and action planning activities. This self-renewing capability was fostered, then tolerated, and now celebrated by various central office managers. The initial and very strongly expressed support of a central office leader provided a safety net for the first three years, and active involvement and consistent support by several principals who were committed to shared decision making was also instrumental. Successes led to greater efficacy, that led to more successes. What we have learned from this instance of shared power is that it requires sharing by all parties—parents, board of education, central office personnel, principals, teachers, and university faculty and administrators. Learning how to share power while working in a power-over culture is also a developmental process with a steep learning curve. We know well the rules and playing field of the power-over game, and thus find it easier to verbalize than actualize the tenets of participatory democracy.

The ethics of participatory democracy were assertively addressed at one PDS site. Key teacher leaders from the school district were asked to meet with their university counterparts—without the presence of school or university line administrators—in order to establish power-sharing "ground rules. " This step became necessary when the reform activities, which were expanding in scope, began to be corrupted by persistent top-down, bureaucratic beliefs and related procedures. Once the school and university faculty had established the ground rules, they were shared with the appropriate line administrators.

At the time of completing this chapter, the impact of this assertive action is not clear. The administrators, either at the school district and/or at the university, may not alter their methods of operation. If this happens, the PDS work may continue at this school district site but on a limited basis. The necessary collaborative foundation for a broader, systemic reform effort will not have been established. Compounding this problem are communication difficulties between a key district office staff member and one of the collaborating university professors. In effect, four years of PDS work at this site is at risk since the personal and social structural obstacles may be too great to overcome.

Predicament Two: From Individualistic Practice to Professional Community

Breaking down the walls of isolation and privatism that are integral to contemporary professional practice in schools and universities is closely related to the development of an organizational culture of shared power. Within the cultures of schools and colleges, staying isolated and keeping professional beliefs and practices private become part of the protective coloration required to survive.

Creating a professional community requires, among other conditions, extensive opportunities to talk with each other about matters of consequence, to publicly review the joys, warts, and knots that necessarily accompany the messiness of pedagogical practice, to be empathic toward others' personal and professional beliefs, and to establish a common conceptual framework and ethos to guide collaborative planning, acting, and reflecting. Creating time and developing the capacity to engage in such substantive and caring dialogue is problematic (Noddings, 1984). Time allocated for this form of deliberation frequently means less time for doing those things deemed most valuable by the achievement test culture. At the Kent State site, we have found time to talk in informal and formal ways. Trips to conferences, hallway conversations, and telephone exchanges typify the informal exchanges. More formal times have been designated for steering committee and task force committee meeting, writing sessions, mini-conferences, and full PDS Consortium meetings. In these varied forums we attempt to obtain a balance in the sharing of practice-based stories, deliberating on how to envision and organize our work, and critically reflecting on both practice and vision.

At another site, a teacher educator has established a series of cooperative learning workshops. The first round of introductory workshops were so well received that, with the direct involvement of now cooperative experienced teachers, he designed and offered advanced workshops. The experienced teachers have become the primary instructors in several rounds of introductory and advanced workshops. It is important to underscore that the workshops, while addressing very useful knowledge and providing excellent training in an area of high interest today, are really as much a device for engaging faculty in dialogue with each other about their practices and the beliefs they carry. What starts out as a focus on a particular model of teaching rather quickly becomes a context for very serious discussions and critical reflections leading toward exploration of alternative ways of thinking about students, teaching, learning, and curriculum in general.

Authentic dialogue frequently places honest disagreements in direct confrontation with a collegially oriented ethic of caring. Part of the conflict stems from our collective ignorance of and/or experience with group process facilitation. There is continuous tension between our individualistic past and our attempts to create community.

Predicament Three: From Technical Rationality to Pedagogical Reasoning

The dominant perspective for framing problems of teaching is technical rationality characterized by the specificity of ends, linear reasoning, measurability, and control of imaginative problem solving (Schon, 1983). In contrast, pedagogical reasoning is a form of praxis in which what is good, right, and just for children actively guides all teaching-learning deliberations. Unlike technical rationality, pedagogical reasoning acknowledges and grows out of the centrality of educational values. It also acknowledges the uncertainty and messiness of the context and problem solving associated with professional educational practice. Finally, pedagogical reasoning acknowledges that because of the uncertainty and value-based nature of professional practice, there is continuous tension over values and related practices.

This leads to a problem with the practice of shared pedagogical reasoning. Who decides what values are to frame the educational vision and define the quality indicators of educational practice? Who decides what the focus of problem solving should be? A related predicament is one acknowledged by Jackson (1968) when he wondered whether the rush of the day-to-day realities of classroom teaching were amenable to reflection-in-action. Can the typical teacher, confronted with the physical, emotional, and intellectual tasks of teaching, transcend it all to critically assess his or her practice? Clearly, the bureaucratic culture of most schools and the approach-avoidance pattern toward the value of teaching expressed in most higher education institutions suggest not. In contrast, PDS work is grounded on the belief that teachers can engage in a rich deliberative praxis.

Finally, there is the predicament that takes the form of an expectation that teacher education faculty are pedagogical experts who teach others how they should address the problems of teaching. The belief that there are best ways to teach that are revealed through research or theoretical reflections conducted by these experts has only recently been challenged openly and effectively. Likewise, it is only recently that the belief that teachers can be researchers of their own individual and collective practice has been granted credibility. This shift from the dominance of technical rationality, which searches for generalizations and predictive control done largely by expert researchers from the outside of the action space, to a pedagogical reasoning in which teachers and teacher educators seek understandings of teaching and learning within the action space of schools is a major change in the culture of the school and in the epistemology of educational practice. There are some wonderful and powerful examples in the literature of such shared inquiry leading to new ways of thinking about practice in the context of practice (McDonald, 1986; Holly, 1989; Eisner, 1992).

In the urban teacher education program for early childhood and elementary education students, a collaborative action research project has recently been established. The focus of the project, which is not yet completed, is on program participants' core educational beliefs. The key participants in the program are the university-based director, several faculty associates (supervising teachers who serve as liaisons between the university and the school sites), the cooperating classroom teachers, and the university interns. The operation of the program requires an enormous amount of dialogue: face-to-face and phone conversations, frequent clinical supervision, and two different weekly seminars. One of the results of all of this professional interaction has been conflicts over the meaning of "good teaching." In particular, there have been fundamental differences over the relative emphasis on classroom discipline and instruction. To paraphrase one participant, "What is more important in the classroom, management or teaching?" Conflicts over this question emerge from the participants' core personal-professional beliefs, which are not in all cases well-formulated. Given the amount of their daily contact, the negotiation of basic beliefs is particularly important for the cooperating teachers and their interns.

The purpose of the collaborative action research project is to examine differences in core beliefs on teaching. The hope is that through deeper insight into this communication problem, a stronger sense of community can be established in the program and better matches can be made between cooperating teachers and their interns. Though the inquiry work may not lead to final solutions, at least basic beliefs will be more openly examined, and the problem of fundamental value conflicts will be more frankly acknowledged.

One of our PDS sites is connected with the college's elementary education Master of Arts in Teaching (MAT) Program. Three research teams are involved in collaborative inquiry at this site, focusing respectively on the topics of inclusion, whole language, and curriculum integration. Each team is composed of an intermediate grade teacher, a primary grade teacher, and a student teacher. The team's action research projects, which are designed in part to enhance faculty dialogue on the targeted topic, appear to be having the desired effect. According to the school district's director of staff development, there has been increased faculty conversation on the three research topics, both within individual schools and between schools in the district. In addition, a number of teachers have asked the director to organize a formal panel presentation on the topics of inclusion and whole language.

Our early childhood education PDS site spans five schools in distinctive rural, suburban, and urban school districts. There are several action inquiry projects under way at this highly diversified site. One of the projects involves collaboration between a college of education professor, who is working at the site, and a doctoral student, who is engaged in dissertation research. Through the use of a narrative methodology, the doctoral student is inquiring into the processes by which PDS projects are convened by university faculty. The goal is to throw light on the following questions: Is there any necessary or sufficient background for this type of reform leadership? How do professors deal with the inevitable role conflicts associated with negotiating two very different organizational cultures? Do professors possess sufficient political leverage to help schools become action research organizations? The most likely result of this collaborative research will be a careful, thorough narrative on the dilemmas associated with convening a PDS site. These dilemmas, which, of course, will be site-specific, will most likely reflect the four predicaments covered in this chapter.

All three of these action research projects are guided by the norm of pedagogical reasoning. The overriding purpose is to foster meaningful dialogue and to encourage the development of a collegial synergy premised on personal and institutional differences. From a radically different perspective, the point of view of technical rationality, there is no need for this type of work. The norm of technical rationality directs attention to a different research agenda, one focusing on measurability and control. If teachers are expected to follow prescribed protocols, or, at the very least, to achieve standardized student learning outcomes, there is no need or time for the messiness of meaningful professional dialogue and collegial trust building. In fact, this type of work would actually inhibit efficient learning production. Furthermore, from this point of view, education professors should not be allowed to distract school employees from their appropriate duties. The professors should stay focused on their proper role, which is to help create and dispense the knowledge base necessary for quality educational outputs.

Predicament Four: From Evaluation of Productivity to Evaluation of Impact

In spite of the emergence of such policies as authentic evaluation, portfolio evaluation, and outcomes-based education in recent years, successful teaching is still defined in terms of student academic achievement as measured by standardized tests, not by indicators of the quality of life or the quality of learning experienced by students. In the university, successful professorship is defined in terms of scholarly productivity and advancement in professional organizations far more than it is by the quality of life or learning experienced by students or the impact of one's engagement in school or teacher education reform. A related and important factor to consider in relation to this predicament is that the majority of teachers and teacher education faculty directly involved in PDS sites are female, and in the case of the university faculty, the males and females most directly involved are nontenured as well. The concern is obvious. How do we address the serious work of teaching, school, and teacher education reform if those who evaluate others' professional lives and actions do not assess the impact of that work on the quality of life and learning and reform in each of the contexts? How might we assess the quality of such PDS work and ensure that the assessment is authentic, rigorous, meaningful, and just?

The teacher education faculty at Kent State have taken a major step forward in addressing this knotty matter. A growing number of teacher education faculty who are invested in PDS values, goals, and processes but are not necessarily engaged in PDS sites outside the College of Education, are members of the pertinent promotion and tenure committee. At the promotion and tenure committee meetings as well as at full departmental meetings, the nature and importance of PDS work and the implications of junior professors being engaged so fully in such work have been discussed. To enhance an understanding of the implications and to render the reviews more comprehensive and authentic, a portfolio assessment procedure has been instituted. The first phase of the portfolio is the individual faculty member's own description and rationale of his or her professorship. The intent is to make public the blend of organizational expectations and individual perspectives on what teaching, service, scholarship, and reform activities mean and how they intertwine to form a holistic conception of the professorship in relation to PDS work.

Beyond the description and rationale of the PDS professorship, faculty arc asked to place in the portfolio the conventional descriptions and assessments of their teaching, service, reform, and scholarly activities. Key to the portfolio are the narrative descriptions and analyses of one's PDS activities and accumulative documentation that illustrate how teacher education field and clinical work has evolved and improved, how professional development work has progressed at the PDS site, and how the processes of inquiry and collaborative problem solving are enacted by the professor and colleagues at the site.

Another important aspect of the portfolio is the section in which faculty develop and present their own in-depth evaluation of their work and its impact. Finally, it is highly recommended that each faculty member work with a mentor over the several years of review and the critical year of tenure/promotion. It is the ongoing development of one' s own professorial maturity on the one hand and the growing understanding of the evaluators about PDS work in general and the faculty members' own integration of scholarship, teaching, professional leadership, and reform work on the other that enables the elusive complexities of initiating PDS collaboration to take on substantive dimensions.

The first faculty members to write and document their portfolios were in their third and fourth years of employment as assistant professors, or were untenured associate professors in their first or second year of review. The amount of time they spent trying to construct what they thought "we" wanted in a portfolio that would best represent the diversity and impact of their work as professors was extensive to say the least. The reactions to the task were twofold: first, frustration and anger. It was universally viewed as a painful, humiliating, and an all-consuming task: "If you really want to know what I do and if I make any difference doing it, come out with me and talk with my school-based colleagues;" and second, awe and appreciation. Those who mentored and those who read the portfolios felt they had a much more comprehensive and in-depth understanding of their colleagues' respective PDS efforts. These are the initial experiences with portfolio assessment of teacher education faculty. Much more needs to be done to expand our conceptions of impact, to develop alternative means to obtain more diverse authentic descriptions, and to evolve and make public a new set of criteria that represent the basis for tenure and promotion judgments. This is essential work if we are to attract and keep faculty in colleges of education who see themselves as key players in the reform of teaching, schooling, and teacher education.

OUR COLLECTIVE NORMATIVE POSITION

Confronting the four dialectics on a daily basis over a two-year period through extensive collegial dialogue, a public normative referent to guide our transitional leadership efforts was derived. Space does not permit the complete reproduction of our policy statement; however, its essence is captured in the following three paragraphs:

> This policy statement is the product of an eighteen month process of participatory democracy. It is not a final definitive statement on our common PDS values and concerns but rather a working document that can be changed at any time through continuing dialogue. The ideas in this policy statement are less important than our continuing commitment to complete participation by all members in the PDS Consortium.
>
> Professional Development Schools are settings in which communities of learners are engaged in professional development relationships that enable best practice through shared inquiry. Within the Consortium, professional development relationships take a variety of forms such as partnerships among individuals within a school or college; memberships from several schools or constituencies; and formal partnerships between the College of Education and particular schools.
>
> PDS Consortium members are engaged in work that is characterized by commitment to the values of collaboration, participative democracy, diversity, active meaning-making through inquiry, building caring communities of learners, life-long learning, willingness to negotiate differences and to undertake change consistent with PDS values and processes.

CULTIVATING CULTURAL AND PEDAGOGICAL PRAXIS

The values and processes of our policy statement serve as the normative referent for two interactive forms of praxis: cultural change praxis and pedagogical praxis. We are using Hodgkinson's (1991) conception of praxis: Praxis . . . implies a duality in action, two 'moments'; one of consciousness or reflection in the first moment and one of action and commitment in the second moment. Praxis involves critical reflection about our pedagogical intentions and practices; it involves the steady recursive rhythm of action, evaluation, further action, further evaluation, and so on.

Cultural change praxis is reflective action that attends to the "ways we do things here" (Deal, 1989). The "things" that define the culture of schools and colleges of education include the organizational structure, climate, teaching, classroom management, curriculum, and evaluation. "The ways we do those things" include our communication patterns, decision-making routines, political behaviors, social interactions, and affiliations with one another. One of the perspectives we are finding helpful in inquiring into and reflecting on our site cultures comes from organizational development. We are using Schmuck's organizational development orientation, because it is based on a commitment to strong democratic principles and processes (Clarke, 1991, 1992). This approach to organizational development is also committed to ongoing inquiry and reflection on the school culture and building the capacity of the faculty to solve their organizational problems and continuously renew themselves as learners.

Pedagogical praxis grounds authentic cultural change praxis. It entails what van Manen (1992) termed a sense of pedagogy, "that one is capable of perceptive insights into the child's being or character. It also implies one has a grasp of what is good for children and for their healthy development" (p. 4). We choose to use the construct of pedagogical praxis to keep our work clearly centered on the ultimate measure of PDS reform: the creation of programs, practices, and contexts that enhance the quality of life and learning of children. Pedagogical praxis involves seeking understanding of our curricular intentions and practices, framing teaching and learning problems from a pedagogical perspective, and reflecting on our intentions and actions in terms of pedagogical virtues. It means systematically gathering data about the ways we teach, developing relations with students, making curriculum decisions, and acting on the full range of educational problems that form the pedagogical substance of our transformational efforts.

As teacher education and college of education faculty members, pedagogical reasoning and the critical reflection and inquiry it represents is not a perspective directed at schools and the attendant problems they address. A clear intent of the Holmes Group, as evidenced in the most recent publication they have produced, titled *Tomorrow's Schools of Education*, is to effect significant reform in teacher education and professional development, and to reform the policy and inquiry posture and programs of schools and colleges of education. Such reform efforts necessarily entail cultural and pedagogical praxis and change in our own College of Education. Accordingly we established ourselves as a PDS site. This meant and continues to mean that as teacher education and PDS faculty we must wear two "hats," one signifying our identity as integral members of a school-based PDS effort, the other signaling our identity as a professor and member of a college of education PDS effort. As suggested earlier, it is much easier to study someone else's context and conduct—to engage in cultural and pedagogical praxis with them in their context—than to turn the focus on one's own context and conduct. There is much to learn as we move past the nascent stages of our own maturity as a PDS site.

RECOMMENDATIONS FOR PDS PRAXIS BASED ON A WORK IN PROGRESS

Our qualitatively focused PDS reform work has undergone several iterative phases as we learn how to transform ourselves. We have established the beginnings of authentic collaboration with colleagues in varied PDS sites. We have taken the time to establish meaningful, reciprocal dialogue over concrete reform efforts and are discovering a common ground. We have conceptualized a demanding transitional leadership associated with a value-added orientation. And we have openly confronted the dialectics associated with our transitional and transformative work. Finally, we have initiated combined cultural change and pedagogical praxis projects at five of our PDS sites and in our College of Education. Based on our experiences to date, we offer the following recommendations for consideration by those engaged in or contemplating PDS reform work.

1. PDS reform efforts must be grounded in authentic dialogue over meaningful qualitative changes. If the focus is not on "the processes of schooling and . . . the context in which those processes occur" (Eisner, 1992, p. 621), change will most likely be superficial.
2. All participants in the reform effort must reject narrow technical solutions. They must readily embrace a moral transformative leadership position. PDS reform cannot be engineered by detached technical specialists. Technical considerations need not be rejected; they simply cannot be allowed to dominate.
3. One clear indication that the reform effort is both honest and value-added will be the emergence of dialectical tensions. If complex predicaments do not emerge, then most likely the transformative effects will be short-lived and faddish in nature.

4. Critical reflection on authentic reform predicaments should be public and ongoing. Without this commitment to a critical praxis, the initial qualitative change focus will not mature into an iterative co-constructivist activity. Reform interpretations will once again be shallow, underdeveloped, and private.
5. Efforts must be made to harmonize cultural change with specific pedagogical change efforts. We cannot ask teachers to engage in more sophisticated pedagogical reasoning without also reforming the social context in which that reasoning occurs.
6. An authentic, long-term PDS focus must include organizational development and pedagogical change efforts within the College of Education. Teacher educators must not function as experts telling others how to change; they must see themselves as part of the complex change problem and as responsible parties in the problem-solving process.

These recommendations can be phrased and ordered in different ways. However, we find the spirit conveyed by them to be pedagogically, morally, and pragmatically compelling as we conduct our PDS reform work.

Our critical PDS work at Kent State University has only begun. We cannot claim that we have made great strides in transforming the organizational cultures or pedagogical practices within the consortium of PDS sites. Nor can we claim that the individuals in these organizations are now more deeply committed to the critical values we espouse in either their educational activities or collegial interactions. We are fully aware that the processes of evolving new belief systems take large amounts of time and energy. We have made a start in honest reform and so far have not settled for cosmetic change. We believe we are embarked on realizing the qualitative transformational potential of PDS rhetoric.

REFERENCES

Barber, B. R. (1984). *Strong democracy: Participatory politics for a new age.* Berkeley: University of California Press.

Clarke, J. (1991/92). Richard Schmuck: Organization development—building communities of learners. *Cooperative Learning, 12*(2), 14–17.

Deal, T. E. (1989). The culture of schools. In L. T. Scheive & M. B. Schoenheit (Eds.), *Leadership: Examining the elusive.* Alexandria, VA: Association for Supervision and Curriculum Development.

Eisner, E. (1992). Educational reform and the ecology of schooling. *Teachers College Record, 93*(4), 610–626.

Greene, M. (1988). *The dialectic of freedom.* New York: Teachers College Press.

Hodgkinson, H. (1991). Reform versus reality. *Phi Delta Kappan 73*(1), 9–16.

Holly, M. L. (1989). *Writing to grow: Keeping a personal-professional journal.* Portsmouth, NH: Heinemann.

Holmes Group (1990). *Tomorrow's schools: Principles for the design of professional development schools.* East Lansing, MI: Author.

Jackson, P. (1968). *Life in classrooms.* New York: Holt, Rhinehart and Winston.

McDonald, J. (1986). Raising the teacher's voice and the ironic role of theory. *Harvard Education Review, 56*(4), 355–379.

Noddings, N. (1984). *Caring: A feminine approach to ethics and moral education.* Berkeley: University of California Press.

Schon, D. A. (1983). *The reflective practitioner.* New York: McGraw-Hill.

Sergiovanni, T. J. (1990). *Value-added leadership: How to get extraordinary performance in schools.* San Diego: Harcourt Brace Jovanovich.

Sergiovanni, T. J. (1992). Moral authority and the regeneration of supervision. In C. Glickman (Ed.), *Supervision in transition* (pp. 203–214). Alexandria, VA: ASCD.

Van Manen, M. (1992). Reflectivity and the pedagogical moment: The normativity of pedagogical thinking and acting. *Curriculum Studies, 23*(5), 507–561.

JAMES L. COLLINS

Chapter Five

Listening But Not Hearing

PATTERNS OF COMMUNICATION
IN AN URBAN SCHOOL-UNIVERSITY PARTNERSHIP

In a recent article examining the "culture of power" in society in general and schools in particular, Delpit quoted a black teacher from an urban elementary school:

> When you're talking to White people they still want it to be their way. You can try to talk to them and give them examples, but they're so headstrong, they think they know what's best for *everybody*, for *everybody's* children. They won't listen, White folks are going to do what they want to do *anyway*. It's really hard. They just don't listen well. No, they listen, but they don't *hear*—you know how your mama used to say you listen to the radio, but you *hear* your mother? Well they don't *hear* me. (Delpit, 1988, p. 280)

In this chapter, I use the metaphor of differences between *listening* and *hearing* to describe how competing channels of communication can co-exist in the midst of a professional development collaboration. My focus is on different perceptions of literacy instruction held by university-based and school-based educators in an urban school–university partnership. I argue that these differences are sustained by a mode of communication in which the university-based educators "listen to but do not hear" the school-based educators. I describe what "hearing" one of the school-based educators would be like by quoting excerpts from interviews with her and by applying what she has said to an interpretation of the differing perceptions of literacy instruction.

In this report, I call the school-based educator from whose interviews I quote Mrs. Donaldson, which is not her real name. The interviews are part of a larger ethnographic study of the same school-university partnership and use an in-depth, three-interview process: personal history, current practice, and reflection on the meaning of the first two interviews (after Seidman, 1991 and Cleary, 1991). In this paper, I present Mrs. Donaldson's perspective on education and schooling in her own words from sections of the interviews dealing with similar themes. The excerpts have been edited only as was necessary to render spoken language in writing.

The interviews, and other data from document analysis and participant observation, allow me to situate Mrs. Donaldson's perception of literacy instruction in its broad social setting. Stoddart (1993) also writes about school and university educators who seem to be "talking at each other but not hearing each other" (p. 14), and her analysis of the problem takes place at the institutional level. She describes tensions in a professional development school in terms of a conflict originating in the opposition between a transmissionist approach to teaching on the part of the school and a constructivist approach on the part of the university. The full ethnographic project from which this report is taken supports her description of competing pedagogical stances, but it also recommends an additional interpretive framework, one based in social dimensions of education, for understanding tensions between school-based and university-based educators. This report is a first step in that direction.

THE COLLABORATION

For four years, the Graduate School of Education at the State University of New York at Buffalo has had a professional development relationship with a public urban middle school. The school serves an African-American neighborhood and has 600 students across two levels: an early childhood center, grades pre-K through two, and an academy, grades three through eight. On eight Thursdays over a six-month period, a professor from the university visits the school with five graduate students in a teacher preparation program, and they work with all of the school's sixth graders, about 50 students in two classes. The collaboration also brings the sixth graders and their teachers to the university campus six times each year. The purposes of the project are to provide school-based pre-practicum tutoring and teaching experiences for the graduate students, and to enhance the literacy learning and college aspirations of the sixth graders.

Each year, the centerpiece of the collaboration is a series of writing tasks culminating in the publication of an anthology of the sixth graders' writing. On Tuesdays during the project, participating graduate students meet with the university professor for about two hours to discuss their work in the project and to design or revise the writing tasks and to make specific plans for using them. On teaching days, they arrive at the school about 8:30 A.M. and share their plans for the day's activities with the two sixth-grade teachers until about 9:15. At 9:30, they start working with one of the classes and continue the work for about 40 minutes. Next, they break from the teaching activities and one of them reads a literary selection to the students. Then they change rooms and repeat the morning's activities with the other class, ending about 1 1:00.

During the third year of the collaborative project, the series of writing tasks began with a brief self-introductory piece and then two pieces about their neighborhood, first in a personal narrative mode and then in a descriptive mode. Members of the university team used a multiple-draft, highly collaborative style of teaching and conferring with writers individually and in small groups. Their approach consisted mostly of modeling writing processes by collaborating and even coauthoring with students. To illustrate how the method worked, I will provide an example consisting of two pieces of writing, the first produced by one of the sixth graders working alone in response to the assignment, "Tell us about something that happened in your neighborhood," and the second written immediately after the first by the same sixth grader in collaboration with one of the university tutors.

First Sample
I almost got shot by a man. He was tall and was wearing a black leather jacket. First I threw a snowball at his car. Second he backed his car to where my friends were. Third he got out the car. Then he had the gun in his hand and when he took me and yanked me by my coat collar and let me go and said go get your father. Finally me and my friends walked to school.

Second Sample
It was really hot in the gym and we were all sweating. I could not believe we had played for two hours. We were tired and it was getting to the end of the game. The score was 166 to 160 and we were winning. In the last minute they scored and got a foul shot to make the lead only two. Then we scored a three pointer and it was 169 to 164 and their coach called a time out. He was mad and told his team to fight. When we came out after the time out, it was their ball and we thought it was over, but they scored a three pointer to get back within two points of our lead. Then, in the last seconds they scored to tie the game!

The game went into overtime and now we were so tired we could barely run. I got hurt and went out of the game and in the last two seconds of overtime Sam[1] missed a three pointer and the coach called a time out and put me in. After the time out, Sam shot a three point shot and the coach jumped in the air and said 'Go in please!' The ball missed and the rebound tipped over to me and I got it and threw it back to Sam. Sam shot it over and made it to win the game!

The other team was mad. When they tried to fight us, we pulled down their shorts and left them standing in front of the crowd in their underwear! Our coach gave me the game ball for playing hurt and still making the big play. Sam and I celebrated by going to Disney World. We went on every ride twice!

In addition to illustrating the instructional approach favored by the university team, these two writing samples can also be used to begin to illustrate the different perceptions of literacy instruction held by the university-based and school-based educators. Field notes show that the two teams of educators tacitly disagreed on the form and function of writing instruction. While the university educators believed strongly in their highly collaborative approach, the school educators saw such close tutor-student collaboration as possibly allowing students to avoid much of the real work school requires. The university team saw coauthored writing as a way of modeling how writers behave and as an efficient, hands-on means of teaching the sixth-grade students to make their writing longer, fuller, more coherent, and more interesting. The school team saw partnership as sometimes substituting friendship for authority, a substitution that can undermine a serious attitude about schoolwork in favor of an overly playful one, as in the example of the basketball story.

Different perceptions of literacy instruction between educators in the same school-university partnership suggest a lack of communication between the partners. To illustrate the patterns of communication operating between the school-based and university-based educators, I will describe the process of creating the specific tasks, the writing the sixth graders produced in response to them, and the school and university educators' reactions to the students' writing. Field notes show that the writing tasks were designed by the university-based educators because the university professor thought that designing the tasks, trying them out in the context of collaborative teaching, and evaluating the results were valuable teacher-preparation experiences for the graduate students. Once the tasks were drafted, the university-based educators shared them at meetings with the school-based educators to make any necessary changes.

At the initial planning session involving both sets of educators at the start of the third year of the collaboration, the university professor met with two educators from the school and told them that he would like to use neighborhood life as the focus of student writing in the project. He described the first writing task as a personal narrative about neighborhood events and as a telling of stories to construct and share an understanding of everyday life. He also described a possible subsequent task in which students would compare their own views of life in their neighborhood to newspaper stories about events in the neighborhood and adjacent sections of the city. One of the school-based educators asked if the students would be allowed to write negative remarks about the neighborhood. The professor replied affirmatively and explained that the primary purpose of the task was to have students use writing as a means of constructing and valuing their own meanings. He also said that he had used neighborhood life as a focus for student writing several times while teaching in an urban high school and that most students had produced long, pleasant reminiscences about growing up in their neighborhoods. His remarks persuaded the two educators from the school to accept, or at least not to object to, the use of the neighborhood topic.

When the university educators subsequently met by themselves to plan the writing tasks, they worked on the precise wording of both the narrative task involving writing about the neighborhood and the descriptive task comparing student descriptions of neighborhood life to published media descriptions. They decided to use a planning sheet to help students get started, and this is reproduced in Figure 5.1.

The planning sheet suggests that the university-based educators expected the students to write about ordinary events of their choosing in a structured way, including a plot with a beginning, middle, and end, and a climax or "most interesting or exciting part." Field notes and other documents suggest two other expectations on the part of the university-based educators: that the sixth graders would portray their neighborhood in mostly positive terms by telling stories of their experiences growing up in a tightly-knit community and that the sixth graders' narratives would show a contrast with media descriptions of the section of the city that includes the neighborhood, descriptions that were almost uniformly negative in their focus on drugs, violence, gangs, break-ins, and shootings. Their idea for the descriptive writing in the second task was to build on the narrative writing by having students compare their neighborhood stories to the newspaper accounts of life on their side of the city. The university-based educators would then have them write about differences between their accounts of life in the neighborhood and newspaper accounts.

When the sixth graders wrote in response to the initial neighborhood writing task, however, they did not portray their neighborhood in positive terms. Many of the stories they told, especially in the longer, better pieces of writing, were every bit as negative as the newspaper accounts, perhaps more so because they were told from a personal point of view. Here are two examples:

> I live on [street name], and our corners are atrocious. There are drug users and drug pushers there. There is trash everywhere, too. My mother does not like me to go to [street name], because ugly men stand on the corners. There are needles on the street.
>
> This is a sad story. This girl named Martha[2] went to the store for her mother. Two men were fighting. One of the men took a gun out of his truck and tried to shoot the other man, but he missed and it hit Martha. She died instantly.
>
> It is sad that people can be so mean to others by using drugs and killing. I wish it would all stop. If they do these bad things in front of kids and we see

Getting Started on Your Neighborhood Story

1. First, think of some things that happened in your neighborhood. They can
   be things that happened to you or things you saw happen. List these as
   "Possible Ideas."

Possible Ideas

2. Now choose one of your ideas to be the one you'll write about. Put it in
   the "Main Idea" box.

Main Idea

3. Next, think about your "story line" by writing notes in the "What happened" boxes.

What Happened First

What Happened at the Most Interesting or Exciting Part

What Happened at the End

Fig. 5.1. Planning Sheet for the Neighborhood Writing Task.

this, our future is going to be bad, too. The cops are on the corners everyday. They don't let anyone stand on the corners if they got three or more dollars in their pockets.

I will like to be a mayor, so I could throw away all the bad people forever.

* * *

There was a male rapist near my neighborhood a few months ago. The rapist was raping girls between the ages of 9 and 16 years old. When he first raped a few girls, the [name of newspaper] started handing out description papers.

When some neighborhood residents, who were the angry mothers of young girls, got together and researched they found out that the man had been at large for over a year. The police thought that by hiding the case they could catch the man easier without alerting the residents.

After awhile a girl across the street from my cousin got raped. She bit the man on the hand as an act of self-defense. The residents were informed that the man was ' using a weapon to force the girls into abandoned places where the victims were raped.

I was scared to go outside after I heard about it. I was only allowed to stay near my street, and I had to inform my mother to where I was going. We haven't heard of any other attacks and people are starting to feel better and safe again.

The university-based educators were surprised by the negative portraits of neighborhood life in the students' stories, and several of them attributed the negative qualities of the finished pieces to the language and structure of the planning sheet, especially the request for a "most interesting or exciting part." They felt in retrospect that the planning sheet caused the students to look for extraordinary, exciting events to write about. The school-based educators, on the other hand, were not surprised by the dominant focus on negative topics; instead, they were disappointed. The two sets of educators did not talk directly about their different reactions to the neighborhood stories during their next planning session. Instead, in brief conversations during class the following week, the university professor learned from the school-based educators that they had expected the negative aspects of neighborhood life to show up in the writing and had wanted the negative aspects to be balanced by positive ones. They felt that the students should have been told explicitly to balance positive and negative descriptions of neighborhood life in their stories. As a result of their concern, the university-based educators revised the sequence of assignments to encourage more positive perceptions of the students' neighborhood. In the process of revising the tasks, as in the original design of the sequence of assignments, the university-based educators did not include the school-based educators. Here are the original and revised assignment sequences:

Original	*Revised*
1. Tell us about yourself	1. Tell us about yourself
2. Tell us about something that happened in your neighborhood	2. Tell us about something that happened in your neighborhood
3. After reading your stories, discuss ways of describing events in your neighborhood	3. Write a 12-bar blues poem in the same manner in which that form is used by Eloise Greenfield
4. Compare your discussion of events in your neighborhood to newspaper reports	4. Write a description of a tour of your neighborhood and include brief descriptions of five places
5. Describe a day in your life as a student at the University at Buffalo	5. Describe a day in your life as a student at the University at Buffalo

The revised sequence of assignments still moved from narrative to descriptive writing and it still had the sixth graders write twice about their neighborhood. The emphasis, however, shifted to encouraging positive portrayals of neighborhood life in the revised Assignments 3 and 4. The university-based educators selected the poetry of Eloise Greenfield in the books *Nathaniel Talking* (1988) and *Night on Neighborhood Street* (1991) to serve as a model of writing which inspires love for family, home, and community in Assignment 3, and they created the neighborhood tour task to call out descriptions of neighborhood places and events in a more dispassionate and positive manner in Assignment 4 than had been true for the original Assignments 3 and 4. The school-based educators told the university professor they were pleased with the new assignments, especially the 12-bar blues poetry modeled after Eloise Greenfield. Still, the tension over the neighborhood writing did not disappear permanently. It surfaced again on the last day of the project when members of the university team distributed the anthologies of the students' writing, including the original relatively negative neighborhood stories, and invited the students to volunteer to read their writing aloud. Two of the school-based educators openly encouraged the students to read only positive selections aloud.

HEARING AND NOT ONLY LISTENING

Throughout this school-university collaborative project, then, communication takes place on two levels. The first level has the character of the "top-down" relationship often typical of school-university partnerships (Clift et al., 1990). An example of top-down communication is seen during the initial planning meeting for the project's third year, when the university professor answers the question from one of the school-based educators about the possibility of the neighborhood assignment leading to negative writing. In his experience, students are allowed to write whatever they want to write, and the neighborhood task has led only to positive kinds of writing. His point of view prevails, as if he has listened to but not fully understood the meaning of the school-based educator's question about negative writing. The second level of communication has the character of a "bottom-up" relationship, such as when the school-based educators make it clear, in brief informal conversations after the students have written in response to the initial neighborhood task, that they had expected negative portraits of the neighborhood from the outset. In their experience, students will not balance positive and negative observations unless they are explicitly told to do so.

The overall pattern of communication throughout the school-university collaboration is two-way, both top-down and bottom-up, but the top-down messages carry more influence because they are expressed at meetings and therefore have the character of "official" decisions. In terms of the metaphor of listening but not hearing, the "listening" message is the one openly expressed at meetings. The "hearing" message shows up briefly and indirectly, after the fact and in private informal dialogues. Meetings are of short duration, owing to the tight schedule of classes at the school, and their brevity allows little in the way of deliberation or negotiation, which in turn encourages the top-down communication pattern. Field notes show that the university-based educators do most of the talking at meetings and that their talk consists mostly of sharing plans for working with the sixth graders. Thus, the "official" decision-making processes operating at planning sessions tend to favor the university perspective. The perspective of the school is listened to but not seriously considered during decision-making processes at the meetings, partly because the university people dominate the agenda by doing most of the talking and partly because the school educators express their points of view as reactions to the plans of the university educators, as in the above question about possible negative writing, and not as designs or plans of their own.

What do we learn if we give our full attention to one of the school-based educators? What if we *hear* what she is saying, and not just listen? The major theme that emerges from the in-depth interviews with Mrs. Donaldson is that school is a place for earnest, business-like attention to learning and to reinforcing normative values and behaviors. Above all, she advocates a seriousness of purpose regarding schoolwork.

The interview data fall into three categories of concern for Mrs. Donaldson. The first is a view that education is larger than schooling and originates in the community, the second is a perceived need for discipline and structure in schooling, and the third is a pedagogy based in knowledge transmission and teacher modeling of work-related, community-sponsored codes and behaviors. The interviews show that the theme of school as a place for serious attention to work originates in social contexts and not only in educational ones. For Mrs. Donaldson, the community itself is a primary educator, a teacher of normative behavior:

> [Our students] really are not the fighting kind. I don't hear about weapons, and I don't hear them doing things that I know [students] do at other schools. Our kids are more silly and more immature than they are anything else. We have very few incidents of violence. Now, they will fight each other, but not to hurt. If we have someone who comes in, and there's a confrontation and weapons are talked about, that's not somebody who has been in our neighborhood all their life. It's someone who has moved in from another part of the city. . . . I've seen a great changeover in the population in the area since I began to teach here up until now, and with each change comes a different breed of kids. [For example,] a family . . . [moved] here and they were really rough and tough. And now that I see the littlest one is in eighth grade, now he is no longer like that. He's sort of adapted to what the neighborhood is. He is not a really rough, tough kid. But when he first came, their family stood out because . . . they weren't like the other kids. They were fighting, arguing, they didn't dress the same. . . . Then, like I said, the youngest one of that family is now in eighth grade and he fits right in. He dresses like the rest of the kids. He's mild-mannered like the rest of the kids. And I think that the neighborhood environment has a lot to do with it. A lot. Like I said, most of our kids, who we really have the problems with are kids who have come into the neighborhood, moved into the neighborhood from someplace else.

Mrs. Donaldson believes the community serves a socializing function by influencing behavior and social roles, influencing even the symbolic representation of codes of behavior in styles of dress. Her motivation as an educator comes out of a sense of commitment she feels to the values and beliefs of the community in which the school is located. She feels herself a part of the community and communicates and represents its values in her work as an educator. This gives rise to her belief that modeling is an important part of teaching:

> I feel a special commitment to the children in this neighborhood because it's home to me, and I try to always present myself in a way where maybe I can make a difference in somebody's life. I try to dress a certain way, I try to act a certain way, I try to present the most positive African-American female image that I possibly can.

Acting as a role model is an important part of any teacher's work in Mrs. Donaldson's view, but it is especially important for her because being a role model is connected with community life because the neighborhood is her home. That is the real justification for sharing with children the qualities and characteristics of a successful role model. This does not mean, of course, that teaching is any less a process of transmitting or co-constructing knowledge.

I had a student who's in Syracuse now, a very good friend of my family. She was telling us last summer how when she was in my room we had homework every night. 'I can't believe it, every single day,' [she said.] 'She'd ease up on the weekend, but Monday through Thursday we had it every night.'

It was something that I [had hoped would give] her a headstart in the seventh and eighth grade because I did demand that they do homework. She did say how strict I was, but [she added] I was fair.

Those are the kind of things, I think, that keep me in education. A success story. The kids that come back to me and say, I'm doing this and doing that.' It makes you feel good to know, even if they never say to me, 'you helped me do this, you helped me do that.' But if they are successful, I feel that maybe there was something that I did that stuck in their minds and steered them in a certain direction.

It is difficult to say if the referent for "something that I did" in the last sentence is teaching or modeling. Indeed, the implication is that it is both: learning from the content of teaching is what sticks in the mind, and acquisition from demonstration by modeling is what steers students in certain directions. High expectations, structured teaching and learning, and the modeling of appropriate behaviors and values comprise Mrs. Donaldson's view of education as a process of acquiring socially responsible, community-sponsored qualities of mind and character. Elsewhere in the interviews, Mrs. Donaldson makes it clear that the absence of these characteristics can make a teacher appear fraudulent:

A few years ago we had a teacher here and the kids instantly told me they thought she was phony, but she always would profess her concern for them. They said she told them she really cared for them, but they really didn't feel that kind of warmth.

With the teacher perceived as phony by the kids, they weren't prepared for [the city-wide final] exams, and they weren't prepared to go on to the next grade because she was too much of a friend and not enough of an authority figure or teacher. They didn't give her any trouble discipline-wise because she would more or less let them do what they wanted to do. When they got to sixth grade and didn't know as much as they should have known, they got the message.

Mrs. Donaldson makes it clear that her belief in structure and discipline is not just for the sake of control in the sense of classroom management. A teacher can manage a classroom in many ways, including management by friendship and letting kids do whatever they want. A parallel may be drawn between the work of the teacher perceived as phony and the collaboration, cited earlier, that produced the basketball story. The friendliness in both has no practical value and suggests in Mrs. Donaldson's view that the teacher in each case does not care about students enough to get them to take their work seriously. For her, caring about student success is shown through authority and

discipline and acquiring the practical value of schoolwork. She is interested
less in control for the sake of order or friendship than in control for the sake of
teaching:

> I think most kids really need structure and guidance. My tolerance of noise
> level was always low, and so my room was usually quiet when the kids were
> working. When we did group things and it got a little noisy I could handle that,
> but I could never handle these kids over here talking while I'm teaching, even
> if they are talking about school. I couldn't function that way. So it had to be
> quiet. Later, I would give them the opportunity to work in groups or go to cen-
> ters and do something involving noise, but when I was giving some directions
> or I was teaching I had to have it quiet.

In Mrs. Donaldson's view, preparation for the world of work is certainly
among the most important objectives of schooling. The guidelines for establishing school as a place for work are manifested in many ways in her remarks.
For example, in another reference to the symbolic value of clothing, she
extends work-related values to norms governing dress:

> I believe that you should have standards and codes in school, and I believe that
> nowadays it is even more important to have a dress code because you get an
> awful lot of backlash from today's society with clothes and sneakers and
> Starter jackets and who dresses the best. Wearing shorts to school is one of my
> pet peeves around here. I don't think that any child above third grade should
> wear shorts to school. I think that because in fourth to eighth grade we are in
> the business of [establishing that] this is school. We are trying to get them
> ready to move on to high school and from there to the work world. I think that
> in these institutions of learning we should teach the kids that this is serious and
> you should dress accordingly. I'm not saying that they shouldn't wear sneakers
> or slacks, but something happens to them, I notice, when they wear shorts to
> school. It's like a party. It's like they are going to the beach, or they are going to
> the playground, or they are going to the park. And that's not what school is
> about. When they come dressed to play, that's what they do, they play. When
> they come dressed to work, they work.

In using these remarks to clarify the nature of the tension between the
school-based and university-based educators, it is important not to take what
Mrs. Donaldson is saying out of the context of her pedagogical beliefs. This
excerpt from one of the interviews, for example, if taken out of the context in
which her educational beliefs are embedded, could be misunderstood—listened to but not *heard*—as making Mrs. Donaldson seem to be arguing in
opposition to the university team's approach to the teaching of writing:

> I'm a person who believes in discipline and structure. I believe that the kids
> want you to tell them, This is what we are going to do next and this is the way
> we are going to do it. 'They want that guidance. They want you to get them
> started, give them a push and then let them expand into what they want to do.

They want to be told what you want from them. They don't want you to give them a piece of paper and say, 'O.K. do whatever you want to do.'

The interviews reveal that Mrs. Donaldson is not simply interested in discipline and structure as a pedagogical stance, and she certainly is not interested in opposing the university team's methods of teaching writing. Instead, she wants school and work to be taken seriously. If we come back to the notion of neglecting the bottom-up channel of communication, the one in which the school-based educators attempt to influence the university team, the meaning of Mrs. Donaldson's remarks is placed in an appropriate context.

A request, for example, from one of the school-based educators to let students know when their writing is supposed to portray serious subjects in a serious way takes on new meaning in the light of Mrs. Donaldson's remarks. At the initial planning meeting involving both sets of educators at the beginning of the fourth year of the project, one of the school-based educators spoke up and said, "When we're doing a serious piece, the kids need to know that." She went on to explain that she was particularly unhappy about some of the humor in the student writing produced in the previous year, such as the basketball story I reproduced earlier. Another example she mentioned is the following piece, written in response to the task asking students to "Describe a day in your life as a student at the University at Buffalo":

> I would wake up at six o'clock so I can eat with Henry[3]. Last time I ate his eggs I think I got food poisoning. He also gave me spoiled milk. After I wash up in a nice hot tub I brush my teeth and comb my hair.
>
> I go to Knox Lecture Hall from eight o'clock until 9:00 a.m. My teacher, Mr. Gold, is fun. He is twenty-five years old and he wears the same clothes that young kids wear. He has a toupee because he lost his hair when he got in a fight with his wife. She burned his hair off with a torch.
>
> I go to the Fine Arts Center to take art. My teacher, Professor Rumpy, is all right. He needs to do more teaching and tell fewer stories. He is a good teacher.
>
> I go to lunch. I eat a ham and cheese sandwich and a donut with sprinkles and glaze. I meet a few friends like Henry and James. We all go and play a game of 'twenty-one.'
>
> I go to Baird Music Hall and practice playing the drums. Our teacher's name is Mr. Ralph. He wears plaid jackets and pants that never match. For his birthday I gave him some breath mints. Henry gave him a toothbrush and toothpaste. His breath really smells and his teeth are so yellow he makes the sun lose business.

What this piece has in common with the basketball story is its irreverent humor. This time the writing goes further, however, because it challenges authority and undermines the seriousness of education. What the school-based educators are saying in asking that serious subjects be treated seriously in students' writing is that it makes little sense to ask sixth graders to imagine themselves in college if college is portrayed in a silly manner. Irreverence belongs on the street or on the playground; it has no place in school.

CONCLUSION

The two levels of communication in the school-university collaboration seem to reflect opposing pedagogical stances, as in the tension between constructivist and transmissionist methods I discussed earlier with reference to Stoddart (1993), but the real issue goes deeper than differing perceptions of literacy instruction. It is true that both channels of communication are carrying messages about the teaching of writing. The top-down channel represents the university educators' position of allowing students to write whatever they please, to discover topics and ways of exploring them by themselves or in close collaboration with the university tutors. The bottom-up channel represents the school educators' preference for asking or requiring students to produce a particular kind of writing, one treating serious subjects in a serious manner, as in showing a balance of negative and positive aspects of neighborhood life. To decide that the opposing viewpoints in the school-university partnership are limited to competing positions on the teaching of writing, however, is to misrepresent the nature of the problem. The teaching of writing, by itself, is a dominant concern only for the university team. Their primary purpose in joining the professional-development relationship was to enhance the preparation of graduate students, prospective English teachers, for teaching writing. Their belief, as indicated in field notes and interviews, is that close tutor-student collaboration produces independent, fluent, critical writers. Getting students to like writing and helping them to become proficient writers capable of generating their own meanings are therefore important objectives, important enough for the university team to persistently make its perspective the dominant one. For the school-based educators, however, the teaching of writing is not a major concern, and writing is not perceived as a separate activity or objective. For them, writing is part of a broad range of educational concerns that center not only around literacy but around general behaviors and values. Whereas the university team views literacy as an individual ability related to academic success, the interviews with Mrs. Donaldson show that both literacy and academic success are part of a larger, social process of adopting community-sponsored, work-related behavior and values.

Just how these two positions are to be reconciled is by no means clear. What is clear, however, is that the two positions are not only about literacy instruction. They are also about schooling and societal structure, social codes and power. The fact that the university educators saw their role more as talking with the students than with their teachers, the fact that humor and irreverence show up in the writing coauthored by tutors and students, and the fact that the university team maintained control over the writing tasks and instruction suggest that they were interested in loosening the controls on student writing at the same time they were maintaining control of the school-university partnership. The underlying issue in the patterns of communication in the partnership is power.

Perhaps it is appropriate for me to end this essay as I began, with a quote from Delpit:

> Many liberal educators hold that the primary goal for education is for children to become autonomous, to develop fully who they are in the classroom setting without having arbitrary, outside standards forced upon them. This is a very reasonable goal for people whose children are already participants in the culture of power and who have already internalized its codes.
>
> But parents who don't function within that culture often want something else. It's not that they disagree with the former aim, it's just that they want something more. They want to insure that school provides their children with discourse patterns, interactional styles, and spoken and written language codes that will allow them success in the larger society. (Delpit, 1988, p. 285) .

NOTES

1. This is a pseudonym for the name of the tutor originally appearing in this sample.

2. This is a pseudonym for the name of the friend originally appearing in this sample.

3. This and "James" later in the piece are pseudonyms for the names of friends originally appearing in this sample.

REFERENCES

Cleary, L. M. (1991). *From the other side of the desk: Students speak out about writing*. Portsmouth, NH: Heinemann Boynton/Cook.

Clift, R., Veal, M. L., Johnson, J., & Holland, P. (1990). Restructuring teacher education through collaborative action research. *Journal of Teacher Education, 41*(2), 52–62.

Delpit, L. S. (1988). The silenced dialogue: Power and pedagogy in educating other people's children. *Harvard Educational Review, 58*, 280–298.

Greenfield, E. (1988). *Nathaniel talking*. New York: Black Butterfly Children's Books.

Greenfield, E. (1991). *Night on neighborhood street.* New York: Dial.

Seidman, I. E. (1991). *Interviewing as qualitative research.* New York: Teachers College Press.

Stoddart, T. (1993). The professional development school: Building bridges between cultures. *Educational Policy, 7*(1), 5–23.

DAVID F. LABAREE

Chapter Six

Why Do Schools Cooperate with University-Based Reforms?

THE CASE OF PROFESSIONAL DEVELOPMENT SCHOOLS

Educational reform has proven to be "steady work" in the words of
Elmore and McLaughlin, because it has been so routinely unsuccessful in
bringing about significant change within schools. As they put it,

> Reforms that deal with the fundamental stuff of education—teaching and
> learning—seem to have weak, transitory, and ephemeral effects; while those
> that expand, solidify, and entrench school bureaucracy seem to have strong,
> enduring, and concrete effects (Elmore and McLaughlin, 1988, p. v).

This is the core insight one can distill from the dismal literature about
American reform efforts: that schools have shown an amazing capacity for
accommodating their organizational form to the latest reform initiative while
refusing to adopt its substance. According to Cusick (1992), the formal organization of schooling responds to such initiatives using standard techniques of
specialization, moderation, and cooptation, which "combine to turn educational reform into organizational reform" (p. 211). And such a transformation
of the original thrust of the reform effort can, in turn, appropriately be interpreted as a failure—what Sarason (1990) called, in the title of his recent book,
The Predictable Failure of Educational Reform. School reformers fail so predictably, in Sarason's view, in large part because of their chronic inability to
tailor reforms to a particular educational context. The message seems to be that
unless you understand the unique structure of relationships that defines a par-

93

ticular school and community, you will never be able to bring about substantive reform in school practices. If reformers in general have a problem of being cut off from context, the difficulty is particularly acute when they hail from the university. School reforms that draw upon the personnel and perspectives of the university, as so many do, run into predictable problems of implementation because of the gap separating the universalistic concerns of university people from the particularistic concerns of school people. Education professors and educational researchers are removed from the necessity of responding to the daily barrage of practical problems that confront practitioners in schools, and at the same time they are constrained by academic career incentives that put a premium on making contributions to the theoretical literature. As a result, they can and must look on schools as sources of data for the construction of general theories about teaching, learning, and the functions of schooling. Meanwhile, teachers and administrators, who cannot escape the practical demands of running classrooms and schools, tend to look on each classroom and each school as a unique site for educational practice that is inextricably embedded in local issues and relationships. Therefore, whereas university people see reform as an effort to apply general principles in schools, school people see such reforms as simply inapplicable to their own problems of practice or as usable only if radically adapted to fit the local setting.

Given these differences, the remarkable thing is not why schools resist university-sponsored reforms but why they ever agree to participate in such reform initiatives in the first place. Yet they continue to do so. Educators still call on university professors and draw on educational research when they consider making changes within schools; they still are willing to sign on, albeit cautiously, to reform efforts supported by the university. Why is this so? What benefits do K–12 educators feel they may gain from such association with higher education? It is these questions that I will explore in this chapter. I will attempt to sketch some of the reasons that motivate administrators and teachers to pursue reform of existing practice within schools and classrooms in cooperation with university faculty and in line with university research. In exploring these reasons I will draw on the example of one current educational reform movement that has emerged recently from the university, the effort by the Holmes Group to professionalize teaching and restructure the school. First, let me provide a little background about this particular reform effort, and then I will turn to the question of why schools might be willing to go along with it, and other university-based reform efforts, at least for awhile.

The Holmes Group is an organization of about 100 colleges of education in research-oriented universities in the United States. It has defined its goals in two reports, *Tomorrow's Teachers* (1986) and *Tomorrow's Schools* (1990). (A third report, tentatively titled *Tomorrow's Schools of Education*, is being released this year.) Arguing that educational research has now developed a solid knowledge base for teaching, the Holmes Group reports propose that teaching should be elevated into a full-fledged profession. The advantage to teachers would be an increase in status, rewards, and autonomy, while the advantage to students would be an increase in the quality and competence of instruction. These reports lay out a two-part plan for carrying out the professionalization process—asking colleges of education to increase the breadth and depth of professional education for teachers and simultaneously asking schools to restructure themselves in order to give teachers a more autonomous and influential role in regulating school practices. The latter aim has become operationalized as the current effort by Holmes Group institutions to create what are called professional development schools (PDSs). As spelled out in *Tomorrow's Schools*, a PDS is intended to be a collaborative project between university faculty members and the teachers and administrators in a particular school for the purpose of rethinking and redesigning the way schools work.

In this chapter, I will be using the effort to create PDSs as a case in point of the larger problem of school cooperation with university-based reform efforts. The Holmes Group initiative is certainly such an effort: the group is made up entirely of university people; its call for teacher professionalization emerged from its own ranks and not from teachers or schools; in like manner, the idea for PDSs also developed initially within the university; and now the Holmes Group institutions have been trying to sell this idea to schools. My question, then, is: Why have some schools been willing to buy?

ADMINISTRATORS AND UNIVERSITY-BASED REFORM

There are at least two reasons why school administrators may feel that it is useful for them to draw on ideas and personnel from the university and even to sign on to a university reform effort. Such a strategy may give them some leverage in dealing with the public, and it may also give them some leverage in dealing with teachers.

Deflecting Public Control

School administrators feel intensely vulnerable to public pressure. Most Americans are comfortable criticizing schools and second-guessing educators, because public education is the most public of all American institutions. Unlike the economy, family, and even perhaps government, public schools are thoroughly open to public view and influence. One reason for this is that they are intensely local, and as such they are both accessible to ordinary citizens and thoroughly integrated in their lives. After all, public schools play a central role in the social, cultural, and intellectual development of most members of the community during their formative years. In their youth, local citizens spend a total of about 15,000 hours in these classrooms, and after graduation the affiliation continues. Schools sit prominently in the middle of every neighborhood, acting as community centers and civic symbols. Adult members of the community go there to vote, to attend public meetings, to see a play, and to learn CPR.

A lifetime of close association with the schools means that what schools do is quite visible and understandable to the public. This point is underscored by the fact that schools are governed by boards of ordinary citizens, not professional educators. School board meetings are places where individuals feel free to come and speak their minds and where administrators have to sit and listen. Superintendents and principals, in particular, as the front-line representatives of the school system, must become accustomed to receiving unsolicited advice and criticism from the general public and doing so with reasonably good grace. These administrators need to keep the public happy. If they fail to do so, citizens reassert their right to reject major actions by the administration with every vote of the school board, every millage election, and every bond issue campaign. As a result, schools are remarkably sensitive to local expressions of concern about how they carry out their functions, or at least they need to appear that way.

This sensitivity is one of the engines driving the continuing waves of reform in American education. Administrators need to deflect public discontent by showing that they are doing something about whatever problem the public sees as currently afflicting the local school, so they subject schools and school systems to one reform effort after another in order to demonstrate their willingness to make necessary changes. Drawing on the authority and expertise of the university can be quite helpful in this effort to deflect criticism. Whether administrators ground their actions in research findings or forge a direct alliance with university faculty, the university connection gives them a powerful political tool. It allows them to tell the public that their reform efforts are not merely examples of political pandering but that these efforts constitute *authoritative* remedial action.

Past failures by local officials, and their identification with an institution as familiar and understandable as public education, may well undermine their credibility with the public as agents of change for schools. But the university retains a distance and prestige that the school administration does not, and it has a reputation for generating expert knowledge that is both obscure to the average layperson and apparently imbued with special authority. Therefore, tapping into the social and intellectual resources of the university can invest actions by local officials with a degree of both authority and mystery that would otherwise be lacking. These qualities serve both to reassure the public that something serious is being done and to block further public inquiry, since the measures taken are beyond the ken of ordinary citizens. Rowan (1984) labeled this use of educational research as a form of "shamanism" in which "the stylized knowledge we call 'science' functions much like magic" (p. 78). When local officials invoke this power in support of reform efforts, the result is frequently a kind of "healing ritual" (p. 79), that restores the community's sense of educational well-being and its confidence in the officials.

One consequence of particular benefit to administrators is that their appeal to the shamans of the university helps to mystify a situation in the schools that may otherwise be all too clear to the average citizen. Put another way, when the kind of expert knowledge embedded in educational research and embodied in the university researcher is applied to a local school concern, it serves to transform a touchy *political* problem into an administratively manageable *technical* problem. This transformation helps to buffer administrators from future interference by the laity. After all, now the problem is no longer amenable to solution through the application of political skills, which are widely held, but instead a solution calls for the kind of technical skills that are only possessed by a few experts—who are already on the administration's side. Instead of having voters make educational decisions based on values, the administration can assert, we need to have specialists make these decisions based on science.

In light of these kinds of considerations, school administrators may well find that allying themselves with the Holmes Group's effort to professionalize teachers is a potentially useful way to allay public fears about the quality of local schools and protect themselves against political intrusions from the community. The first Holmes report spelled out that the professionalization movement is firmly grounded in the science of teaching as developed by the experts at the university (Labaree, in press). Led by the most prestigious and research-oriented colleges of education, the movement offers administrators a chance to link themselves to the full authority of the university and of science itself. By agreeing to collaborate with the university in the construction of a professional development school within their district, administrators can make a dramatic statement to the public about the technical wizardry they are bringing to bear on the problems in the local schools and their willingness to go beyond minor forms of incremental remediation. They are vividly demonstrating their willingness and ability to build one of "tomorrow's schools" right in their own community, based on the latest in educational technology and overseen by the high priests themselves.

Promoting the Control of Teachers

University-based reform can be useful to administrators not only because it helps them blunt efforts by the public to control schools but also because it helps them sharpen their own efforts to control teaching. As Lortie (1975) and others (Bidwell, 1965; Weick, 1976) have pointed out, school administrators have considerable power in dealing with the noninstructional realm of schooling but have remarkably little ability to shape the way teachers teach. In part, this is the result of the difficulty administrators have in acquiring direct knowledge on how instruction is being carried out. The way schools are spatially organized, instruction goes on in relative privacy behind the doors of the self-contained classroom. The problem is also the result of the weak mechanisms available to administrators for the control of teacher behavior. Standard forms of reward and punishment used by supervisors in other organizations to regulate how employees do their jobs—the promise of pay increases for the compliant and the threat of firing for the noncompliant—are simply unavailable to the school administrator, who is bound by union contracts and tenure rules. Thus, administrators often do not know how well a teacher is teaching and cannot do much about it even if they have this information. The result is that administrators often experience chronic frustration, feeling that they are being held accountable by the public for carrying out the competent instruction of students when they do not have the direct power required to fulfill this expectation. Curriculum mandates, standardized testing, and merit pay plans are all methods they have used to gain some control over teachers and teaching, but these methods have not been very successful. One key reason for the relative ineffectiveness of such methods is that they are often seen by teachers, quite accurately, as efforts to reduce teacher autonomy and therefore lead to various forms of active and passive resistance, such as when a merit pay proposal meets union opposition or when a new curriculum package ends up in the teacher's desk drawer.

However, drawing on the expertise and authority of the university in support of a local effort to reform instruction offers administrators the possibility of augmenting their own modest powers in this area. This approach allows the administration to present the proposed reform as something other than a bald effort to gain top-down control over the classroom. By grounding the reform in educational research and drawing on university personnel to help in its implementation, school administrators help to establish the idea that this reform is a simple application of the latest and best ideas about effective pedagogical practice rather than another example of bureaucratic intrusion in the classroom. The administrator takes the role of facilitator in this scenario, in which reform is presented as an effort to aid the teacher in carrying out what "research says" are the most effective means of accomplishing the teacher's own educational goals.

The advantages of the university's involvement for school administrators come not only from its authority and its expertise but also from its image as a disinterested party. Since university people are not part of the school system's power structure, they can make suggestions (directly as consultants and indirectly through their research findings) without appearing to take sides in the local power struggle over the control of the classroom. Teachers might be willing to take advice from this neutral corner that would be greeted with suspicion if backed only by the bureaucratic authority of the superintendent or principal. However the effectiveness of the university's involvement in reform in this regard depends on its credibility—both as a source of useful knowledge about teaching and schools and also as a neutral party in the organizational politics of a particular school or school system.

The teacher professionalization movement fits these kinds of administrator concerns quite nicely. It focuses attention directly on the problem of teacher quality and the need to upgrade the way that teachers teach, yet it does so in the name of supporting teacher autonomy and improving teacher status. If there is ever going to be a reform effort that can convince teachers to accept outside guidance in rethinking their own methods of teaching, this may be it. After all, the Holmes Group is offering to do its magic for the benefit of the teachers themselves (what occupational group does not want to be considered professional?) and to involve the university directly in the process (thus helping to allay suspicions about another administrative gambit). It presents teachers with a very attractive opportunity to become deeply involved in the construction of a school dedicated to professional development. But for administrators, this potential for enlisting teacher involvement in PDS development creates the opportunity to tear down the walls protecting teachers from instructional control and to institute a new system that defines acceptable norms of teaching practice and establishes mechanisms for enforcing these norms—all under the banner of professionalism.

Of course, teachers and administrators both may well ask the university reformer (and the PDS proponent) two key questions: How helpful is your knowledge going to be in resolving our educational problems? And whose interests are you really serving in your intervention in the schools—the community, the administration, or the teachers? These are issues I will take up later. But first let us examine some reasons that teachers might have for finding value in the university perspective on schools and for welcoming university involvement in local reform efforts.

TEACHERS AND UNIVERSITY-BASED REFORM

There are at least two reasons why teachers may feel that it is useful for them to draw on ideas and personnel from the university and perhaps to become involved with a university reform effort. Such a strategy may give them some leverage in dealing with the educational bureaucracy, and it may also give them a useful perspective in thinking about their own practice.

Deflecting Administrative Control

Whereas administrators may think of research and researchers as mechanisms for gaining control of classroom instruction, teachers may see them as mechanisms for deflecting such control efforts. One of the problems facing teachers is that they are trapped within the school's micropolitical structure, where the administrative bureaucracy claims a monopoly over the definition of appropriate curriculum and good teaching. They enjoy instructional autonomy, but this is accidental rather than intentional. The administration has difficulty knowing about and influencing their teaching, but that does not mean that teachers are recognized as having the right to teach as they wish. Far from it. The superintendent is still charged by the public with the responsibility for governing instruction within the schools. He or she has the right, if not the means, to establish what teachers teach and how they do it. Thus teacher autonomy lacks public legitimacy, and teachers find that their only structural link to both the political and curricular base of public education runs up against the school system's hierarchy. Through the production of curriculum guidelines, the control of curriculum materials, and the generation of staff development programs, the administration asserts (formally, at least) its organizational ascendancy over teachers.

Goodson and his colleagues argue that teachers, trapped within the micropolitics of the school, may reach out to researchers from the university as an alternative source for legitimate ideas and views about teaching and schooling (Goodson & Mangan, 1991; Fliesser, 1991). Since university professors are not beholden to the educational bureaucracy and are invested with their own legitimate claim to knowledge about schools, teachers may find association with them potentially valuable. This relationship may not only give teachers access to ideas that are different from the official administrative position, but it may also give them independent and authoritative allies who could help advance their educational concerns within the school system. Thus, affiliation with university personnel and reform efforts may help teachers offset and even deflect administrative control over teaching.

The creation of a professional development school is a situation that appears to offer precisely these kinds of benefits to participating teachers. The Holmes Group's rhetoric about PDSs represented them as an effort to restructure the power relationships within the school and in the process create new and legitimate ways for teachers to take part in curriculum formation, instructional supervision, and school governance. If realized, this would mean a significant improvement over the limited and negative autonomy of the average teacher—who is "administratively subordinate but instructionally autonomous, disempowered within the school and school system but all-powerful in the classroom" (Labaree, 1988, p. 133). Reinforcing the attractiveness of this possibility for teachers is the promise of establishing long-term collaborative relationships with professors, whose continuing role within the PDS promises to buttress the position of teachers relative to the administration.

Promoting Reflective Practice

Not only can university researchers intervene providentially in the relationship between teachers and administrators, but they can also play an important role in helping teachers to reflect on their own instructional practice. The theoretical and decontextualized character of educational research can make this research useful for teachers, since it gives them access to a view of teaching and schools that is not wholly bound up in their immediate context and the demands of daily practice in that setting. This allows teachers to examine which elements in their classrooms are situationally unique and which are ones they have in common with other teachers in other places. Research gives them a general picture of teaching that they can compare with the particulars of their own practical setting. Reflective practice would seem to require a good sense of both and an ability to move back and forth easily between the two. In a recent paper, Fliesser (1991) describes his own experience as a teacher moving back and forth "between two worlds" (the school and the university). His testimony provides powerful witness to the potential benefit that contact with research and researchers can have on one's perspective about one's own teaching.

The PDS initiative would seem to provide extensive opportunities for teachers to engage in close collaborative contact with researchers and thereby gain an invaluable perspective on their own teaching. In PDSs now under way, professors and teachers work in teams to develop curricular and pedagogical goals and then jointly try to put these goals into practice in their school. It is not hard to understand why many teachers might find this kind of involvement personally and professionally gratifying.

PROBLEMS POSED BY COLLABORATION
BETWEEN SCHOOL AND UNIVERSITY

The preceding account suggests two kinds of problems that may confront school people when they draw on the knowledge and personnel of the university to support local efforts at educational reform. One is a problem of determining the credibility of the university as a useful ground for reform: When university research findings are applied in schools, how well do they work and what is the effect of this result on the reputation of the researchers? The other is a problem of determining the interests served by this collaboration: Who benefits when the university becomes directly or indirectly involved in school reform?

Credibility of the Researcher

The core of the credibility problem facing the researcher turned reformer is the basic incompatibility between the theoretical aims of educational researchers and the practical needs of school practitioners. Buchmann (1984) puts the issue this way:

> Scientific authority is based on competence in inquiry, which means seeking and asking, not answering and prescribing. The tentativeness of [research] knowledge is like a safety catch that a pretension to usefulness tends to remove. This is so, in particular, because the public accepts scientific findings not because it shares the scientific conception of reality but because of the social authority of science. Scientific knowledge and judgment are opaque and indisputable to most people (p. 431).

Researchers seek to establish general relationships between variables, and this quest presses them to abstract from particular contexts and remove extraneous variables for the sake of conceptual clarity and methodological precision. However, practitioners must deal daily with the distinctive features of their own context and the complex mixture of issues that shape what goes on there.

The result is a mismatch between precision and utility, which makes it impossible to effect any sort of simple application of research findings in a practical setting (Cohen & Garet, 1975; Lindblom & Cohen, 1979). In fact, attempts at "[i]mproving applied research ha[ve] produced paradoxical results: knowledge which is better by any scientific standard, no more authoritative by any political standard and often more mystifying by any reasonable public standard" (Cohen & Garet, 1975, p. 33). The consequence of this mismatch between researchers and school people is what Slavin (1989) called the "pendulum" swing of reform fads in schools—characterized by "early enthusiasm, widespread dissemination, subsequent disappointment, and eventual decline" (p. 752). Early research results are translated into school reforms (the example he uses is Hunter's "Instructional Theory into Practice" program) that then run into two kinds of credibility difficulties.

First, the effort to translate theory into practice leads to predictable implementation problems in schools because of the complexities and peculiarities of each practice setting. So practitioners begin to question the usefulness and applicability of this theory. And second, further research, employing refined variables and more arcane methodology, leads to a predictable narrowing and qualification of the claims made from the research. So researchers also begin to question the scientific validity of the reform's assumptions. In short, over time, the credibility of research-based reformers tends to come under increasing fire from both practitioners and researchers, who grow to doubt both the reform's practical usefulness and its theoretical validity. Thus the ability of academic shamanism to bring about the ritual healing of a school system's ailments collapses as soon as voices in both school and university begin to suggest that the shaman is wearing no clothes.

The Holmes Group effort to professionalize teaching finds itself in the middle of its own credibility dilemma. The initial report grounded the reform firmly in the scientific research on teaching that came out of the university, using what Buchmann calls "the social authority of science" to establish the credibility and feasibility of its proposals for improving education. Colleges of education that are members of the Holmes Group have drawn on this credibility to convince administrators and teachers to cooperate with them in the establishment of professional development schools. Some of these PDSs are still in the formative stage while others have been in operation for several years. If Slavin is right in his characterization of reform cycles, the former may well be enjoying a stage of "early enthusiasm," while the latter (whose early success stories led to widespread "dissemination" of the PDS model) may be entering the stage of progressive "disappointment."

What are the likely signs that the credibility of the PDS effort might be in decline in these established settings? One might well expect that after several years of strenuous effort in a PDS site, teachers and administrators (and the public) would be asking for proof that the university's promises of educational improvement are coming true. But given the enormous complexity of education as an enterprise and the difficulty of adapting general academic principles to a particular setting, it is likely that there is little progress in educational outcomes that one can point to at these sites. Process changes are going to be abundantly evident because of all the restructuring taking place, but it may be less evident that the restructuring has led to improvements in the educational deficiencies that spurred school people to embrace the reform in the first place. If old reform patterns hold, teachers and administrators are likely to grow weary of the sustained effort that is required in a PDS site given the minimal or equivocal results.

After a PDS has been in operation for a while, funding agencies are likely to ask the same kinds of outcome questions that educators will. Creating and maintaining a PDS is a very costly proposition, in money as well as in time and effort. Having paid for all the effort and heard all the promises, funders (like school people) are going to want to see some sort of definable results. Also at this stage, academics who are not involved in the PDS movement are going to be asking questions about the movement's assumptions, its theoretical rationale, and the connection between its procedures and its effects. School people have an advantage over outsiders in establishing the credibility of the PDS effort because they have direct empirical knowledge about how it is going, while others learn about PDS progress only through the movement's official reports. Relying on insiders to produce the evaluation of the PDS success temporarily protects the movement from outside criticism, but this can hardly last for long. (Slavin (1989) noted that reformers typically try to limit information about how things are going to the kind of success stories that help spur imitation rather than sober evaluation.) Academic acceptance of the credibility of the reform can only come when evidence appears in a suitably academic form—such as scientific studies of these sites performed by disinterested researchers. However, continuing reluctance to allow these sorts of studies will only serve to discredit the whole enterprise within the university. Meanwhile, funding agencies are likely to demand outside evaluations of how their money is being spent and what the consequences are. All of these tendencies suggest that credibility problems are already brewing for the PDS movement.

Interests Served

In addition to the credibility issue, there is another and even more obvious problem that emerges from this analysis of why school people enlist in a university-based reform effort: everyone cannot be right in their assessment of the benefits of cooperation. Given the contradictory expectations that different groups have about the fruits of university involvement in district affairs, someone has to be mistaken. The university cannot simultaneously serve the public interest and serve to protect administrators from the public; and it cannot both give administrators more control over teachers and give teachers more power in dealing with administrators.

The source of confusion about the university's role in reform is its claim of neutrality. This is also a key source of its authority. People of all sorts who seek to affect public policy tend to call on the university to support their position, and the reason is that this institution projects an air of disinterested expertise that is a useful commodity in the rhetoric of reform. If you can cite university research to back your policy proposal, you can assert that this proposal is not then just an expression of your own partisan preferences but a logical deduction from the realm of scientifically certified truth. Having research to back your position means in effect having the facts on your side, since, as Buchmann noted, "[s]cientific knowledge and judgment are opaque and indisputable to most people." The phrase "research says" is thus a conversation stopper, a trump card, because it calls in the authority of science and the objectivity of the expert to vanquish an opposing position, making that position appear to consist of nothing but conjecture and self-interest.

As I noted earlier, the credibility of the university's claim to have answers to the practical problems of schooling is dubious at best, but equally dubious is its claim of objectivity. My contention is that the university has its own interests that it advances through its interventions in schools, and, to the extent that these interventions tend to benefit anyone in the school system, it is to reinforce the position of school administrators against both teachers and the public. Consider the example of the Holmes Group.

As I have argued at greater length elsewhere (Labaree, 1990; 1992; in press), the Holmes Group's vision of teacher professionalization arose from the status needs of teacher educators within the university and from the formal-rational worldview that fueled their status attainment effort. Since the days of the normal school, teacher educators have always been at the low end of the academic prestige ladder. During the course of the twentieth century, normal schools evolved into teachers colleges that in turn rose to the status of universities, and teacher educators rose with them. Arriving in the university relatively late and bearing the stigma of the normal school, these professors found themselves ill-equipped to compete for professional standing within this environment. Yet the rules of academic status were well defined. To gain prestige within the university, professors needed to pursue a vigorous agenda of research activities, especially those framed in the methodology of science. Throughout this century, educational researchers have tried to develop a viable science of teaching, with little success (Tom, 1984). But starting in the 1960s, teacher educators launched a remarkably successful effort in this vein that drew on the behavioral scientific paradigm pioneered by educational psychologists and set off a landslide of research publication. The quantity of output since then has been so great that it has taken three large handbooks just to summarize the recent research on teaching and another to summarize the research on teacher education (Gage, 1963; Travers, 1973; Wittrock, 1986; Houston, 1990).

In the form developed by the Holmes Group, the teacher professionalization movement is a projection of the worldview and the status concerns of the education school faculties that make up its leadership.[1] From this perspective, a teacher's professional knowledge should be grounded in the scientific knowledge about teaching generated in the university, and the primary beneficiaries of the movement will be the same education professors who performed this research in the first place. They gain enhanced prestige in the university for their research productivity and they also gain enhanced influence in the schools. The ones with the most to lose in this reform effort are the teachers themselves, despite the movement's rhetoric about teacher empowerment and status enhancement.

The problems posed for teachers are multiple. The Holmes Group undercuts the strongest claim teachers can make to professionalism—their practical knowledge of teaching acquired through clinical practice—by promoting university-generated research knowledge as the authoritative basis for professionalism. To acquire this knowledge will, of course, require extended instruction at the hands of education professors (through an upgraded professional education requirement). Fundamentally, the Holmes vision of professionalization will call for teachers to accept the authority of theoretical knowledge and to acknowledge their professional responsibility to reconstruct their own class-room practice in order to fit it into the rationalized notion of practice defined by this structure of knowledge. Finally, teachers in professional development schools will find themselves working closely with those same education pro-fessors, who potentially will be looking to see if the teachers are in fact demon-strating professional (that is, research-based) practices in the classroom. This is far from the vision of collaboration and reflection that teachers may have been hoping for in the PDS environment; rather it looks like a case of subordi-nation to both the university and its vision of schooling.

For administrators, however, the Holmes Group and PDS involvement offer some substantial benefits. The alliance with the university seems to offer help in keeping the public at bay, by allowing the administration to project an image of doing something authoritative to improve schools (the healing ritual) and by building a wall of expertise between schools and the ordinary citizen. In addition, the vision of professionalized teaching that emerges from Holmes is compatible with the administrator's vision in many ways, since they both seek to overcome the idiosyncratic autonomy of teaching practice fostered by the present organization of schooling. Holmes is trying to do this by setting research-based standards for professional practice, which provide legitimate criteria for outsiders to get past the door of the self-contained classroom and reshape the way teachers teach—something administrators have been trying to do for years without much success. In this sense, the university-bred brand of teacher professionalization may help bring about what bureaucratization could not—the rationalization of teaching.

CONCLUSION

The question I asked at the beginning of this chapter was: Why do school administrators and teachers choose to go along with university-based reform efforts? The short answer is that they both hope to gain something from the involvement, and, in the case of administrators, this assessment may indeed be accurate. At least in the case of the Holmes Group's initiative to professional-ize teaching, administrators seem to have something to gain, even though the biggest beneficiaries of that initiative seem to be the Holmes Group's own membership. This gain may be real even if the credibility of the professionaliz-ers fades as a result of what promises to be a weak demonstration of their prac-tical effects on schools. After all, the benefits to administrators do not necessarily come from the improvement in student learning but instead from the improvement of the administration's position in relation to the public and teachers. However, my analysis suggests that teachers are likely to get the short end of the stick, even from a reform movement named in their honor and supposedly dedicated to their advancement.

Let me qualify that conclusion, however, by pointing to an important counter-current in the PDS project. While the leadership of the PDS effort promotes the kind of rationalization of teaching and subordination of teachers that I have identified here,[2] the faculty members serving as the footsoldiers in this enterprise are frequently working out their own agenda on the ground with teachers in individual professional development schools. These professors are taking collaboration seriously—developing close relationships with teachers, listening as much as talking, teaching as well as observing, acting as teacher-advocates within the PDS effort more than as PDS agents to the teachers. At the ground level, the PDS experiment may be producing for some teachers the kind of reflective experience they had hoped for, by giving them contact with a sympathetic outsider whose independence and theoretical framework may provide useful insights into the nature of their own situated practice. The problem, however, is that this ground-level reform effort is at odds in many ways with the agenda of the official reform movement. The money, the institutional prestige of the university, and the social authority of science are all on the side of the leadership. Ironically, the benefits to teachers from the teacher professionalization movement are more likely to come in spite of this movement rather than because of it.

NOTES

1. Another branch of the teacher professionalization movement, that emerged at the same time as the Holmes Group, is now taking what appears to be a different road. The National Board of Professional Teaching Standards, which was set up in response to the Carnegie report on teaching (Carnegie Forum, 1986), seems to be moving away from a research-based model of teacher professionalism and toward a practical-knowledge model, valuing clinical skill over university training. The key reason: a majority of the Board and each working committee within its jurisdiction is made up of teachers not university professors.

2. When I say that the efforts of Holmes Group and PDS leaders bring negative consequences for teachers and serve their own interests, I am not arguing that they intend to bring about these outcomes. Far from it. My strong sense is that the aims of the teacher professionalizers are to improve the conditions for teachers and to elevate the quality of schooling. However, their actions and the scientistic intellectual framework that guides these actions are, I suggest, nonetheless harmful in their potential because they are unintended.

REFERENCES

Bidwell, C. E. (1965). The school as a formal organization. In J. March (Ed.), *Handbook of organization* (pp. 972–1022). Chicago: Rand McNally.

Buchmann, M. (1984). The use of research knowledge in teacher education and teaching. *American Journal of Education, 92*, 421–439.

Carnegie Task Force on Teaching as a Profession (1986). *A nation prepared: Teachers for the 21st century*. Washington, DC: Author.

Cohen, D. K., & Garet, M. S. (1975). Reforming educational policy with applied social research. *Harvard Educational Review, 45*, 17–43.

Cusick, P. A. (1992). *The educational system: Its nature and logic*. New York: McGraw-Hill.

Elmore, R. F. & McLaughlin, M. W. (1988). *Steady work*. Santa Monica, CA: Rand.

Fliesser, C. (1991). Between two worlds: Discovering the importance of reflection to action. Paper presented at Spencer Hall Conference, University of Western Ontario.

Gage, N. L. (1963). *Handbook of research on teaching* (1st ed.). Chicago: Rand McNally.

Goodson, I., & Mangan, J. M. (1991). An alternative paradigm for educational research. In I. Goodson and J. M. Mangan (Eds.), *Qualitative educational research studies: Methodologies in transition* (pp. 9–48). London, Ontario: Faculty of Education, University of Western Ontario.

Holmes Group (1986). *Tomorrow's teachers*. East Lansing, MI: Author.

Holmes Group (1990). *Tomorrow's schools*. East Lansing, MI: Author.

Houston, W. R. (Ed.) (1990). *Handbook of research on teacher education*. New York: Macmillan.

Labaree, D. F. (1988). *The making of an American high school: The credentials market and the Central High School of Philadelphia, 1838–1939*. New Haven, CT: Yale University Press.

Labaree, D. F. (1990). The politics of teacher professionalization in the 1980s. Paper presented at the annual meeting of the American Sociological Association, Washington, DC.

Labaree, D. F. (1992). Doing good, doing science: The Holmes Group reports and the rhetoric of education reform. *Teachers College Record, 93*(4), 628-640.

Labaree, D. F. (in press). Power, knowledge, and the rationalization of teaching: A genealogy of the movement to professionalize teaching. *Harvard Educational Review*.

Lindblom, C. E. & Cohen, D. K. (1979). *Useable knowledge: Social science and social problem solving*. New Haven, CT: Yale University Press.

Lortie, D. C. (1976). *Schoolteacher*. Chicago: University of Chicago Press.

Rowan, B. (1984). Shamanistic rituals in effective schools. *Issues in education,* 2, 76–87.

Sarason, S. B. (1990). *The predictable failure of educational reform.* San Francisco: Jossey Bass.

Slavin, R. E. (1989). PET and the pendulum: Faddism in education and how to stop it. *Phi Delta Kappan, 70,* 752–758.

Tom, A. (1984). *Teaching as a moral craft.* New York: Longman.

Travers, R. M. W. (1973). *Handbook of research on teaching* (2nd ed.). Chicago: Rand McNally.

Weick, K. (1976). Educational organizations as loosely-coupled systems. *Administrative Science Quarterly, 21* (1), 1–19.

Wittrock, M. C. (1986) *Handbook of research on teaching* (3rd ed.). New York: Macmillan.

Part III

Culture Changes

When cultures clash, they also often change. All of the selections in this part echo the themes of culture clash that we have seen in Part II, and they also begin to describe the changes that sometimes take place.

Charles Case, Kay Norlander, and Timothy Reagan describe the evolution of their professional development centers precisely as an instance of cultural interaction and transformation. The University of Connecticut belongs to both the Holmes Group and Goodlad's Network for Educational Renewal, so the description of the professional development schools established here shows the large degree of compatibility between these two approaches. This careful, self-conscious attempt to transform the cultures of the school and university was largely successful, but another culture clash—with the State Education Department—surfaced as state officials took a more technical approach to professionalization than the empowerment approach taken by the authors. Both university and school faculty have come to see their roles differently, and more cooperatively, with new forms of inquiry and teaching infusing both school and university. Students in the preparation programs, too, have begun to see themselves more as future empowered professionals. Finally, the discussion of the largely, but not entirely, successful changes in the nature of the school of education confirm the systemic effects postulated to result from work in professional development schools.

A deep concern for the necessary changes in power relationships in both organizational decision making and in collaborative research characterizes the contribution by Jane Stallings, Donna Wiseman, and Stephanie Knight. This selection emphasizes the critical role played by the process of working out a shared vision among the parties for the simultaneous restructuring needed by both schools and universities. The professional development school serves as the locus for these restructurings. The authors also sound the theme of the needed changes within both the university at large and more specifically within the school of education.

In her chapter, Michelle Collay introduces us to the world of rural education and the attempt to form partnerships with universities to provide "boundary-spanning" facilitators to improve the teaching and learning in rural areas. In attempting to develop a professional culture among the rural teachers, the university facilitators found themselves both challenging the traditional top-down administrative culture of the schools and reflecting on and changing their own practice as university professors. They became not only ambassadors from the university to the field, but also bridge-builders back to the university.

The importance of traditional ways of doing things as an inhibitor of change is explored by Jeanne Ellsworth and Cheryl Albers in their description of the integration of clinical school-based teachers into a university teacher education program. Despite a great deal of collaborative effort, traditional conceptions of student teaching and the roles of cooperating teacher and university supervisor tend to persist. Furthermore, the issues of power and authority are never far from the surface. Who is ultimately responsible for grading the student teaching experience? Who ought to be? Should the student teacher be considered a more active contributor to the process? This selection reminds us that culture change is never easy and may not always occur as smoothly as we would wish. Nevertheless, the professional development school concept provides a basis for continued work.

CHARLES W. CASE, KAY A. NORLANDER,
and TIMOTHY G. REAGAN

Chapter Seven

Cultural Transformation in an Urban Professional Development Center

POLICY IMPLICATIONS FOR SCHOOL-UNIVERSITY COLLABORATION

Given the national interest in restructuring, reform, and change in education, many from schools, universities, communities, and businesses are searching for ways to collaborate in the redesign of schools for the next century. Conceptual frameworks must be established, implemented, and evaluated on the basis of their contributions to the revitalization of schooling and the teaching profession. University-school partnerships that surpass traditional arrangements in which student teachers simply complete apprenticeships with a single teacher in one school can play a significant role in school and university change (Case, Lanier, & Miskel, 1986; Goodlad, 1988). However, establishing the kinds of collaborative relationships between and among professionals from different disciplines and roles, which are central to such change, is often hindered by their differing cultural perspectives (Cuban, 1992; Goodlad, 1991; Goodlad & Soder, 1992; Sarason, 1982, 1991).

Original was first published in *Educational Policy, 7* (1), March, 1993, © 1993, Corwin Press, Inc. Reprinted here by permission of Corwin Press, a Sage Publications Company.

What distinguishes change in the teacher preparation program at the University of Connecticut from the typical is the degree to which this need for change has been taken seriously by a wide array of individuals with vested interests in change versus maintenance of the status quo (both at the university and in the schools). Second, the focus on and commitment to urban education clearly differentiates this program from many others. The restructuring of the teacher preparation program at the University of Connecticut was based on a reconceptualization of what preparation ought to entail, including inquiry as the base for practice and preparation, and in changes in the work life of university faculty as well as in school teachers taking on quite different roles in working with the university.

Our focus in this chapter is on the nature of the relationship between the university and the public school as an instance of cultural interaction and transformation. We believe that meaningful and successful university-school partnerships can develop only where such cultural interaction and transformation take place in a collaborative manner, and where all of the various constituencies involved in the partnership are willing to attempt to overcome traditional barriers and conceptual frameworks. As Cuban (1992) noted,

> The notion that professors and practitioners are engaged in the same enterprise, sharing common purposes, has been shredded into finely chopped specialties, distracting dichotomies such as theory and practice, and an abiding hunger for higher status by increasing the distance of scholars from public school classrooms. We are known by our degrees and publications. In being known, we have gained a crippling rigor in our research and kept potential colleagues at arms' length (p. 8).

This chapter, therefore, explores the development and operation of one urban Professional Development Center (PDC) in which such cultural barriers have been largely overcome by both university faculty and public school personnel and examines the policy issues that have driven program design.

THE TEACHER PREPARATION PROGRAM

In response to these challenges, the School of Education at the University of Connecticut undertook a thorough examination of its programs. This analysis led to a redesign of professional preparation across all grade levels and teaching disciplines. Central to the restructured program are strong partnerships with a number of school districts that represent the diverse, multicultural population within the state. These PDCs are collaborative efforts involving school professionals, university faculty and administrators, and students from both environments. Activities in many of the PDCs go well beyond traditional school-university interactions in which the student teaching experience often consists of little more than an apprenticeship with a single teacher in one school. The PDCs seek to play a significant role in professional development at all levels and in promoting school and university change.

Instituting large-scale comprehensive change can be a difficult and often emotional process. Values, beliefs, and habits deeply held by the various players often hinder the process of change. In the University of Connecticut experience, breaking barriers that have traditionally kept the profession stagnant was initially made possible by a dedicated core of faculty, department chairs, and the dean of the School of Education. Committees consisting of school administrators, teachers, university faculty, and students were formed to design a new program. Teams were established to work on the core curriculum, clinical experiences, master's year internships, integrative seminars, and case study approaches to problem analysis and reflective practice. It was an intense process that required much labor and goodwill on the part of many people, but after considerable debate and dialogue, at times heated, a broad, general consensus was achieved about the nature and structure of the program. Debate and discussion continues as specific program objectives are refined and as program evaluation data are analyzed.

This is not to suggest that the process of developing the new program was either easy or without problems. Indeed, there were a number of major problems that had to be faced and addressed. First of all, in the redesign of the teacher education curriculum, interactions of a far more involved and intense sort with liberal arts faculty were needed. Although such interactions were successfully achieved for the most part, they came at a significant cost in terms of faculty and administrative time and energy and were not uniformly successful. In fact, in one case, liberal arts faculty members chose to eliminate their certification program rather than accept the more rigorous new program.

Another area in which resistance occurred was in our interactions with the State Department of Education and the regional educational service agencies that fall under its quasi-control. During the same period when we were redesigning our teacher education program, the State Department of Education, acting under legislative mandate, was engaged in widespread reform of public education, which included significant changes in teacher certification requirements (BEST Program, Education Enhancement Act of 1986). Underlying much of the State Department of Education reform effort was an essentially simplistic competency-based model of teacher preparation and evaluation, that inevitably led to conflicts with respect to the nature, purposes, and goals of our teacher education program, which was based on a reflective-analytic model of the teacher as a professional and educational leader.

Although the potential for conflicts with the State Department of Education continues to exist, a modus vivendi has been reached in which our program is seen to go beyond the minimal mandates of the state, as is demonstrated by the recent full accreditation of our new program by the State Department of Education. Although our model emphasizes university-school collaboration and assumes such collaboration as a necessary component of the program, many teachers and administrators in the public schools were initially understandably skeptical about our intentions. As one of our faculty members commented in an early meeting in one of the PDCs, "I know that you're thinking that one of the all-time big lies is, 'I'm from the university and I'm here to help you,' but we really are here to try to help and be helped—and to learn from each other." Neither teachers nor administrators in the public schools were accustomed to the number of both students and faculty that would be present in our PDC model, and in the beginning, we were not always entirely welcome in the schools. Consequently, we moved slowly and cautiously to develop professional and personal relationships with school-based personnel. Gradually, as it became clear that we were in the schools for the duration, and as both students and teachers in the public schools came to take our presence as a natural part of the school milieu, collaboration became both more natural and vibrant. It is important to note here, however, that it has not been possible for us to "rest on our laurels" in the schools; new faculty, students, and administrators (both in the schools and at the university) must be socialized into this collaborative culture for it to continue every year. It is the age-old dilemma of bringing new people on board with an opportunity to experience the developmental process that those previously involved had experienced without having to return to square one.

Another issue concerned traditional university practice and the agreements between the State Department of Education and the teacher unions that involved cooperating teachers treating student teachers as chicken feed to be spread widely. Our Holmes Group PDC model called for a few partnerships where both partners wanted mutual change (Goodlad, 1988) so that cohorts of students and faculty in sizable numbers could have an impact on each other; also, programmatically having sizable numbers of students in a few locations means more faculty could spend more time there. Consequently, many school districts, schools, principals, teachers, and professional associations were angry because they were not selected.

Finally, our own faculty members have been divided over aspects of the new program. Although decisions related to the new program were made democratically and publicly over a five-year period and involved extensive discussion, debate, and dialogue and pilot efforts, a small group of faculty have continued to resist the changes. This is, of course, a normal part of university politics and is only to have been expected. Even so, one faculty member chose to publish an editorial essay in the local newspaper in the midst of our preparations for both National Council for Accreditation of Teacher Education (NCATE) and state accreditation visits, attacking the content and assumptions of the new program as well as the process by which it had come about. In response to this essay, a number of other essays and letters to the editor were published, including letters from faculty members, students in the program, superintendents, and principals involved in the program. In the various PDCs, teachers and administrators voiced shock, outrage, and frustration about the essay. In short, the essay, intended to challenge and critique the program, ended up demonstrating the strong sense of ownership and pride in the program held by all types of participants.

The program that emerged from this process was intended to address a number of the major criticisms of traditional teacher preparation programs, including concerns about the subject matter preparation of students, the need for extensive and varied clinical experiences throughout preparation, the importance of student exposure to and familiarity with a well-articulated knowledge base, and the development of critical, reflective, and analytical reasoning skills. The components of the program were designed and pilot tested over a three-year period and fully implemented in fall 1991. In articulating program direction, the following tenets of professional preparation were adopted and followed:

1. A broad liberal arts background with a specific subject matter major would be part of each student's educational plan.
2. Every student would participate in progressively challenging clinical experiences, including a mandatory urban placement.
3. A common core of pedagogical knowledge would be offered to *all* education majors, regardless of final area of certification, in addition to subject-specific pedagogy.
4. Teaching competence would be built across six clinical experiences.
5. More critically, the analysis and reflection of classroom behavior and school and community situations would be recognized as essential in preparing teachers to be decision makers and leaders in their chosen profession.

The University of Connecticut was an early member of both the Holmes Group and the National Network for Educational Renewal; the tenets of both were guiding forces in the resulting programs. This model of teacher preparation integrates the bachelor's and master's degrees, with students spending their first two years in a liberal arts program. This is followed by two years in the School of Education, during which students take pedagogical course work, spend time in clinical settings in various school environments, and continue their study in liberal arts. Finally, students complete a fifth (master's) year that includes an internship and a school-based research project. Enrollment limits are established in each program. Most entering students have at minimum a 3.0 grade point average from their first two years in liberal arts and a score of

1,000 or better on the Scholastic Assessment Test (SAT). This student profile contradicts many reports that the quality of the educational work force is declining and that schools of education are unable to attract academically qualified students (Darling-Hammond, 1984). All students are required to complete a liberal arts major, as well as the university's general education requirements.

It should be noted that for individuals wishing to make a midcareer change to teaching, based on a liberal arts degree in a discipline appropriate to the public schools, we have insisted on degrees relevant to the subject matter taught in schools, as opposed to majors in psychology, sociology, family studies, and communications. While it is indeed possible for such a person to enter the program as a graduate student in the School of Education, he or she must complete two full years and a summer of course and clinic work; previously it took 18 months. Needless to say, easier options are readily available at other state and private institutions. We have never claimed that our program is either easy or fast; our concerns have been rather on the quality and rigor of the educational experiences that we provide.

The teacher education program is organized in four strands: core, clinic, seminar, and subject-specific pedagogy. Core is the educational content that the faculty have collectively determined to be essential for all students regardless of certification area and consistent with state and national standards. Clinic is a carefully designed and sequenced set of experiences in the PDCs in which students view, practice, and analyze the content of core. Seminar is designed to bridge the gap often found between theory (core) and practice (clinic). More specifically, seminar focuses on the analysis and reflection of experiences encountered in the field in juxtaposition to learning in content course work. Every phase of the program emphasizes analysis and inquiry in an effort to develop professional decision-making abilities and ethical behavior. Students keep journals, complete case studies, prepare critical incidents, and engage in dialogue throughout the program. The fourth and fifth years of the program feature subject-specific pedagogy deemed essential to individual teaching disciplines. Thus, while students have a broad set of theoretical and practical experiences, they also spend significant time studying, analyzing, and practicing the craft of their chosen teaching discipline.

The series of clinical experiences lead students through progressively challenging and focused fieldwork. Students rotate in rural, urban, and suburban settings, as well as experience educational organizations and classrooms from elementary grades through high school. All students are placed at least once in an urban school district, and every student has the opportunity to work with students with disabilities. The multicultural nature of this approach allows students to better understand the diversity of the school population and to view education from an individual-needs versus group-needs perspective.

Again, it is important to note that the diversity of experiences does not result in a diminution of clinical preparation in the subject matter specialization in a certification area. In fact, the actual time spent in the student teaching experience in the student's certification area is at least as extensive as it traditionally would have been.

The content and direction of the master's year is critical in the overall development of professionals who will be capable of implementing models for teacher and school change, taking lead positions, conducting action research, and mentoring novice teachers. This advanced year of study is designed to expand the professional's skill and knowledge in the areas of curriculum development, instructional design, research, consultation, and leadership. During this fifth year, students complete 20-hours-per-week internships each semester in PDCs. The configuration of these internships varies, depending on the need of the school or school system and the student's individual interests and professional needs. Some students might be involved in direct classroom planning and instruction, others might act as supervisors and mentors for junior year students, and still others might be engaged in the design and implementation of school research and development projects. All master's interns must complete a school-based research project.

THE ROLE OF THE PROFESSIONAL DEVELOPMENT CENTER

It is the intent of the PDCs to move beyond traditional university-school relationships toward the creation of centers dedicated to change within schools and to the enhancement of the teaching profession. Although the PDC allows for supervised and sequenced clinical experiences in the preparation of prospective teachers and other educational professionals (e.g., school counselors, school psychologists, and principals), it is also an environment in which research-based instructional practices and programs can be observed and experienced by those preparing for professional careers in education. Additionally, this arrangement provides for the ongoing professional development of university faculty and school personnel. University and school colleagues work together to identify educational dilemmas and propose and test joint solutions. Dialogue on all levels, research on current educational practice, and continued questioning and reflection constitute the philosophical basis for the PDC. The PDC is not an add-on to the preparation program or the project of one or two faculty members, rather; it is central to the operation and success of this model of professional preparation.

Currently, the School of Education has established such relationships with schools in eight school districts. Although the configuration of each of the PDCs is unique, due to location (urban, suburban, or rural) and local culture, common to all PDCs are several underlying principles for development. First, we seek to provide the best possible environment for student learning and personal self-fulfillment. Second, through the interaction of university and school faculties and administrations, we are better able to provide challenging opportunities for preservice teachers and professional development for teachers, administrators, and university faculty. Last, collaborative research and development projects can be planned and carried out, advancing both educational theory and practice. University faculty and students, teachers, school administrators, and support personnel work together in teams to address particular goals, problems, and research questions. All clinical preparation takes place within these PDCs.

Our experience with PDCs, and with one urban, culturally diverse secondary school in particular, has from the start been implicitly guided by the work of Michel Foucault. Foucault (1972), writing about the study of archaeology, suggested that

> archaeology tries to define not the thoughts, representations, images, themes, preoccupations that are concealed or revealed in discourses; but those discourses themselves, those discourses as practices obeying certain rules. It does not treat discourse as a *document*, as a sign of something else, as an element that ought to be transparent, but whose unfortunate opacity must often be pierced if one is to reach at last the depth of the essential in the place in which it is held in reserve; it is concerned with discourse in its own volume, as a *monument*. It is not an interpretative discipline: it does not seek another, better-hidden discourse (pp. 138–139).

The nature of discourse was a continuing theme in Foucault's work. As Ball (1990) has noted recently,

> Discourse is a central concept in Foucault's analytical framework. Discourses are about what can be said and thought, but also about who can speak, when, and with what authority. Discourses embody meaning and social relationships; they constitute both subjectivity and power relations (p. 2).

This emphasis on discourse and on the embodiment in discourses of power relations was reflected early in our experiences in the PDCs. Our contact with the PDCs began with a desire to increase the university's presence in the public schools and to ensure that our students experienced a variety of different, "real work" educational environments, especially multicultural environments. These concerns were largely the result of our academic background and our familiarity with the compelling literature on the need for school reform in the United States (see, e.g., Goodlad, 1991; Sarason, 1991). Beyond these relatively simple concerns, we had no specific agenda to speak of, nor were we consciously attempting to make sense of what we saw and experienced from any particular theoretical framework, perspective, or latest "fad." Further, we deliberately avoided the adoption of a single model of school change, relying instead on a more open, eclectic approach to reform. We and our colleagues in the schools were (and still are) well aware of the complexities and barriers to be faced. But we have slowly constructed new relationships of trust, caring, and mutual goals. This has been accomplished through many small successes. Teachers, administrators, or we ourselves would identify a problem or an opportunity and tackle it together. We insist that our faculty and students keep whatever promises they make. Thus, apart from an intellectual curiosity and a general commitment to inquiry in the school context, the development of our relationships with the PDCs was guided by events, issues, crises, and the personalities of and in the schools. We functioned, and continue to function, as members of the school community, but this does not mean that we ceased also to be members of the university community. We have, in short, participated in an ongoing, multidirectional process of cultural transformation, in which we as university faculty members, our students, public school teachers and administrators, and high school students have all been players. Initially, some faculty members and students feel a dissonance between their school life and their university life, but as time passes, that dissonance lessens, although, of course, it never completely fades.

CHANGES WITHIN THE UNIVERSITY
AND SCHOOL COMMUNITY

Changes for Faculty and Teachers

The discontinuity between how teachers think about and engage in class-room-based inquiry and how university faculty think about and conduct "research" contributes to the chasm between these two groups of professionals (Bracey, 1990; Cochran-Smith & Lytle, 1990). Bridging this gulf has been one of the central goals of the PDC model of teacher preparation. In our own case, there has been a strong commitment to inquiry, and especially inquiry in the context of the PDCs, on the part of university faculty, students, and school-based personnel. This commitment to inquiry has been manifested in a variety of ways, including a concern with the development of reflective practice and a focus on ongoing, collaborative research among university faculty, students, and teachers. Much of the research that has taken place has been classroom- and school-based action research of various types, but more traditional studies, including detailed ethnographies of school culture, have also been conducted. Perhaps most important in this regard has been the emergence, among members of all of the different cultural constituencies, of an orientation and predisposition toward inquiry.

In our endeavor to encourage a "culture of inquiry," university faculty members have been very careful to ensure that the primary motivation for collaborative studies has come from school-based personnel, with research agendas being driven by classroom teachers or school administrators rather than by the university faculty. We have taken this position because of our recognition of the tendency for collaborative research efforts in schools to be controlled by and disproportionately benefit university faculty (Miller & Martens, 1990). In accomplishing this, it is quite noticeable that the interactions among teachers, administrators, faculty, and students have changed significantly. Although a few teachers remain who want to talk only about the university's basketball team, most engage in discussions about particular students or groups of students and about efforts at mainstreaming, the development of curriculum for global education, alternative teaching methods, or classroom research projects. These discussions occur in staff lounges, department chair offices, the faculty dining room, the library-media center, and elsewhere. Most often, the discussion begins on an informal basis and proceeds to a jointly planned effort.

If "scholarly inquiry and excellence in teaching and the preparation of teachers are interlinked" (Soder & Sirotnik, 1990, p. 402), then faculty must be willing and able to commit both time and resources to the endeavor of teacher preparation. Further, such activity must be valued and encouraged by the university. This has been the case at the University of Connecticut and has made possible much of what has transpired in the creation of working partnerships. A large number of faculty members have invested considerable time and effort, changing not only the way they individually and collectively view their own work but also the way in which they are viewed and understood by their school counterparts. When the PDCs began, teachers, based on past experience, clearly believed that the university faculty were there for the moment— to supervise a student teacher or to give "advice." Four years later, we are seen as true colleagues by many of our partners. The changes in university faculty members and teachers began with a few, and thereafter, each semester more were welcomed aboard. Some will never join in, but a critical mass has. The time spent has been worthwhile; it has allowed for change in ourselves as well as in the practice of education. Individual lives of students have been changed, and classroom teachers are conducting research about problems that are important to them. Finally, university faculty members have found renewed faith in the efficacy of research and its ability to directly affect classroom practice and the preparation of teachers. Examples of such collaborative research include a large-scale ethnographic and statistical study of school dropouts, the chronicling of a math-science team-teaching and curriculum-planning undertaking, the joint exploration of a global studies program, the examination of the effects of incorporating language arts into the content area of social studies, the tracking of the effectiveness of a computer-assisted writing project for a number of at-risk urban high school and middle school students, and the examination of the success of team teaching in the integration of students with disabilities into mainstream settings.

Throughout the planning process we recognized that the concept "critical mass" would be a necessary element of the new program. For faculty members to devote more time to particular schools in the partnerships and to allow them to do more of their teaching there as well as to conduct more of their research in schools, it was necessary to have all of our students in a few locations. As a result of careful planning, many university faculty members, as well as the dean of the School of Education, spend at least one day per week in PDCs. Typically, faculty members supervise students, participate in research and development projects, join teams of teachers who are revising curriculum or instructional practices, or assist in the planning of new programs. The university faculty member thus has an opportunity to carry out a large part of his or her academic responsibility (teaching, scholarship, and service) in a school or set of schools in an integrated fashion. This has been a vast improvement over the traditional model for university faculty, in which these three types of responsibilities have typically been quite separate. University faculty members who participate in the teacher preparation program come from every department within the School of Education, thus ensuring that teacher preparation is a schoolwide responsibility. Prior to the institution of the revised program, an estimated 30 percent of the faculty was involved in undergraduate teacher preparation. Approximately 75 percent of all School of Education faculty members now participate directly in the teacher preparation program, often in courses and seminars on campus as well as in various roles in the PDCs.

In the Hartford PDC, for example, there are typically 40 juniors and seniors (one day per week), 25 student teachers (full-time), 20 graduate interns (20 hours per week), and nine faculty members (one day per week). In addition to the clinical portion of the preprofessional program, there are weekly on-site analytical seminars for students, that are conducted by university faculty members and classroom teachers. There are also a number of research and development projects under way, staffed by the university faculty, students, and teachers, most of whom directly serve public school students (e.g., computerized writing labs, cross-age and peer tutoring, and a Future Teachers of America club). Faculty and teachers have designed an interdisciplinary, ninth-grade house plan and a global studies program; others have worked to link regular and special education teachers to increase mainstreaming, and other projects are in place or in the design phase. In this setting, undergraduates, master's-level interns, and doctoral students, along with teachers and the university faculty, are conducting a variety of research projects that address concerns relevant to urban education. Most important, many have become colleagues, with distinctions or barriers of perceived job roles removed. There are many friendships and much respect.

The dialogue among students, faculty, teachers, and principals reaches deeper levels every year, as it continues examining purposes and structures. The willingness of all to challenge what has been and the desire to create anew is a steady evolutionary growth. Further, it is important to note that collaboration has taken place not only between the School of Education and the PDCs but also within the university community. Strong relationships with the College of Liberal Arts and Sciences and the School of Human Development and Family Relations have been critical in the overall design of the preparation program. In the university context, one of the unintended but very positive outcomes of this restructuring process has been that many faculty members have developed cross-departmental commitments, interests, and relationships. As one junior faculty member recently commented, "I don't really know where I fit—and it doesn't bother me at all. The colleagues that I work most closely with are almost all in other departments, but we really feel that we're making a difference—that's what counts." Many faculty members have also become deeply involved in community-based activities tied to the PDCs and have become advocates for the communities and groups that the PDCs (and thus the university) serve.

Much faculty development has taken place from the planning stage through implementation and revision. Faculty members have assisted one another in the planning and delivery of each phase of the program. A series of professional development seminars has been held for them. These sessions have focused on the integration of core with seminar and clinic experiences. Faculty members have been encouraged to work together and learn from one another. Sessions have been held to critique and revise particular segments of the program. Faculty members conduct seminars for other faculty members on how they teach particular concepts or skills, how they supervise students, and how to conduct a seminar. This too has evolved from wariness to openness and mutual support. Typical departmental lines have been blurred in this process. For example, in the school context, a faculty member from special education might work closely with a faculty member in reading to assist a school team in the redesign of a language arts curriculum.

Professional development extends well beyond the university itself into the school setting and affects school professionals and university faculty on a continuing basis. In-service activities are no longer "one shot" lectures delivered by the "experts." Rather, in-service needs are planned and delivered jointly by school and university personnel. The lecture format is rarely used; instead, seminar sessions designed to explore problems and suggest solutions are the most common approach. Typical of such activities has been an ongoing series of in-service meetings concerned with both multicultural and global studies in the context of an urban secondary school and planning sessions for a new urban elementary school.

Another major shift that has taken place in the Hartford PDC has been in university faculty members directing their grant and project development activities toward the PDC rather than creating artificial environments or spreading their activities across the educational landscape. By directing grant monies and developmental thrusts into the PDCs and by basing such efforts on existing problems and needs in the PDCs, opportunities for school change, research on innovative teaching methodologies, and the viewing of and participation in these practices have become part of the novice professional's development. These activities also add significantly to the professional development of all involved. Sometimes the grants are initiated by teachers and administration, at other times by university faculty, but most culminate in partnership activities.

Changes for Students

The teacher preparation program is sequenced, analytical, and rigorous. It provides experiences in differing settings with a variety of learners. Student diversity is stressed and issues of multiculturalism are embedded throughout the curriculum. Clinical experiences that span rural, suburban, and urban environments ensure exposure to the diverse populations that future teachers must be prepared to instruct. Students are actively involved in a course of study that allows them to view the practice of teaching from a "school as organization" perspective rather than from a singular classroom, cutting across teaching disciplines. How the prospective teacher views students who might be considered "different" is central to much of the core content as well as to his or her clinical experiences. The university student is directed to analyze his or her own behaviors, learn methods for research, and begin to take a leadership role whenever possible. Observing students' progress through these experiences has allowed for more active mentorship of novice professionals by both university and school faculty and administration. In several cases, students have early on in their preparation made directional shifts in their intended area of certification. The place of the PDC in virtually all aspects of the teacher preparation program, in short, is one of centrality.

Changes in the educational experiences of high school students are also seen on a regular basis. These students often become instructors for the university student. Consider the case of David and Mark (pseudonyms). David was in the teacher preparation program and wished to be a secondary English teacher. For his junior year, he was assigned to a computer-based writing lab in the Hartford PDC, working with a group of students of whom approximately 60 percent were Hispanic. One of the students in this "special education" class was a young man with cerebral palsy named Mark. He has limited speech and poor motor control and was in a wheelchair. David perceives Mark as "retarded." Despite their educational, socioeconomic, cultural, and racial differences, these two young men began to work together, learning the computer, the software, and the writing process. A number of weeks later, Mark printed out the following story:

My Life Story

I was born on June 10th, 1982 in St. Francis Hospital to Regina Chavis and to a father I don't know about and have never met. I wonder what it would have been like to have had a father figure in my life. The reason why he left was because when I was two years old I was found to have Cerebral Palsy. My mom said times were hard when he left. She also said she wanted to give me up because the doctors told her that I was going to be retarded. But she didn't let that happen. It took a lot of years before I could actually walk. The first of many operations were performed. It was long and hard but I did what I had to do to achieve the first goal and my best goal I think. There are still a lot of obstacles I have to overcome. But I am determined to achieve all of my goals in life. (presented in Sweeney, 1991, p. 23).

It was fascinating to watch these two young men, who have affected each other's lives forever. As Mark says, "I'm not retarded—I wish all my teachers knew that," David has tears in his eyes. David's life as a teacher has been inextricably altered as a result of his contact with Mark. In the future, David will be far less likely to form opinions about his students based on casual observation or labels of disability. In fact, David has gone on to work toward dual certification—in English and special education.

POLICY, PROCESS, AND NORMATIVE CHANGES

The policy issues embedded in the program rationale and changes described earlier can be categorized as those that directly affect the work life of faculty members, curriculum and student matters, and institutional relationships. In many instances, the process of change, the changes in norms, and policy issues are wedded. Some of these issues and matters were determined by formal faculty votes, some by consensus as changes evolved, and some by informal understanding. The changes described herein began with general commitments to the overall premises and framework put forth by the Holmes Group (1986, 1990) and by John Goodlad's (1991) National Network for Educational Renewal. The Holmes Group framework provided goals and structure for a complete revamping of the teacher preparation program that included liberal arts majors, more extensive clinical preparation, clinical practice based on reflection and inquiry, and preparation based in PDCs: This resulted in the integrated bachelor's-master's degree program previously described.

The National Network for Educational Renewal premises and framework provided a new cultural paradigm that suggested that significant and ongoing change in teacher preparation and in schools can occur only if both change together, with collaboration functioning as the essential component. It was this belief that led the program change to begin with the identification, formation, planning, and implementation of PDCs. From the beginning, teachers, principals, and central office staff from the schools met with faculty members to discuss, debate, dream, and design a range of clinical preparation experiences. As these changes were being implemented, evaluated, and refined, the teacher preparation program was being designed and phased in. Hence for two years the faculty were straddling the old and the new programs—the common denominator being the PDCs, in which about 90 percent of the clinical preparation took place for both programs. The transition was aided by the fact that a policy decision had been made that the new program would be a responsibility of all departments in the School of Education, so that many areas of faculty knowledge that had not traditionally been part of teacher preparation would be so in the future. This decision was also seen as a way to involve a greater percentage of the faculty in schools and a way to encourage more school-based research on the part of university faculty members.

As the partnerships began building, trust and role modeling were seen as critical to ensure significant, rather than cosmetic, changes. In urban settings, the distrust of universities was powerful and widespread. How many times had deans and faculty members come in with soft-money projects and disappeared when the money dried up? How many times had university presidents promised undying commitment to the city schools with great media fanfare and then two years later had only one or two faculty members in the schools? How many faculty members wrote about how horrible the teachers and teaching were in the city schools? How many university faculty members feared contact with the poor and with minorities? How many faculty members had proclaimed they knew how to save city schools? At the same time, how many teachers and administrators saw no benefit in fresh observations and knowledge beyond the repetitious knowledge of practice? How many believed theory was irrelevant? How many believed research results were useless? How many believed university students would be a burden rather than providing assistance in formulating new patterns of instruction?

The answer to all of these questions, of course, was "many." As we met with the entire faculty of a 1,600-pupil inner-city high school for the first time and explained the changes we wanted to make in teacher preparation and how we needed their help, we endured some uncomfortable silences. Slowly, some of the points made in the foregoing questions were expressed, often in a hostile fashion. We maintained that we were in for the long haul and that we did not arrive with "the answers." We wanted a partnership. We were willing to work out and sign an agreement for a five- to 10-year collaborative endeavor. We would be making these changes with our existing resources—faculty and student time. We needed large numbers of students in a few locations to accomplish this. We decided that if significant changes were to occur in the norms affecting faculty and if deep changes were to occur in our program that it was necessary to change how both the faculty and the students used their time. Like many schools of education, 93 percent of our budget is tied to the salaries of personnel; the alternative was to fund PDC activities through external grants and contracts. We, the university and school people, had experienced too many projects that disappeared once the soft money disappeared. These arguments and policy decisions, and, most significantly, our commitment that every teacher preparation student must have an urban experience, won the day. We also made the decision that the two faculty co-coordinators of the Hartford PDC would be present in the school at least one day every week and that other faculty members would also be there to supervise and others would be available to work on collaborative projects. Slowly, more and more teachers and faculty joined in, and each year the number of participants and projects has grown. This continued commitment of time and resources is clearly contributing to the overall success of this program.

The new teacher preparation program is dedicated to reflective practice and school-based inquiry. University students keep journals and field notes; they conduct classroom experiments; they prepare critical incidents. These materials and others are used in weekly in-school seminars headed by university faculty. Teachers are invited to participate; most do so. During the sessions it is difficult to determine who is who. The teachers and faculty alike praise these sessions as being invaluable, changing, through dialogue and reflection, their teaching and research practice. This has, of course, also been an evolutionary process.

POLICY ISSUES RELATED TO FACULTY WORK LIFE

It was noted earlier that a decision was made early on to effect program changes and to establish new institutional relationships using existing resources. University-wide, the budget is 93 percent personnel costs. To effect changes of the magnitude described meant changing the work life of faculty and students. The analogy used while revamping faculty roles and expectations was that of professors in a medical school who are able to instruct students while involved in clinical practice and simultaneously conducting research on the clinical practice in which they were engaged (Case et al.,

1986). Granted, the analogy is a loose one; nevertheless, it contained enough reality to stimulate and sustain change. Hence the concept of critical mass was essential: For faculty members to more fully integrate their responsibilities—teaching, research. and service—they must have enough students in a school or cluster of schools so that some of their teaching can take place there as well as their supervision responsibilities and that they also are able to conduct their research there. Service is a natural fallout from their involvement in the schools on curriculum and program design teams, technical assistance, and in-service education.

As this evolution occurs, in-school projects jointly determined to be desirable and for which existing resources of the university and the school system are not adequate are identified. It is around these shared dreams that the university and school have submitted proposals and received numerous grants. These activities have attracted support from local business, industry, and local foundations; federal grants have been written by faculty, teachers, and community services personnel. Much of this grant writing has been collaborative, with two or more of these parties teaming in the writing process. These monies do not support university faculty members or teachers. The monies buy equipment, materials, graduate students, and summer tutors. Our base of support continues, then, to be ourselves, the university faculty and school personnel.

These changes in faculty work life have a direct impact on hiring decisions. For example, when hiring an assistant professor in English education, we search for an individual who is not only expert in that field, from a major university, a researcher with a few good publications, and a proven teacher but also one who has some history and commitment to field-based teaching and field-based inquiry and to urban education. Weight is also given to certain research skills and methods as we attempt to represent a variety of inquiry and research methods. The retirement of almost one third of the faculty during the past five years, much of which was due to three state retirement incentives, was both costly and advantageous. The hiring of new faculty members committed to the precepts of the new program added needed strength and expertise.

As the new program was implemented, a staff development program for the faculty was instituted. Obviously, this had to be done with great care and sensitivity so as not to insult the faculty and yet at the same time to increase the use of a variety of instructional forms and continuous refinement of curriculum. This has become an ongoing process that has been successful: Many more instructional forms are evident than was previously the case. The use of the lecture–multiple-choice format of instruction and evaluation has decreased significantly. Student evaluations are regularly sought and highly positive, and faculty members have a deep understanding of and commitment to the entire program. These changes in faculty behavior have contributed to the overall success of this program.

The final policy area for the faculty is the matter of criteria and policies for promotion and tenure. It is our belief and experience that much myth and manipulation surround this issue. Often, we hear faculty members at national and regional meetings assert that if nontenured faculty members become involved in schools they will not meet the criteria for promotion and tenure. Our position is that a school of education is a professional school, not a liberal arts department; therefore, we have a major responsibility to schools and must conduct much of our work there. Our promotion and tenure criteria have changed only slightly. Teaching is still a very serious matter for us, and ample evidence is required to satisfy this criteria as well as strong supervision and advising skills. It should be noted that 80 percent of our faculty is involved in both undergraduate and graduate education. Doctoral students are about equal in number to the students in the integrated bachelor's-master's degree program in teacher preparation. The requirement for scholarship now gives equal footing to field-based research and qualitative research with the more quantitative, non–field-based research that has tended to dominate in the past, although some faculty still resist this change. Refereed publications and outstanding teaching practice are still the coin of the realm. As mentioned earlier, the service responsibility is more easily and significantly accomplished in the PDCs. Possibly those who decry university promotion and tenure requirements as an impediment to school-based activity do so as a convenient excuse not to change.

The key policy decision beyond the previously described curriculum and program change for students was to insist on a liberal arts or fine arts major that represents a subject matter taught in schools. Enrollment limits were established for each area (15 per secondary subject area, 25 special education, 45 elementary education). This was necessary to have faculty members responsible for clinical experiences and to have clinical experiences throughout the program. A liberal arts grade point average of at least 2.7 (most are over 3.0), SAT score of at least 1000, intensive interviews by the faculty, and the decision to admit students only once per year were the decisions made to guide the admissions process. This has resulted in very strong student cohorts that are respected on a university-wide basis. In fact, students in the School of Education are academically among the strongest on campus. School of Education students are a major presence in the university-wide honors program. By limiting enrollments, we ensured a faculty-student ratio that allows for a strong field-based program. Moving through the program in cohorts initiates the students in a culture of collegiality that was rare in the past—especially in the current integrated cohorts of secondary, elementary, and special education students.

Finally, as noted in our earlier examples, the changes in institutional relationships between the university and the partner school districts are much more changes in the culture of both than policy changes. The changes are based on mutual goals and aspirations, mutual commitment to children and schools. Collegiality, respect, and trust are essential to these partnerships.

CONCLUSIONS

Partnerships that address the changing needs of the educational community while simultaneously preparing future educators are essential in ensuring the success of schooling across the country. In this article, we have discussed the development of university-school partnerships that are pivotal to an integrated bachelor's-master's teacher preparation program. Our experience strongly indicates that these partnerships have enhanced the education of individual students; have provided professional development for teachers, faculty, and administrators; have fostered research activities within school environments; and are successful in building a new cohort of teachers who will be better prepared for the challenges of the next century. Entrenched organizational policies that have traditionally kept our educational cultures stagnant have been discussed openly, put to the test of change, and, in many instances, replaced with more effective, collaborative arrangements.

Evaluation of these changes is now taking place. It is not always easy to look at what you have done, predict the future impact of these changes, or develop a level of comfort with new ways of viewing the world of education. As Rose (1989) commented, "Having crossed boundaries, you sometimes can't articulate what you know, or what you know seems strange. . . . What are the gaps and discordances in the terrain? What mix of sounds—eerie and compelling" (pp. 241–242). We have tried to look at some of these gaps, to articulate what we believe we have seen, and to suggest directions in which we, and others, can now go. Our goal has been, and remains, the dream that all children can learn and that all teachers should be able to teach. To value difference—to sense when something is wrong and to have enough skill and fortitude to do something about it, and to not be afraid to question what is or to take a risk— that is what teaching should be about.

REFERENCES

Ball, S. J. (Ed.). (1990). *Foucault and education: Disciplines and knowledge.* London: Routledge.

Bracy, G. W. (1990). Rethinking school and university roles. *Educational Leadership, 47*(2), 65–66.

Case, C. W., Lanier, J. E., & Miskel, C. G. (1986, July–August). The Holmes Group report: Impetus for gaining professional status for teachers. *Journal of Teacher Education, 37*(4), 36–43.

Cochran-Smith, M., & Lytle, S. L. (1990, March). Research on teaching and teacher research: The issues that divide. *Educational Researcher, 19*(2), 2–11.

Cuban, L. (1992). Managing dilemmas while building professional communities. *Educational Researcher, 21*(1), 4–11.

Darling-Hammond, L. (1984). *Beyond the commission reports: The coming crisis in teaching.* Santa Monica, CA: Rand.

Foucault, M. (1972). *The archaeology of knowledge.* New York: Harper & Row.

Goodlad, J. I. (1988). The national network for educational renewal: Past, present, future (Occasional Paper No. 7, Center for Educational Renewal). Seattle: University of Washington, College of Education.

Goodlad, J. I. (1991). *Teachers for our nation's schools.* San Francisco: Jossey-Bass.

Goodlad, J. I., & Soder, R. (1992). *School-university partnerships: An appraisal of an idea* (Occasional Paper No. 15, Center for Educational Renewal). Seattle: University of Washington, College of Education.

Holmes Group. (1986). *Tomorrow's teachers.* East Lansing, MI: Author.

Holmes Group. (1990). *Tomorrow's schools.* East Lansing, MI: Author.

Miller, J., & Martens, M. (1990). Hierarchy and imposition in collaborative inquiry: Teacher researchers' reflections on recurrent dilemmas. *Educational Foundations, 4*(4), 41–59.

Rose, M. (1989). *Lives on the boundaries.* Middlesex, England: Penguin.

Sarason, S. B. (1982). *The culture of the school and the problem of change* (2nd ed.). Newton, MA: Allyn & Bacon.

Sarason, S. B. (1991). *The predictable failure of educational reform.* San Francisco: Jossey-Bass.

Soder, R., & Sirotnik, K. A. (1990). Beyond reinventing the past: The politics of teacher education. In J. I. Goodlad, R. Soder, & K. A. Sirotnik (Eds.), *Places where teachers are taught.* San Francisco: Josscy-Bass.

Sweeney, J. (Ed.). (1991). *Wings.* Storrs: University of Connecticut, Special Education Technology Lab, A. J. Pappanikou Center on Special Education and Rehabilitation.

JANE A. STALLINGS, DONNA L. WISEMAN,
and STEPHANIE L. KNIGHT

Chapter Eight

Professional Development Schools

A NEW GENERATION OF SCHOOL-UNIVERSITY PARTNERSHIPS

Throughout the 1980s, considerable national attention and criticism have been focused on the processes and products of public schools and on schools or colleges of education where teachers and administrators are prepared. This scrutiny has resulted in a wave of reforms, one of many in the long history of American education. While the first reforms encouraged more testing and additional requirements for students and teachers, the second wave of reform has concentrated on changing or "restructuring" these organizations (Maloney, 1989). A major proposition of the most recent reform efforts involves the simultaneous restructuring of schools and colleges of education.

Past efforts at reform in either schools or colleges of education have been initiated and implemented separately despite the seeming interconnectedness of the goals and needs of the two entities. For example, early laboratory schools, located primarily on college campuses, focused mainly on pre-service education, but were isolated from the public schools. As a result, lab schools lacked "real world" relevance. The portal schools of the 1970s, on the other hand, were designed to serve as a focus for school-university interaction in order to establish a point of entry for promising new curricula and practices (Stallings & Kowalski, 1990). Schools and universities signed written agreements and created plans for sharing responsibility for program development. While there was much rhetoric and elaborate planning, there was little action or institutionalization of ideas. By 1980, the term "portal schools" had disappeared from the literature (Stallings & Kowalski, 1990). Both models, the lab school as well as the portal school, lacked the focus on simultaneous restructuring that is a characteristic of the current reform movement.

One of the ways to accomplish simultaneous restructuring is embodied in the concept of professional development schools (PDS). A term initially used by the Holmes Group, the PDS has many of the characteristics of earlier partnership initiatives sponsored by schools and universities. However, instead of merely a partnership with parallel, but separate goals and activities, the PDS resembles a symbiotic relationship that is in place long enough to allow a "lasting, powerfully productive relationship to develop" (Goodlad and Soder, 1992, p. 12). Current conceptions of PDSs, are characterized as organizational structures that include new flexible roles and rotating assignments for teachers; strong connections with parents and community organizations; new varied ways of assessment; and teacher decision-making powers (Holmes Group, 1990). School-university partnerships are supported through stable, mutual governance, enduring budget allocations, new positions that span institutional boundaries, integration of school and university faculty, new rewards and incentive structures, and recruitment of faculty committed to collaboration (Holmes Group, 1990). The PDS offer the promise of improvement of not only in-service and pre-service education but also the education of elementary and/or secondary students attending public schools (AACTE, 1991).

Although the current conceptualization of PDS incorporates aspects of school-university cooperatives of the past, (Holmes Group, 1990), it should be considered a new model of teacher education. A major difference between traditional partnerships of the past and the more recent PDS model is the focus on parity or true collaboration. The consistent focus on parity between schools and universities and the goal of a mutually beneficial reciprocity produces an entity that is very different from past models of school-university collaboration. The parity associated with a PDS, based on shared respect and joint decision making, exhibits the following characteristics: (1) The common goal of dual, simultaneous restructuring of schools and college curricula for preservice teachers and the expectation that mutual benefit will result from all joint activities form the basis for partnership. A shared vision of improving schooling for all participants undergirds all activities; (2) Power, authority, and decision making regarding the partnership are shared by participants and are based on consensus agreements. Implicit in the shared decision making is the empowerment of all participants; and (3) A commitment to collaborative inquiry and evaluation of the processes and products of the PDS is evident.

When the parity issue is considered in relation to these characteristics, school-university relationships look very different from simple partnership relationships of the past. Additional differences can also be more clearly delineated by reviewing the developmental processes associated with PDS.

A MODEL FOR SIMULTANEOUS SCHOOL-UNIVERSITY RENEWAL

Professional Development Schools are more than a superficial partnership, and reflect a difference in the type of collaboration that has occurred between schools and universities in the past (Goodlad & Soder, 1992). In fact, current PDSs share several characteristics in process and form that make the subtle rhetorical differences appear quite large when operationalized.

The differences between PDSs and traditional school-university relationships first become noticeable during the development phase. While there are several ways that schools and universities can approach formation of a PDS, the process must embody the idea of shared, mutually beneficial, activity. The following model (See Figure 8.1) suggests some common components of simultaneous school-university restructuring but does not eliminate the possibility that a flexible process exists depending on the context of development. The model describes common elements necessary to establish a PDS, provides a framework to delineate the differences between the PDS concept and other school-university partnerships, and suggests indicators for identification and evaluation of PDS activities. Each of the components is discussed in more detail in the sections that follow.

Recognition of a Shared Context

An awareness and acceptance of the context the institutions share is inevitable and important. Shared contexts are those elements that are common to both the school and the university, such as geographical areas, similar populations, history, and political and economic climate. The total context can affect the ultimate goals of partnerships (Knight, Wiseman, & Smith, unpublished manuscript) as when national, state, and local mandates and societal demands provide the initial impetus for joint meetings to explore partnership possibilities. For example, the state of Texas has recently legislated funding to support school-university partnerships established to provide professional development based on technology. The funding is based on the premise that the planning teams who conceptualize the school-university partnership must represent an equal distribution of school, university, business, and community contributions.

Most universities and schools entering a partnership share a history of both formal and informal past interactions. For the most part, these activities are carried out with minimal interaction and collaboration between the institutions. The interactions may have been based on traditional pre-service teacher

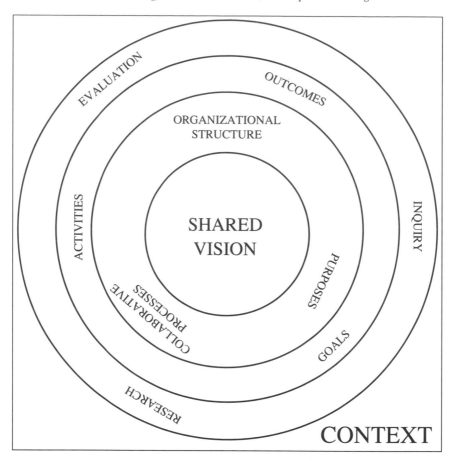

Fig. 8.1. Model for Simultaneous School-University Renewal.

education field experience arrangements and/or individual research projects. While these activities do not represent the type of interactions desired in a PDS, small scale collaboration can engender ties of mutual respect across the schools and universities (Hange, 1992) and provide the foundation for more complex relationships required by the PDS. These past collaborations become a part of the contextual makeup of a PDS.

The context forms the backdrop for the development and implementation of a PDS. The remaining components of the model are embedded in the context. As a result, all parts of the model are sensitive to variations in contextual elements that are amenable to change. For example, changes in funding may impact the resources available to carry out the proposed activities of the PDS. Or rapid shifts in demographics, such as the southwestern United States is currently experiencing, will affect the goals of a PDS associated with student learning and teacher preparation.

A Shared Vision of School-University Restructuring

At the heart of the model is the concept of a shared vision of school-university restructuring. Both the school and the university must establish expectations of what can occur as a result of school-university joint planning and activity. The vision moves beyond one that represents a single institutional view of what can be accomplished to a shared vision of partnership possibilities. As the vision evolves, it must be based on what is desired, not what is currently in place. In contrast, traditional partnership models often maintain existing and separate visions.

Negotiation of the shared vision requires both parties to consider two essential questions. First, as educators, what are our goals for our students and ourselves? Second, how does a partnership move us both closer to meeting our goals? To answer these questions, the school and university must identify areas of interest and concern that intersect, realizing that there are areas unique to each institution. The intersection of commonalties form the basis for a shared vision. Since neither partner can assume that initial, unspoken visions are congruent, this necessarily involves interaction and negotiation between partners. Often a philosophy, approach, or model can serve as the basis for establishing a shared vision. For example, institutions may focus on the middle school concept as a unifying theme, or on the implementation of an approach such as Accelerated Schools (Levin, 1987) to form the basis for the joint pursuit of common interests.

The context is the backdrop while the vision is the core of the model. The comparison of two PDSs in Texas (Knight, Wiseman, & Smith, unpublished manuscript) reveals that the context can produce similarities due to shared political and economic factors and differences due to histories and interactions at each of the settings. In one instance, the shared vision of the partnership, focused on the middle school philosophy and activities, was initiated in a "grass roots" manner based on informal discussion between two administrators. In a second example, the partnership vision revolved around a school restructuring philosophy, and activities were preceded by the development of a formal organizational structure by a large group of representatives from each institution. The context and vision may stay relatively intact as the development proceeds, but the remaining components may be characterized as interactive, flexible, and much more dependent upon the unique context and the shared vision of the partners.

Establishment of Organization and Structure

Each PDS must develop an organization and structure to support the ongoing activities initiated by schools and universities. As in other components of the process model, organization, structure, and decision making are based on parity between the two institutions. Parity can be affected by many different variables, but the type and level of initiation may impact the subsequent institutionalization of the partnerships, as well as the nature of interactions between the institutions. As in the examples given above, PDS initiations can range from grass roots project development to the establishment of sweeping district and university policies. Regardless of the initiatives' origins, a partnership eventually requires an explicit agreement between the leaders and administrators of the two entities that will provide the framework for subsequent organization and structure development.

Several factors must be considered relative to the development of a formal structure. These factors include, but are not limited to, reallocation of resources by individual institutions and issues related to shared resources and salaries within the partnership. Other factors may involve new role definition, rewards systems that support differing professional requirements, and recognition of shared responsibilities.

While the context in which the partnership occurs and the nature of the shared vision of the partners has a great impact on the structural development of a PDS, it also influences the process and products. In addition to creating the structure and organization, the partners must identify common goals based on the vision and initiate activities to move them closer to their goals.

Shared Process and Products

The shared processes and products include goals, activities, and outcomes associated with collaboration. While the processes and products associated with PDSs in general may have certain common characteristics across sites, they also will reflect the unique contexts of the two institutions. In other words, a PDS reflects general characteristics as well as site-specific characteristics. One of the general characteristics of the new generation of PDSs involves the notion of joint restructuring. The success of collaboration depends on the institutions' simultaneous commitments to the goals of educational renewal. In other words, both the school and the university must work together to change the way they educate their respective learners. The new generation of school-university partnerships will move beyond just one more iteration of rhetorical reform only if they are as committed to the outcome of school renewal as to the process and only if that outcome involves dual as opposed to traditional unilateral restructuring.

At another level, the joint purposes will yield measurable objectives that both parties feel are important and reflect the context of the shared agreements. For example, a collaboration might be based on the implementation of the middle school philosophy into a middle school and teacher education program. The school-university team must identify the objectives that they will want to measure. They may establish the delivery of an interdisciplinary unit to both sixth graders and college pre-service teachers as an objective. To accomplish these objectives may involve the resolution of a series of value conflicts that require extensive discussion and compromise by those involved. The ability of the collaborators to establish common processes based on parity may determine their success at working together to achieve their common goals. However, a constant appraisal of collaborative processes and products is necessary in order to determine the progress the partnership is making toward stated goals. This inquiry must also be a collaborative effort.

Collaborative Inquiry

The area of inquiry, research, and evaluation could potentially produce the greatest source of conflict in the collaboration. Participants must be critical of collaborative efforts as they establish the PDS and be constantly aware of the balance that must be established between the reflective proclivity of the university and the activity preference often associated with public schools (Cuban, 1992; Knight, Wiseman, & Smith, unpublished manuscript). In their role as self-appointed reflectors, university collaborators often must initiate the cooperation of schools in the analysis and evaluation of processes and products of collaboration. But the role of inquiry is imperative particularly as the new generation of partnerships evolves. The success of future generations of partnerships depends on systematic study of the patterns, promises, and pitfalls of those currently being implemented. Otherwise, the PDS may join portal and laboratory schools as merely a footnote in the history of educational reform.

Even after the importance of inquiry is recognized by the two parties, the process evolves differently than traditional university research. Conceptualization of the inquiry process for PDSs must necessarily reflect parity and shared interests. Inquiry can no longer be viewed as the domain of the university alone or framed by outside parties conducting unrelated studies in schools. However, the compilation of anecdotal information with the unstated intent of validating the collaborative effort will also be counterproductive. In order to add to our knowledge of the process and outcomes of PDSs, the two partners are obligated to jointly participate in the design and implementation of studies to investigate the processes and outcomes at the school level, the university level, and the collaborative level. This process will provide formative information for revising and improving the process and outcomes of the partnership and contribute to a spirit of scholarly inquiry on the part of all involved.

The Interactive Nature of the Model

While many parts of the PDS model can be delineated and described separately, in fact, they are interdependent. If there is an adjustment or revision in any one of the components, the other components may change as a result. If, when the partners take stock, they realize that the structure must change in order for teacher education courses to reflect what is happening at the school, then the overall process might adjust and the inquiry process could change. The impact of changes made is dependent on where the adjustment occurs in the model. If the vision changes, then the entire model must make substantial adjustments. However, if the inquiry process changes, it might not be as apt to change all the other entities in the process. This suggests that the model is dynamic, flexible, and responsive to changes and differing contexts.

There are also multiple ways of building or linking the components of the model. While all the components of the model must be present and consistent, the context may suggest different arrangements and linkages, therefore suggesting differing processes and results.

The Houston Teaching Academy

One early example of the PDS is the Houston Teaching Academy (HTA) established in the late 1980s (Stallings, Bossung, and Martin, 1990). The HTA serves as an excellent example to demonstrate the components of the model (see Fig. 8.1). The vision of the partnership revolved around the need for excellent teachers for disadvantaged inner-city schools. The inner-city multicultural school involved in the project mirrored the demographic diversity of the community shared by the university and school. This shared context influenced the goals and activities pursued by the partners. The long-range goal was to improve the instruction of teachers and student teachers so that inner-city students could prosper academically. One goal of the partnership was to develop teachers who were effective teachers of the inner city population, were self-analytical, and shared in the decision-making responsibility for carrying out the goals of the program. Goals for children in the school included active participation in their own education.

The organization and structure of the partnership was based on collaborative decision-making councils that established the policy for the HTA. For example, the council sought and received school board approval to close a school and create a professional development school for teachers; decided upon the qualifications for the HTA principals and teachers; and established a shared budget. Activities focused on the development and delivery of the weekly seminars whose purpose was to bridge the gap in communication existing among the college supervisors, the classroom teacher supervisions, and the student teachers. An essential element of the inquiry component of the PDS was the observation of student and supervising teachers at the beginning and end of each semester. Participants were taught to analyze their own observation profiles or behavior, and they set the goals for behavior change. At the end of the semester they assessed their own change in behavior and set new goals.

The HTA is a successful example of a PDS, and it relied on the support and energy of many individuals in the project. It provides insights and understandings of the benefits derived from a PDS. However, even when there are individuals committed to the development of a PDS, there are certain factors that must be considered to ensure its success and continued evolution. These factors often become the challenges related to maintaining a healthy PDS.

CHALLENGES TO PDS COLLABORATION

While the notion of PDS appears to be positive and the benefits are numerous, there are several challenges that must be recognized during the process of initial school-university partnerships.

1. *Danger of superficiality.* A PDS may look like a collaborative model on paper, but it may not include the elements that identify the partnership as part of the new generation. The elements necessary for the new generation of partnerships include dual restructuring, shared vision, and parity. This challenge can be met by incorporating inquiry into PDS processes and outcomes in order to detect and remedy superficiality. Collaborative inquiry will reveal instances where there is only structure and no true change.

2. *Threat of fragmentation.* Partnerships may exhibit only parts of the model. For example, schools and universities may work together to implement pre-service field experiences, they may develop in-service training models, or they may design school-based research, but they may not engage in all of these activities. To truly exhibit the new generation of PDS, a partnership must engage in elements of all these components. Although there have been isolated and successful examples of school-university partnership, such as evidenced in the Houston Teaching Academy (Stallings, Bossung, & Martin, 1990), to date, there are few representative models illustrating the complex interrelation of all of these components (Goodlad, 1991). While one model may have one or two components, few models combine use of all the elements.

3. *Difficulties due to cultural clash.* Schools and universities are very different entities. They differ in "purpose, function, structure, clientele, reward systems, rules and regulations, ambiance, ethos" (Goodlad, 1988, p. 14). In particular, the reflection orientation of university professors and the action orientation of school personnel, often characterized as a theory and practice dichotomy, are in direct conflict in collaborative endeavors (Goodlad, 1988; Schlechty & Whitford, 1988). Recognition of the differences and possible contributions that each entity can make is necessary in order to overcome the conflicts that will arise. However, conflict resolution will depend on the redefinition of leadership at both school and university levels.

CHALLENGING TRADITIONAL NOTIONS OF LEADERSHIP

The previously described process model for establishing a PDS suggests many changes in the ways that schools and universities conduct their businesses. The parity that characterizes the PDS and sets it apart from previous school-university partnerships requires changes in the structure, organization, and roles of existing school and university entities. Restructured schools and colleges of education require a change in the traditional notion of all roles; in particular, the roles of university leaders are drastically different in a PDS as opposed to traditional school-university relationships (Stallings, 1992). College administrators must extend their leadership function to facilitate the school-university partnership necessary for joint renewal. School-university partnerships are labor intensive and require total commitment from those involved in the process. An administrator cannot mandate the commitment, but he or she must foster it.

Fostering commitment to school-university partnerships produces serious philosophical, theoretical, and practical discussions among faculty. The leaders of the colleges of education may need to allow the issues related to school-university partnerships to become the focus of debate for the college. There will be faculty members who feel that the prime mission of a college of education, the generation of knowledge, is impeded by partnerships. Other faculty members may argue that the PDS is no different than what had been going on in field-based programs of the past and still others in the college may believe that the PDS is not part of the mission of their department or division. The debate should be viewed as healthy and encouraged by the college leadership with the recognition that the interaction could result in a restructured vision for the college of education.

Extending the leadership roles of university administrators may produce differences in the way they view their domain and influence. The concept of extending leadership functions could result in two major paradigm shifts. These two conceptual differences are embodied in soliciting and encouraging input of school-based leaders and acting as a catalyst that promotes interaction and restructuring of both entities.

Extending leadership may mean that there is more contact with school superintendents, involvement with pilot schools, reassignment of an associate dean or other dean's staff to take responsibility for the development of school-university partnerships, encouragement of faculty to participate in teams, and participation with principals, faculty, and the college of education in developing a shared vision for the partnership. Much interaction between schools and universities is necessary to promote the partnership. It may be sometimes necessary for university leaders to act as catalysts to enable two very different organizations to get together to accomplish joint restructuring.

Providing ways for the two entities to interact can include engineering structures for initial contact between schools and colleges of education as well as maintaining the avenues required for continual interaction long after the first excitement of the partnership has vanished. The leadership in colleges of education will need to devise methods of communication between the partners as well as encourage maintenance of the vision. Many times this vision is lost in the day-to-day operation of school-university activities.

Often, the development of a PDS requires the dean to meet with other colleges in the university and elicit their participation in school-university partnerships. This may involve the identification of liberal arts and science faculty who devote a portion of their professional time contributing to the educational renewal efforts in the schools or the university setting. In other words, liberal arts and science faculty can be encouraged to become directly involved with public schools or to assist in the development of a collaborative teacher education curriculum.

College of education leaders are key in ensuring that all elements of the model are considered during the development and implementation of the PDS. They must facilitate the negotiation and maintenance of the shared vision, establish mechanisms for communication and inquiry, encourage institutionalization of the model, and create school-university families. This requires creative and supportive administrative procedures that ensure win-win situations, encourage all partners to learn and grow, and develop team players instead of game players.

REFERENCES

American Association of Colleges for Teacher Education. (1991). *Restructuring the education of teachers: Report of the Commission on the Education of Teachers in the 21st Century.* Washington, DC: Author.

Cuban, L. (1992). Managing dilemmas while building professional communities. *Educational Researcher, 21*(1), 4–11.

Darling-Hammond, L. (1989). Accountability for professional practice. *Teachers College Record, 91*(1), 59–80.

Goodlad, J. (1988). School-university partnerships for educational renewal: Rationale and concepts. In K.A. Sirotnik & J. I. Goodlad (Eds.), *School-university partnerships in action: Concepts, cases, and concerns* (pp. 3–31). New York: Teachers College Press.

Goodlad, J. (1991). A study of the education of educators: One year later. *Phi Delta Kappan, 73*(4), 311–316.

Goodlad, J., Soder, R., & Sirotnik, K. (1990). *Places where teachers are taught*. San Francisco: Jossey-Bass.

Goodlad, J. I. & Soder, R. (1992). School-university partnerships: An appraisal of an idea. Occasional Paper Series. Seattle: Institute for the Study of Educational Policy. University of Washington.

Hange, J. (1992). Fostering change through college-school collaborative mini grants. Presented at the American Association of Colleges of Teacher Education Annual Meeting, San Antonio, TX.

Holmes Group. (1990). *Tomorrow's schools: Principles for the design of professional development schools*. East Lansing, MI: Author.

Knight, S. L., Wiseman, D. L., & Smith, C. W. (Unpublished manuscript). The parameters of school-university partnerships: Considering the reflectivity-activity dilemma.

Levin, H. (1987). Accelerated schools for disadvantaged students. *Educational Leadership, 44* (6), 19–21.

Maloney, W. J. (1989). Restructuring. *The Executive Educator, 11* (10), 21–23.

Schlechty, P. C., & Whitford, B. L. (1988). Shared problems and shared vision: Organic collaboration. In K. A. Sirotnik & J. I. Goodlad (Eds.), *School-university partnerships in action: Concepts, cases and concerns* (pp. 191–204). New York: Teachers College Press.

Sikula, J. (1990). National commission reports of the 1980s. In W. R. Houston (Ed.), *Handbook of research on teacher education*, (pp. 72–82). New York: Macmillan.

Stallings, J. A. (1992, February). School-university collaboration for change: Challenging traditional notions of leadership. Paper presented at the Annual Meeting of the American Association of Colleges of Teacher Education, San Antonio, TX.

Stallings, J. A., Bossung, J., & Martin, A. (1990). Houston Teaching Academy: Partnership in developing teachers. *Teaching and Teacher Education, 6*(4), 355–365.

Stallings, J., & Kowalski, T. (1990). Research on professional development schools. In W. R. Houston (Ed.), *Handbook of research on teacher education* (pp. 251–263). New York: Macmillan.

Zimpher, N. (1990). Creating professional development school sites. *Theory into Practice, 29*(1), 42–49.

MICHELLE COLLAY

Chapter Nine

Creating a Common Ground

THE FACILITATOR'S ROLE IN INITIATING SCHOOL-UNIVERSITY PARTNERSHIPS

The Professional Development School (PDS) is an organization which, as Candide sings, "is the best of all possible worlds." Built on the strengths of the best educational practice and honoring a partnership of teacher educators, the PDS can and should provide a forum for teacher growth as well as student learning, a place where new teachers are nurtured and veteran teachers reinvigorated. The reality of the PDS, however, could remain as elusive as the dreams of Candide. The two partners, public schools and universities, are themselves complex bureaucracies with different sets of priorities and values. University-based people believe their hard work with pre-service teachers is washed out by the rigorous socialization of an archaic school system, and new teachers decry their inadequate university preparation for teaching after first steps in their own classrooms spawn the painful realization that they have just begun to learn. While the two worlds seem quite separate from one other, the ground where educators meet provides the potential to restructure both. The parallels between how both organizations function may actually allow optimism for change in each. In this chapter, I consider the role of teacher educators who move between the two systems and their ability to create a common ground.

The PDS concept emerged from debates about school restructuring, reform in teacher education, and new models of teacher preparation. The PDS is a learning community where innovation is welcome, research on best practice is conducted, and new and experienced educators collaborate toward reform of the educational system. Winitsky, Stoddart, and O'Keefe (1992)

reviewed the reemergence of clinical settings for teacher education, highlight-
ing recommendations from the Holmes Group:

> Critical to the Holmes reform agenda and the PDS idea is a systems view of
> education. . . . To improve one part of the system, one must improve all of it . . .
> the locus of reform has broadened to include the educational system, not just
> the individual classroom teacher (p. 5).

The educational "system" is at least two systems, each housing a group
of educators from different classes, ethnic and cultural backgrounds, and life
experiences; the organizational climate and rules for success in schools and
universities are markedly divergent and often conflict with each other; and
notions of restructuring are further confounded in each by shifting expectations from all segments of society. Restructuring either system proves almost
impossible, given the scope of the project. David (1991) told us, "Restructuring requires all parts of the education system to change, from students and
teachers up through the myriad bureaucratic layers to the nation's capital" (p.
11). Sarason (1990) wrote compellingly about the interconnectedness of systems for decades, with special concern for school reform. How can a partnership between two such complex organizations as schools and universities even
begin? In this chapter, the potential of university-based facilitators to mediate
change in both settings is evident. The PDS is conceptualized as a community
of educators, rather than a third bureaucracy that might limit its potential for
reform.

Organizations don't behave, people do! People create, work in, and
move between organizations and are ultimately responsible for success and
failure of institutional partnerships. In this study, I examine the role of university-based educators responsible for facilitating change in schools. Rather than
focusing on the structure of schools and their potential to professionalize
teachers, create curriculum, or determine policy, I focus on the individuals
who mediate change within them. The perspective presented is an organizational change process viewed through the eyes of the facilitators. People
change, and structures reflect their changes. A group of teachers turned
teacher-educators present their practice as one model of rethinking professional development schools.

The requirements for facilitators were straightforward, although people
who met them were not easy to find. In their roles as change agents, facilitators
had to understand first-hand life in schools, have real access to and respect for
teachers, and agree to carry the word from practicing teachers to professors in
higher education in order to inform teacher preparation within the academy.
The successful facilitator was required to have the cultural understanding of an
anthropologist, the leadership skills of a teacher, and the diplomacy of a mar-
riage counselor. These catalysts of change were people who understood both

worlds and were willing to place themselves on the boundary between them. It was they who created the common ground.

BACKGROUND

The context of this study was a new teacher induction grant funded by the Bush Foundation in St. Paul, Minnesota, implemented to reduce attrition of first-year teachers in rural schools. The incentive for staffs was retention of new teachers, and the reward for participation was opportunities for all teachers to seek individual professional growth. The potential influence of individual school staffs on the socialization of new teachers (Collay, 1988; Jordell, 1987; Lortie, 1975; Sarason, 1982; Zeichner & Tabachnick, 1985) led to a concept called "group mentorship." (Harris & Collay, 1990). A key player in catalyzing small school staffs to engage in professional development activity was the university-based facilitator.

The focus shared by this rural project and many PDSs in urban settings is the focus on new teacher education. There is both historical interest in and renewed study of the effects of schools on the professional socialization of teachers. In a classic work, *Sociology of Teaching*, Waller (1932) says of the induction process, "a landmark in one's assimilation to the profession is that moment when he decides that only teachers are important. . . ." (p. 389). Lortie (1975) reviews the factors that influence teachers throughout preprofessional and professional life. Other studies emphasize the diversity of individual school environments and implications for teacher socialization within them (Blase, 1986, Feiman-Nemser & Floden, 1986; Lieberman, 1992; Popkewitz et al., 1979; Rosenholtz, 1987). It was the philosophy of this team of facilitators that the community of the school is *the* place where teachers are made, first as child and adolescent observers. As pre-service teachers at the university, their existing knowledge of what it means to teach is founded in powerful memories of life in schools. Upon return to the classroom, they reenter a once-known world feeling like a "teacher as stranger" (Greene, 1973). This lifelong setting of socialization, therefore, is the place where change must occur. The PDS must provide a learning community, a powerful place where memories are made and beliefs about good schooling born.

New teachers are a powerful catalyst for educational change, often unwittingly so. They reenter a world that is truly a model of socialization. The creation of a professional learning community cannot take place without revisiting authority and decision-making practices in schools. The institution is autocratic, built on a powerful combination of traditions and assumptions, and often stymies efforts to build professional communities. Teachers in schools challenge this system when they attempt to provide real learning for students.

They meet with resistance when they challenge outmoded practice, and creative teachers who refuse to follow tradition are often rejected by the system. As goes one system, so goes the other. Parallel efforts to change outmoded practice in universities can be seen in education faculty who choose to work directly with teachers. They meet with another form of resistance, a merit system that seldom rewards school-based activities. They, too, are often rejected from the system or forced to speak in two languages to survive. Faculty members choosing this role have a natural empathy for teachers with whom they work, as both share lives on the boundary of their workplaces. The partnership is established as individuals in both organizations seek out support from like-minded people from the other world.

This case study details the efforts of university facilitators to carry out roles of boundary-spanners, to find a common ground on which they might support teaching staffs in rural schools. Their attempts to improve the professional climate in eight rural schools provide insight to stages of organizational change and the creation of a professional common ground. Three aspects of facilitating the school-university partnership are expressed in this study: making facilitators for school-university partnerships out of university-based teacher educators; implementing school-based activities; and returning to the university with informed notions of practice. The facilitators reflect throughout on their assumptions and beliefs about their role, observe changes in the schools in which they worked, and envision potential reform for university-based teacher preparation.

THE MAKING OF A FACILITATOR

This facilitator team was made up of three faculty members, five graduate students, and the grant director. All of us had rural teaching experience, had studied teacher education formally, and were active in other forms of school-university partnerships. Facilitators first met as a group to examine their own assumptions about schools, study the specific context of grant activities, and define their new roles within this particular school-university partnership. To do this, a simulation was conducted at a two-day retreat 90 miles from anywhere, in which the facilitator experience was ironically parallel to those of rural teachers. Many of us struggled to find colleagues to cover our classes, some met with resistance from superiors, and the tone was decidedly unsympathetic. Spoken and unspoken, we heard, "Whose idea was this, anyway? These school outreach projects take too much time and energy. You should stay at the university and write."

The facilitators conducted a simulation of "outsider university-type entering a rural school." Our goal was to emulate the disruption of school norms caused first by the new teacher and then by the grant facilitator. We first recalled anecdotes from our first-year teaching experiences, and the telling of these stories provided a shared understanding about our own beliefs. Next, the simulation called for each member of the team to adopt the role of a teacher, staff member, or administrator. In our scenario, Vera, the school secretary, and Hal, a sixth-grade teacher-coach, played out a power struggle we found disquieting and all too familiar. Vera calmly chastised Hal for never bringing food to the potlucks, while he criticized her for not patching a phone call through to the teachers' lounge. The facilitators had a vast store of firsthand experiences on which to draw as we relived vignettes of school culture. Practicing teachers know the power of the school secretary, yet her role is seldom taken seriously by outsiders. University-based people make errors in organizational change processes because they assume the school principal controls all school activity. Time-honored reactions emerged throughout the simulation as we lived the experience of breaking in a new teacher. Those behaving as experienced teachers found themselves saying, "this isn't my job, it's the principal's job," and, "this new teacher will move on to another job after we get them trained." Finally, "What's in it for me?" Our disillusionment with our charge as facilitators also emerged as the power of these sentiments sunk in: "Why should they accept a university-based person?" None of us could remember much success from our teaching days when outsiders came in. Each of us asked, "How will I become credible?" We agreed that most new teachers would want little association with an outsider, being outsider enough. And another realization, "What if the staff doesn't want us anymore than they want that new teacher?"

Individual facilitators shared thoughts about the role itself after the simulation. David mused: "Until recently I have been rather stuck in the assumption that only a teacher, someone who just yesterday was in the teacher's role in a small rural school, could do justice to the facilitator's role. Only a teacher could really empathize with another teacher. As such a person, I would have automatic credibility." We knew that an outsider, however, is an outsider, however recently he was in his own classroom. We would be crossing boundaries to do the work, whatever our affiliation.

George reacted to the complexity of the role, and said, "I'm also struck by the difficulty of the task we're preparing to take on. We hope to move into a group of teachers as a stranger and we expect to provide some leadership and direction, but we are as new as the first-year teacher is to this school." This comment reminded us of the parallels between the new teachers and the facilitators—both individuals were new to the school community, without history or credibility.

Lavonne remarked: "Faculty development as we were discussing it will be difficult to sell to many rural schools in North Dakota, since they tend to be set in their ways and satisfied with the status quo for the most part." She spoke from many years of experience as a rural teacher and a rural teacher educator. Would the school staffs welcome us?

Helen reflected on the process after the simulation: "The use of recollections of our stories and lives created both the common ground and the unique within us at the same time. I like the role-playing—it gave a lot of ideas on things I hadn't thought about." Those ideas we had not thought about became the focus of our beliefs about our roles in schools. Our jobs would be to support teachers in their own learning so they, too, could explicate their assumptions and determine the degree to which they might involve themselves in school change. Our own agenda must be their agenda. This powerful simulation served our group by eliciting our assumptions about the role of the university-based facilitator. No longer would we enter their world believing our good ideas would deserve consideration. Our experience in the prairie winter fishing camp during those two insightful days was hardly disillusioning; rather, we returned to our homes in higher education a little wiser about the challenge before us. Our experience prepared us to do the work required to enter another culture and create a common ground.

INTRODUCTION OF "THE PROFESSIONAL CULTURE"

School-based management language and the growing curriculum reform efforts of "outcome-based education" are two movements that have prompted continued research on decision making in schools. These notions of organizational change, however powerful and seductive on paper, are not easily introduced in schools or universities. McLaughlin's and Marsh's (1979) discussion of the Rand "Change Agent" study made clear the complex relationship between staff development and educational reform. Working collectively toward change is complex, politically charged, and demands longevity. If a learning community is to emerge in schools, it must be organized and implemented by teachers. Our grant implementation was tied to the notion that the creation of a school-based management team or advisory council might be less threatening to administration and more likely to succeed if the task were addressed in three stages. These three stages of implementation are derived from our own brainstorming and the organizational development practices of Schmuck and Runkel (1972); they provide a useful framework from which to build a professional culture in schools. The following activities were introduced by the university-based facilitator assigned to each school.

Stages of Development

The first stage focused on the nurturing and retention of new teachers. This perspective builds on the research of Gehrke (1988), who described mentorship as "the giving of gifts." This process requires the veteran teachers to reflect on their own strengths as teachers and imagine ways those strengths could serve the needs of the newest member. Our notion of "group mentorship" combined our beliefs about organizations and mentorship. Focusing on the new teacher provided a safe topic around which teachers could initially meet to brainstorm appropriate activities for the newest member of their community. It also provided a forum for individual teachers to identify potential gifts to share. The task of the facilitator was to gather teachers on their own behalf, thus breaking old norms of top-down decisions about administrator-directed teacher "in-service." This focus also removed the stigma of one experienced teacher being singled out by a principal to look after a greenhorn.

The second stage of development of a professional culture was based on the assumption that veteran teachers could not merely assist new teachers in acquiring needed skills and resources; rather, they must also model a professional culture by seeking such opportunities themselves. "Experienced teacher as learner" required self-assessment, the weighing of one's own skills and hopes for further development, and attention to the planning required to address specific needs There was initial reluctance by teachers to choose individual learning opportunities "just for themselves," and the facilitator had the task of creating a safe place for those conversations. Neither was there a norm in schools of individual choice and behaviors toward seeking individual growth. None of our schools even considered professional release time before our funding was made available.

The third stage of development of the professional culture in the school was the emergence of a collective agenda from the needs of the individual teachers. All teachers were assured of individual support should they seek individual opportunities. In a very natural way, needs for professional development that were common to the majority of teachers became a shared agenda. With the facilitator convening the teachers, personal agendas could emerge, especially in settings where administrators had previously controlled teacher professional development. It was in this stage that notions of authority to make decisions were challenged, and the greatest demands placed on the outside facilitator.

While the new teacher was the catalyst that attracted grant support, the university-based facilitators focused on professional growth opportunities for the entire school staff, thus reflecting the research that demonstrates staff influence on new teacher induction. The first reaction felt by facilitators was their role in disrupting assumptions about who makes decisions in schools. The establishment of advisory committees at schools previously without such governance had an immediate effect on teachers, administrators, and the community. The compelling need to "rethink power in schools" (Dunlap & Goldman, 1991) became the context that surrounded each decision made by the committee. Their research points out the challenges in changing perceptions of power. The effects of this shift in balance of power were further described by Darling-Hammond (1988) in her chapter "Policy and Professionalism:"

> Establishing a professional culture within schools may produce teaching that is more knowledgeable and responsive to students' needs; it will also disturb the delicate balance between state, community, and parental interests as they are currently configured and deployed in defining schooling. (p. 55)

In addition to the external structures that shape practice in schools, the internal structure is quite powerful. The bureaucratic traditions that drive schools can reduce teachers to cogs in a machine. Teachers are seldom asked about their needs, desires, or ideas, but rather to respond to the myriad of stakeholders who grow ever more demanding of school people. Challenging this perspective, Clark and Meloy (1989) asked:

> Suppose the object were to figure out what the teachers need rather than what the school needs? 'Need' to do what? Need to tap into each one's truest, unique self; to reach so that he or she has a chance to succeed; to become what every person desires to become—an effective, recognized, rewarded individual in the work setting. (p. 273)

An example of the shift in power and authority became evident in the acknowledgment of other teachers. Advisory committees often chose teacher colleagues from their own schools or neighboring schools to provide expertise. This can only happen when teachers make the decision based on teacher-identified need, rather than administrators or university facilitators determining what teachers "need." Teachers also value honoring peers for their knowledge, rather than paying large sums to strangers with advanced credentials.

Sharing Authority

The notion of shared authority is one that strikes terror into the hearts of many administrators and community members, but in reality teacher authority is already a fact of life. When teachers close their doors and do what they believe is right, they take a large share of autonomy. The quality of instruction may be excellent or poor, but a healthy professional interaction that might determine this is almost nonexistent. Beyond the limited flow of ideas and information created by the closed-door policy, a more pervasive problem teachers face is overcoming the demoralization of being denied a place at the formal decision-making table. The facilitator played a key role in creating a place for all teachers at the table.

The facilitator walks a fine line between willingness to respect and empathize with life in schools and still advocate for change. Rushcamp and Roehler (1992) identified six characteristics that support change in schools. While the university facilitator plays an important role in all six, this particular aspect of the role is captured by Number 5:

A balance needs to be struck between supporting and challenging professional development at the school. As teachers made decisions about professional development initiatives, the university facilitator and the principal helped arrange the environment to provide participants with two tools critical to their work: time for dialogue and the resources necessary to do their work. (p. 24)

The decision makers in the advisory committee process were community members, administrators, and teachers. As interested constituents, they helped define current practice and determined direction for individual and schoolwide activities, contributing to an improved professional climate. In all eight schools, administrators retained some authority, some formally and some by subverting teacher planning efforts. Authority was delegated to teaching principals in three schools because superintendents were not interested in participating. They continued to be part of the dialogue and debate, however, hardly adopting a hands-off policy. Administrators in the other five schools involved teachers in the decision-making process with various degrees of ambivalence. The struggle for power cited by several respondents to an advisory council survey indicates that authority is at the center of the conflict. There was evidence in the conflicting responses to the surveys that many teachers had mixed feelings about the authority of administrators. This need for shift in power and responsibility is addressed by Lambert (1988) in her efforts to rethink staff development:

> Professional development means developing the profession. Using such a definition, the teacher has the responsibility to contribute to the profession through the redesign of schooling to better meet the needs of all concerned, to contribute to the knowledge base of the profession, and to share in the enculturation of new teachers. (p. 666)

Individual teachers were encouraged to seek specific opportunities to enhance their own growth and to help set schoolwide agendas to improve the professional climate in each school. This invitation to be "selfish" and address their own needs first was a welcome change for most of our participants. They often chose colleagues from nearby schools as experts, sometimes identified by teachers and other times by the facilitator. Staffs were encouraged to seek out local experts rather than bring in outsiders. One staff asked a high school teacher with computer expertise to train an elementary staff with little background. This had the added bonus of improving the scope and sequence of curriculum at both levels.

Facilitators did share their own expert knowledge. They modeled group decision-making skills in meetings. At times, teacher meetings were literally moved to rooms with tables instead of straight rows of desks. Facilitating change involved setting up advisory councils with heavy teacher representation, resisting requests to "solve the problem" for staff, and distracting administrators who became uncomfortable with the emerging teachers' voices.

Finally, monitoring committee behavior became critical, as those used to making all the decisions were persuaded to share their power. Facilitators were willing to share curriculum ideas in their specialty areas, such as math education and whole language, but remained devoted to facilitating the leadership of those based in schools.

INFLUENCING UNIVERSITY PRACTICE

The eight members of the facilitator team were housed in a research university, two state colleges, and a private college. Their interactions with teachers across the state influenced their thinking about schools and awareness of the challenges of organizational change and renewed a desire to restructure pre-service teacher education. Seeing real teachers in real schools on a weekly basis forced an honesty in university teaching that can be overlooked by isolated faculty. Abstract theorizing about schools was not necessary, because the instructor had returned from a school the day before. Examples of improved university-based teaching followed.

Jane took her introduction to elementary education classes to the tiny school district in which she was a facilitator. The pre-service students corresponded with the staff, arrived in car pools to take over the school for "Earth Day," conducted the entire curriculum, evaluated each other on their teaching, and developed friendships with veteran teachers who were their hosts. Their "intro term" in teacher education was a case study in both teaching children and participation in the creation of a unique school-university partnership. In a second example, a facilitator shared anecdotes told to him by first-year teachers in an effort to stimulate pre-service students to think about what teaching would be like. Pre-service teachers recalled their own days as students, gaining a deeper understanding of their own assumptions about teachers. Several facilitators cited examples of revised curriculum for pre-service training that would more adequately reveal the realities of practice. In my own case, an archaic "microteaching" was completely revised to reflect the findings from an ethnographic study of new teachers (Collay, 1991). Using simulation, role play, and anecdotes from school settings, students on campus struggled to solve real problems encountered in real schools.

Once facilitators attain the status of a part-time member of a school, they must invest time and energy to build bridges *back* to the university, not only outward *from* the university. To build partnerships requires speaking the language of the academy. If practice is to inform theory, university faculty must listen to teachers and other school people. Rather than bemoan the lack of transmission of their theoretical knowledge to recalcitrant teachers, faculty must come to terms with their isolation and enter a true dialogue. This means respect for one's self as a learner, for veteran teachers long isolated from colleagues, and for other faculty. This means respect for the people who do their work in the field—often nontenured junior faculty who were former teachers. This means respect for the undistilled message they carry to the academy, directly from the voices of teachers. And finally, members of the academy must admit they are part of the problem as they remain behind their podiums, lecturing pre-service students about the goodness of cooperative learning. New roles as change agents require support from the academy. One of Lieberman's (1992) colleagues addressed the emergent role this way:

> "Calling us 'boundary spanners,' 'linkers,' 'marginal,' or 'translators,' depending on one's orientation, helped, but just a little. Because although we were making things happen in the schools and trying to write it all down, we didn't yet have a way of explaining it to others." (p. 6)

We are learning to name what we do as we go. Without a shared understanding of process in the academy, the facilitators living their professional lives on the boundary are at great risk of remaining strangers in their own land—the university.

THE INHABITANTS OF THE PDS

In our model, university-based facilitators were guests in schools far from the reaches of the academy. From their positions as outsiders, they had some efficacy in disrupting old norms and patterns of behavior. But as guests, they were never true members of the community. They came with a quiet mission, a respect for teaching, and a clear understanding of the social forces shaping lives in schools. The movement toward an organizational partnership began with a focus on the needs of new teachers who, like the facilitators, were by their mere presence disruptive. This process was followed by individual decision making about each teacher's needs as a learner. The forum established by a university-based facilitator for these conversations allowed school-wide conversations, teacher priority-setting, and examination of constrictive policies to take place around relatively safe topics. University people were required to be learners, apply new knowledge, and share their authority.

These early opportunities for teacher decision making about new teacher and veteran teacher needs were helpful building blocks for the organizational development that occurred later. For example, decisions about a broader-based staff development agenda took place after teachers became aware of the shared objectives already in place. The choice to implement whole-language curricula throughout one elementary school or the decision for teachers in another to improve their computer skills are examples of activities that emerged from real needs of all teachers.

The key players in a professional development school must be the teachers. They conduct business, create norms, influence children, serve as role models for new practitioners, and hold an historical knowledge base that drives practice in schools. If the PDS is to be truly effective, it must represent a sharing of knowledge by teachers within the supportive context of a community of learning. University-based facilitators are challenged to create a common ground for the sharing of knowledge, not to carry truth from the university to the school. The creation of professional development schools is an exciting and challenging prospect for teacher educators, whether they are practicing teachers or housed in universities. Perhaps it is not possible to restructure one institution or the other—it may only be possible to restructure the relationship between them. On this common ground, new models of thinking about schooling can emerge.

REFERENCES

Blase, J. (1986). Socialization as humanization: One side of becoming a teacher. *Sociology of Education, 59*(2), 100–113.

Clark, D., & Meloy, J. (1989). Renouncing bureaucracy: A democratic structure for leadership in schools. In T. Sergiovanni & V. H. Moore (Eds.) *Schooling for tomorrow* (pp. 272–294). Needham Heights, MA: Allyn & Bacon.

Collay, M. (1988). *Dialogue as a language of learning: An ethnographic study of first-year teachers.* Unpublished doctoral dissertation, University of Oregon.

Collay, M. (1991). Microteaching revisited: Through the looking glass and what Alice saw there. Paper presented at the American Educational Research Association annual meeting, Chicago.

Darling-Hammond, L. (1988). Policy and professionalism. In A. Lieberman (Ed.), *Building a professional culture in schools.* New York: Teachers College Press.

David, J. (1991). What it takes to restructure education. *Educational Leadership, 48*(8) 11–15.

Dunlap. D. M. and Goldman, P. (1991). Rethinking power in schools. *Educational Administration Quarterly, 27*(1), 5–29.

Feiman-Nemser, S., & Floden, R. (1986). The cultures of teaching. In M. C. Wittrock (Ed.), *Handbook of research on teaching* (3rd ed., pp. 505–526). New York: Macmillan.

Gehrke, N. (1988). Toward a theory of mentoring. *Theory into Practice, 27*(3), 190-194.

Greene, M. (1973). *Teacher as stranger: An educational philosophy for the modern age.* Belmont, CA: Wadsworth Publishing Co.

Harris, M., & Collay, M. (1990). Teacher induction in rural schools. *Journal of Staff Development, 11*(4), 44–48.

Jordell, K. (1987). Structural and personal influences in the socialization of beginning teachers. *Teaching and Teacher Education, 3*(3), 165–177.

Lambert, L. (1988, May). Staff development redesigned. *Phi Delta Kappan.*

Lieberman, A. (1992). The meaning of scholarly activity and the building of community. *Educational Researcher, 21*(6), 5–12.

Little, J. (1988). Assessing the prospects for teacher leadership. In A. Lieberman (Ed.), *Building a professional culture in schools.* New York: Teachers College Press.

Lortie, D. (1975). *Schoolteacher.* Chicago: University of Chicago Press.

McLaughlin, M., & Marsh, D. (1979). Staff development and school change. In A. Lieberman & L. Miller, (Eds.), *Staff development: New demands, new realities, new perspectives* (pp. 69–94). New York: Teachers College Press.

Popkewitz, T., Tabachnick, B., & Zeichner, K. (1979). Dulling the senses: Research in teacher education. *Journal of Teacher Education, 30*(5), 52–60.

Rosenholtz, S. (1987). Workplace conditions of teacher quality and commitment: Implications for the design of teacher induction programs. In G. A. Griffen and S. Millies (Eds.), *The first years of teaching: Background papers and a proposal* (pp. 15-34). Chicago: University of Illinois at Chicago Press.

Rushcamp, S., & Roehler, L. (1992). Characteristics supporting change in a professional development school. *Journal of Teacher Education, 43*(1), 19–27.

Sarason, S. (1982). *The culture of school and the nature of change.* Boston: Allyn & Bacon.

Sarason, S. (1990). *The predictable failure of educational reform.* San Francisco: Jossey-Bass.

Schmuck, R., & Runkel, P. (1972). *Handbook of organization development in schools.* Palo Alto, CA: Mayfield.

Waller, W. (1932). *The sociology of teaching.* New York: Russell & Russell.

Winitsky, N., Stoddart, T., & O'Keefe, P. (1992). Great expectations: Emergent professional development schools. *Journal of Teacher Education, 43*(1), 3–18.

Zeichner, K., & Tabachnick, R. (1985). The development of teacher perspectives: Social strategies and institutional control in the socialization of beginning teachers. *Journal of Education for Teaching, 11*(1), 1–25.

JEANNE ELLSWORTH
and CHERYL M. ALBERS

Chapter Ten

Tradition and Authority in
Teacher Education Reform

Doyle (1986) commented that increasingly the "epicenter of teacher education lies somewhere between higher education and the elementary and secondary schools" (p. 39). Using the language of seismic activity may be particularly appropriate in this case, since the space between the school and the university can include some shaky ground. Since the late 1940s, universities and colleges have placed student teachers in the public schools for student teaching (Clark, 1988). In effect, practicing teachers have collaborated in teacher education by providing, sometimes with very limited university support or involvement, field experiences for student teachers. Rather than building a tradition of fruitful collaboration, however, field experiences have often been fraught with uncertainties, conflicts of interest, and suspicions about expertise and authority between and among university and school personnel (Guyton & McIntyre, 1990).

The most recent generation of teacher education reform literature has stressed the wisdom of practice, the acquisition of craft knowledge, and the value of apprenticeship (Holmes Group, 1986; Carnegie, 1986), and so has moved reformers to consider increasing or lengthening field experiences, broadening the role of practicing teachers in teacher education, and developing school-university partnerships for teacher education. Achieving these goals would appear to involve replacing traditions of mistrust with collegial responsibility for teacher preparation, which may be a tall order. In this chapter, we examine the implications for roles and relationships among players in student teaching that can arise in school-university partnerships for teacher education, particularly in regard to field experiences. First, we briefly review the traditional student teaching structures and the implications of change initiatives for student teaching roles and relationships. Next, we describe a partnership program undertaken by the Buffalo Research Institute on Education for Teaching (BRIET) as it played out in the dynamics of roles and relationships in the student teaching triad. We conclude the chapter by considering the implications of the BRIET experience for teacher education reform. Throughout, we focus on the interplay of student teaching traditions with initiatives for change and on issues of power and authority in teacher education.

While there are reasons to celebrate the progress and successes of the redesigned BRIET program, our examination of the BRIET teacher education reform effort in this chapter provides perspectives beyond celebratory reports of teacher education reform initiatives. First, the data for this report were gathered in process during the first two years of the pilot program, as part of an ongoing and larger project of monitoring and evaluating BRIET's teacher education program. Therefore, the complexities and challenges of change in progress are revealed. Second, we concentrate purposefully on difficulties, tensions, and unresolved issues—our appraisal of the program is made under the assumption that educational change is, in the words of Elmore and McLaughlin, "steady work" (1988, p. v.).

TRADITIONS IN STUDENT TEACHING

Traditionally, there have been three key players in the student teaching experience, often referred to as the student teaching triad—a representative of the university (supervisor), primarily charged with overseeing the experience in terms of university requirements; the classroom teacher, in whose classroom the field experience is based (cooperating teacher), and who serves as a mentor to the student teacher; and a teacher education student (student teacher), whose primary role is to carry out the field experience according to the directives of the other two triad members and their institutions.[1] However intuitively simple these traditional arrangements may seem, research consistently shows that student teaching roles and relationships are characterized by difficulties, miscommunications, and mistrust.

First, student teaching roles are often unclear,[2] in part because school and university personnel rarely confer about goals, practices, and responsibilities in the field experience (Clift & Say, 1988). Second, teacher education often is not the primary commitment of teachers, who are occupied with teaching their students, or of university supervisors, who are similarly occupied with teaching, research, and/or graduate studies. Hence, cooperating teachers' and supervisors' roles as members of the triad may have low priority and limited professional rewards or remuneration, or they may conflict with other roles and responsibilities within the school or university (Richardson-Koehler, 1988; Nolan, 1985; Yee, 1968).

Furthermore, university- and school-based teacher educators tend to harbor mutual suspicions about the validity of each other's knowledge of teaching—for example, university research is often harshly critical of schools and teaching, while practicing teachers criticize university-based teacher education as narrow and irrelevant. So, the triad is often characterized by strained relationships and competitive rather than cooperative interaction (Richardson-Koehler, 1988; Emans, 1983; Yee, 1968). Cooperating teachers can feel threatened by visits from a university supervisor, particularly when the supervisor's purpose is perceived as assessing the cooperating teacher as well as the student teacher (Fields, 1988, Richardson-Koehler, 1988). On the part of university-based teacher educators, an adversarial relationship is indicated by their dismay when, during student teaching, student teachers appear to reject university-based knowledge and perspectives (Zeichner, 1980).

Conflict between school and university faculty may also arise from disparities in their perspectives toward purposes and practices in student teaching (Cochran-Smith, 1991). And supervisors, as representatives of the university, may be viewed as "outsiders" or "guests" rather than contributing members of the triad (Niemeyer & Moon, 1988). As reformers of teacher education, university faculty may be perceived as missionaries.

Much of the concern for roles and relationships in the student teaching triad, however, has centered on the school and university faculty—the cooperating teacher and university supervisor. The student teacher's role is rarely at issue, except when questions are raised about "effects" or "outcomes" of the experience, and their role remains largely as educational objects. Expectations are that student teachers comply with university requirements and standards and, at the same time, with their host schools' norms and expectations, submitting to the educational experience arranged for them.

TEACHER EDUCATION REFORM AND THE STUDENT TEACHING TRIAD

Clearly, the relationships among the players in the student teaching triad, both in terms of day-to-day functioning and broader perceptions of expertise and authority, have been less than ideal. Now, reforms stress constructing or reconstructing bridges between the universities and schools, between campus-based and field-based teacher preparation, between theory and practice, demanding that some long-held suspicions regarding expertise and authority in educational matters be broken down.

Teacher education program rationales and reports speak of seeking a "fuller partnership" with public schools, offering "a genuine sense of shared ownership" or "joint ownership" for teacher education, and striving to gain the "front-line voice" or the "different perspective" or the "expanded involvement" of classroom teachers.[3] Toward these ends, cooperating teachers may receive new titles and/or perquisites that suggest conferment of a status closer to that of the university professor. While on the one hand confirming the existence of hierarchy in teacher education, such renaming of cooperating teachers also strives to represent, create, or facilitate a sense of social and intellectual parity between teachers and university teacher educators, presumably in the name of fostering collaborative rather than competitive relationships.

Initiatives have also included the development of new, altered, or expanded cooperating teacher roles. Rather than merely working with student teachers (an assignment of considerable responsibility), cooperating teachers may be also expected to participate in special projects designed by the university (McDaniel, 1988–1989), to collaborate with or initiate research projects (Oja, 1988), assume the role of university supervisor (Richardson-Koehler, 1988), teach or participate in university methods courses (Cornbleth & Ellsworth, 1994), or serve on a field experience coordinating committee (Arends, 1990).

At the same time, expansion of field experiences often has resulted in a need to establish a sizable corps of experienced, suitable, and willing cooperating teachers. Some universities have attempted to meet this demand by "upgrading" the quality of cooperating teachers through seminars, courses, and "training" (Cornbleth & Ellsworth, 1994), thereby adding new dimensions to the cooperating teacher role. Further education and enhanced status for cooperating teachers certainly have the potential to dignify the role of the practitioners in teacher education. On the other hand, the suggestions that cooperating teachers need reeducation or that "improvement" will result when cooperating teachers become more like university faculty (by doing research or teaching at the university level, for example) raise a fundamental doubt about the efficacy and validity of teachers' roles in teacher education.

Role changes for cooperating teachers create corresponding role changes for supervisors. Depending on the specific circumstances of the program, supervisors' roles may be fully assumed by cooperating teachers (Emans, 1983); limited to that of university liaison (MacNaughton, Johns, & Rogus, 1982); or expanded to include co-supervision with cooperating teachers (James, Etheridge, & Liles, 1991), membership in a supervisory team (Bush, Moss, & Seiler, 1991), or leadership of such a team (McDaniel, 1988–1989). Other alterations of the supervisor role can include the additional responsibilities of researching their practice (Cochran-Smith, 1991; Gore, 1991) or even serving as "the major change agent for schools and for teacher education" (Emans, 1983).

Notably, efforts at role change conspicuously omit considerations of how to extend the benefits of collaborative professional relationships to student teachers, leaving them to continue the difficult negotiations of the "two worlds" of university and public school (Feiman-Nemser and Buchmann, 1985). However, some attention has been given to the possibility of changing the student teacher role from one of passive educational object. This change can be inferred in programs whose goals include, for example, "for students to become reflective teachers who question and assess the origins, purposes, and consequences of schooling and work," under the assumption that the "wisdom of practice . . . needs to be gotten around, exposed, or changed" (Cochran-Smith, 1991, p. 108). Specific attention to the role of the student teacher, however, is rare. Also, while programs may contribute to a more strongly articulated and active student role, these changes also have the potential to undermine collaboration by devaluing or denigrating the perspectives of practitioners (Cochran-Smith, 1991).

In sum, teacher education reform directives have initiated or implied role changes that often hold contradictory messages and may either improve or exacerbate tensions in the student teaching triad.

THE BRIET EXPERIENCE

We now turn to the 1989–1992 development and implementation of a pilot program of teacher education at the Buffalo Research Institute on Education for Teaching (BRIET). The ongoing monitoring and evaluation of the teacher education program provided the following sources of data on which this chapter drew: meeting minutes dating from the planning stages of the pilot program from spring 1989 through June 1992, observation and interview fieldnotes prepared in connection with an ongoing BRIET research project that focused on field experiences, institute documents and drafts, and interviews and surveys conducted with university and school personnel.[4]

Planning for the redesign of the university teacher education program began in the spring of 1989, when BRIET hired seven outstanding experienced teachers from two local school districts as clinical faculty to collaborate with the Institute.[5] Clinical faculty drafted a proposal for the redesign of the teacher certification program. The proposal outlined a program that reflected aspects of national teacher education reform directives and also the clinical faculty's extensive experiences as cooperating teachers. The resulting pilot program sought, among other things, to capitalize on practitioner knowledge, improve communications (and, conceivably, smooth relationships) between school and university, and conduct the field experience through a collegial system of planning, mentoring, and evaluation.[6] Each of these aims of the new program was supported by changes in program structures and practices and held implications for triad role changes. The language of the opening paragraphs of the proposal reveals strong feelings about the validity of the expertise of practitioners:

> [I]n order to redesign American education in ways that are cogent, practical, cost-effective, and likely to succeed in the long run, American teachers must be involved at the "drawing board" stage. After all, teachers know more about what goes on in classrooms, which instructional strategies work and which don't, the merits and inadequacies of the curricula they follow, the strengths and weaknesses of the textbooks they use, the impact of academic policies on students—in short, everything which they as 'purveyors' of education must deal with daily—than anybody else in the business. (Dell, et al., 1989, p. 1)

Clearly, a first concern of the clinical faculty was to assert the validity and exploit the wealth of practitioner wisdom. Supporting the ability of practitioners to shape the program, the proposal allowed for significant variability and flexibility in how it was carried out across schools, so that "possibilities will be explored by each team for the greatest benefit of the student teachers" (Dell, et al., p. 6). So, many of the specifics of roles and responsibilities were not spelled out in the proposal in order to encourage and allow cooperating teachers to "design the optimum plan for field experiences and student teaching" (p. 9).

More generally, cooperating teachers were to be involved more fully as "partners in teacher education." This involvement was to be achieved largely through a series of on-campus "Cooperating Teacher Seminars" at which program goals and practices could be communicated, cooperating teachers and BRIET staff could address issues of student teaching, and cooperating teachers could plan for field experiences at their sites. The seminars added to the cooperating teacher role a new demand on their time—attendance at the seminars, as well as a further intellectual-social demand—acting and reacting with field teams from other schools and districts, clinical faculty, methods course instructors, and BRIET staff.

To improve communications and guide the new program, the program added the role of "BRIET liaison," who would serve as "the university 'voice'" (Pilot Proposal) at each participating school. This individual would be the primary communicator between the university and the site, and would "ensure that while field experiences may vary from site to site depending on the academic program and student population of each school, an overriding consistency will prevail" (Pilot Proposal, p. 8). Some of the liaison positions were undertaken by clinical faculty; at other sites, cooperating teachers served as liaisons.

Collaboration among university faculty, practitioners, and pre-service teachers was a third key concept in the proposed pilot program. The primary unit of operation in the field was to be a structure larger than the individual student teaching triad—a field team of at least two practicing teachers and two student teachers in a particular school working closely with a BRIET liaison and a university supervisor. The intent of this change included an altered relationship among triad members—toward a more collegial system of planning, mentoring, and evaluation. For the roles of each of the traditional triad members, this structure implied an additional intellectual-social responsibility— acting and reacting with other field team members—as well as an additional time commitment in order to schedule and attend field team meetings.

ROLES AND RELATIONSHIPS: 1989–1992

With the substitution of the field team for the traditional triad and the addition of the BRIET liaison, roles and relationships in student teaching were in flux. Overall, individuals were at least intrigued by the possibility of developing new roles. However, the influences of traditional roles were strong, and perennial issues of power and authority for teacher education were not entirely resolved. The following section describes role changes and conflicts during the first three years of the new BRIET program.

It is not surprising that difficulties ensued where perceived role responsibilities overlapped, were unclear, or had unforeseen dimensions. During the first two years of the program, a brief "Teacher Education Field Activities Overview" stood as the only written role statement available to participants in the program, and there were few set structures for sharing or working through these expectations with participants. Not surprisingly, role confusion surfaced. The most frequently noted set of difficulties devolved from an overlap in the perceived roles of the BRIET liaison and the supervisor—each felt responsible for communicating with cooperating teachers. Communications breakdowns were fairly common, and a general sense of "who should I ask," and "who does what" often was at the root of these. As one supervisor described her feelings,

> It's like an insecurity—you don't know what you're supposed to do, you don't know who you're supposed to be. . . . I don't know whether I should say 'I want everybody here and I want them after school'—I don't know if I have that—I don't know what my boundary is. (supervisor 3:2-22-91)

Other role conflicts ensued when players' own role perceptions failed to coincide with others' expectations. The most prominent and persistent of these disjunctions was in regard to the supervisor's role in the field team. Supervisors were either unsure about the extent to which they should become involved in the meetings or convinced that they should adopt a "hands off" attitude. While about half of the cooperating teachers and BRIET liaisons were content with supervisors' limited participation and/or thought that the more distanced role was appropriate, the others believed that supervisors should be active and key members of the field team—planning, attending, and contributing to meetings. Unfortunately, these cooperating teachers sometimes interpreted supervisors' "hands off" attitudes as lack of commitment to their field team and/or their supervisory responsibilities.

Even when roles were clear and agreed upon, it was sometimes difficult for individuals to stay within their role boundaries. For example, supervisors made frequent reference to not wanting to be or be seen as directive in regard to the operations of the field team. As one described it, she saw herself not as an authority, but as a facilitator, to "help the student teacher and cooperating teacher define what is acceptable for them, not to impose things." (supervisor 4:6-5-91) Another supervisor referred to the student teaching experience as "their territory," and although she did not always agree with the way things were handled, she tended to "keep out of it" (supervisor 2: 2-20-91). However, while all of the supervisors preferred to be nondirective, three made comments about their behavior in the supervisor role that suggest that they were not always able or willing to remain so. Supervisors sometimes found themselves feeling an obligation, when no other player appeared to be doing so, to see that basic pilot guidelines were followed. For example, one supervisor felt that the student teachers were not being encouraged to work collegially, so, she stated,

> I keep stressing the working together, trying to organize and plan things that the student teachers do together, that the teachers do together . . . whenever I talk to them, trying to emphasize a collegiality atmosphere, and to have the teachers try to be more collegial, talk about what they'd like to have the kids do together.

Lack of clarity was not the only influence on role confusion; BRIET liaisons' roles included unforeseen responsibilities. Commitment to the idea of working in field teams varied, including one group of cooperating teachers who rejected it outright. So, some BRIET liaisons needed to "sell" other field team members on the notion that field team meetings were a worthwhile investment of time and energy and not an encroachment on their autonomy as cooperating teachers. As one BRIET liaison described her situation, the "veteran" cooperating teachers on her field team were "skeptical and defensive," viewing the meetings as an "invasion of their territory," that territory being their conduct of the student teaching experience (BRIET liaison 1:2-27-91). In some senses, then, the BRIET liaison was more than a communications link with the university. They often found themselves acting as arbiters of two sets of preferences and perspectives: the clinical faculty–university expectations regarding field teams and those of the cooperating teachers.

Interacting with role confusion and unforeseen circumstances, however, was the persistence of traditional roles. First, as suggested above, while field teams became, at most sites, one unit for conducting student teaching, they were often not the primary or preferred unit. That is, the traditional one-to-one relationship of the student teacher with his or her "own" cooperating teacher, the cooperating teacher with his or her "own" student teacher, remained primary in the minds and experiences of most cooperating teachers and student teachers. The language of "my co-op" and "my student teacher" was pervasive.

Second, both cooperating teachers and student teachers, while they applauded the idea of field team meetings, tended to resist the idea of conducting the meetings with prearranged (or what they often called "formal") agendas, preferring that topics arise from the immediately preceding moments and days of classroom experience. This preference suggests that another traditional role was persevering—cooperating teachers appeared to be applying the mentor model of one-on-one, experience-based advising and problem solving to the new structure of the field team, rather than significantly restructuring their role toward that of the teacher educator, linking particular events with broader concerns and working with more general issues as a group. However, a few cooperating teachers in certain field teams had begun to see their roles more as teacher educators than as simply "placements" for student teachers. It may be that the mentor model of the cooperating teacher, dealing with one student teacher on particularistic and local questions of teaching, began to be expanded to an instructor model in field team meetings, with one cooperating teacher responsible for a presentation or sharing of information with a group of others, both cooperating teachers and student teachers.

Cooperating teachers' discontent over field team agendas also speaks to the underlying question of "Whose field team is it?" and encloses broader issues of authority and power. Several of the relationship snags, while they have roots in programmatic loopholes and communications lapses, suggest issues of authority and power between the university and the schools. One way in which these issues surfaced was in the conflict of interest over field team agendas. Student teachers and cooperating teachers viewed the BRIET liaisons and/or supervisors, in their roles as conduits for university ideas to the field team, as overriding the particularistic and local concerns of the team and its individual players. Cooperating teachers almost uniformly believed that the preeminent determiner of how they executed their roles should be what they perceived to be the needs of the student teachers. This was strongly articulated in cooperating teachers' views about field team meeting agendas. The most important aspect of field team meetings, as expressed by the majority of cooperating teachers, was "meeting the ongoing needs of student teachers and cooperating teachers" (cooperating teacher 22). In addition, the most commonly expressed reservation about field team meetings, aside from scheduling difficulties, was that setting agendas rendered the meetings "too formal" and not flexible enough to respond to the events and concerns immediately at hand.

At the same time, some supervisors and liaisons perceived that part of their role was to define topics for or lead field team discussions in order to reflect broader issues in teaching and learning.

In another case that speaks of power and authority struggles, the relationship of the supervisor and the cooperating teacher became problematic in the area of student teacher evaluation. Decisions about student teachers' grades were to be made collaboratively, and during the first three years of the program, there were few major disagreements. Still, cooperating teachers raised the issue again and again—who "has the final say" in the decision of a course grade for the student teacher? Notably, the debate was clearly over who would decide, not on the criteria on which student teachers would be evaluated. This debate also exposes a power issue—that of whether the university or the field is the authority on issues of teaching—whether the scholar or the practitioner "knows best." Cooperating teachers stressed that they were in the best position to evaluate student teachers, since they saw their performance so much more regularly than supervisors. More broadly, they exhibited the traditional suspicions of the quality of supervisors' knowledge of the realities of today's school and classroom life, as in these concerns raised at a 1992 seminar:

> How can BRIET insure that the [supervisors] each year have a realistic view, based on *teaching experience* . . . that can be brought to the supervision situation along with the obligatory theoretical background? We should have some input in the criteria for [supervisors] and teaching *experience* should be one of them. . . . *Successful* teaching experience is needed.

On their part, supervisors, often sensitive to their "outsider" status and to possible power imbalances, wanted to be perceived as nonevaluative, but often revealed that they were indeed strongly critical of practitioners.

> For example . . . the teacher ignores this one eighth grade boy because he's helplessly—well, helpless. Okay, she told [the student teacher], "Don't waste your time with this kid." One of the concerns I had about this [student teacher] was, 'why aren't you addressing the issue of this boy coming in with no books—he turns around, he doesn't expect to learn—he's in eighth grade, he's going to ninth grade, tenth grade, eleventh grade, twelfth grade—so, in other words, he's done?" No, I didn't agree with that. But I couldn't say anything because then I'd be messing with [the cooperating teacher].
>
> I would have liked to say, 'Get rid of your ability groups! Every time I come I see the high group and the whole group is in the hall with the reading teachers doing dittoes!' But I didn't, I couldn't, I *shouldn't*. (supervisor 2:6-5-91)
>
> What happens is that they [student teachers] get taken over by the school, by the norms of the classroom teacher and by the expectations. That doesn't mean they accept it—some do, some don't. But they pattern their behavior after it, it's demanded of them. They see teaching in very technical terms. Their responses to why they do things have very much to do with techni-

cal responses such as "There's a test on this next week," or "They need to know this to understand the next chapter."

Clearly, while supervisors professed and attempted to enact a nonevaluative role, they continued to notice teaching with which they were uncomfortable. Such criticisms, then, while voiced only in interviews, did not simply disappear because their roles were reconceived.

Virtually all of the role and relationship contests, however, were played out, negotiated, and discussed among teachers and university faculty student teachers, those with ultimately the largest stake in the program, who did not appear to perceive themselves as playing active or definable roles in the program. Rather, they perceived themselves to be acted upon by other players. This generalization could be tempered by two trends over time in student teachers' interview responses. First, there was a growing sense among student teachers that they were part of a team. While no pre-service teacher, in initial interviews, mentioned expecting to become part of a team during their student teaching, in final interviews, over three quarters in 1991 and all but two in 1992 stated that they did feel themselves to be contributing members of a team. The most consistently mentioned and most strongly defended sense of team membership was among fellow student teachers. In fact, several student teachers expressed a desire for more time for student teachers to talk "without the cooperating teachers around" (student teacher 52).

In addition, those student teachers who felt themselves part of a team suggested that they felt some responsibility for making a contribution to meetings. For some student teachers, then, membership on their field teams was considered as part of their role, suggesting that they were beginning to construe their roles less as isolated recipients of education and to some degree as participants in a collegial educative process. While some lip service appears to have been given to changing the traditional role of student as passive recipient of education, there was very little sustained or systematic attention to that role change.

Other players in the partnership program attested, in various terms, to feelings of empowerment through the pilot program. While these positive benefits and attendant issues have become a focus of interest, rarely, if ever, have the possibilities of seeking student teacher involvement and empowerment been suggested. For example, while "student-teachers' needs" were cited as the most important determiner of field experience activities, these needs appear to have been consistently determined by players other than the student teachers themselves.

RETHINKING AND REVISING

Roles and relationships in the BRIET teacher education program have undergone and will continue to undergo modification. A wide range in field team constitution and functioning produced concern among some clinical faculty that roles and relationships as they were being interpreted in some sites were not consistent with program intentions. Role statements were not sufficiently clearly defined or monitored to preclude, for example, a field team's decision that the most effective way to provide field experiences at their site was not through the field team structure but through the traditional one-coop–one-pre-service teacher arrangement. Clinical faculty, uncomfortable with site practices that they viewed as having strayed too far from their original intents, began to consider establishing stronger or clearer guidelines for field teams and sites affiliated with the new program. So, a committee of clinical faculty, cooperating teachers, and BRIET staff rethought and redefined roles and relationships.

First, efforts were made to clarify roles in written statements, including a field experiences guidebook and letters of expectation between supervisors and cooperating teachers. Second, supervisors, and later student teachers, were invited and encouraged to attend cooperating teacher seminars, so that role expectations could be worked out and individuals get to know each other. Third, there were concerted efforts to establish forums in which responsibilities and possibilities could be worked out.

One of the most successful of these was the reformatted biweekly supervisor staff meeting. The BRIET assistant director for program and faculty associate decided to use supervisor staff meetings to better delineate and work through the supervisor–cooperating teacher relationship. Meetings were held more frequently, and they were increasingly focused on goals and procedures of the program and on issues of supervision and politics in student teaching. These meetings were coordinated by BRIET staff who, as regular participants in clinical faculty meetings and cooperating teacher seminars, were able to communicate concerns across role groups. They also provided some new forms of intra-program consistency, for example by distributing readings and initiating discussions on the same topics at meetings with different role groups. As a result of the new meetings, supervisors reported more role clarification:

> The meetings have been very informational, so it's a forum where we can ask very specific questions. . . . Sue has given us readings and this helps us to reflect and decide where we fit in, and to think about it more than we might otherwise do. They [supervisor meetings] were helpful certainly in dealing with and addressing the practical questions—that as a first-year [supervisor] are very natural for you to have, such as expectations of student teachers, clarifications of that role between the [supervisor], the coop, and the student teacher. I think that what we did in terms of reading the articles, getting a sense of the whole picture in the country of teacher ed programs, that to me is very valuable. . . . They [supervisor meetings] were helpful in the sense that you always knew you had the support system but also in terms of the intellectual challenge of understanding this whole role.

Roles and relationships became a primary focus of the 1991–1992 year, as did attempts to encourage the acceptance of the idea of field teams. Resistance to the field team as the primary unit of student teaching interaction continued to be considerable—in fact, during that year, in one new program site cooperating teachers rejected the idea outright. Teams that had no choice but to meet before or after school hours began to assert that they could not or would not continue to devote personal time to the project. At the time of this writing, such constraints as time, school ethos, and compensation factors were reconsidered. For example, cooperating teachers with advanced degrees and little use for tuition waivers as compensation began to state their case, wondering whether alternative compensation might be investigated.

CONCLUSIONS AND IMPLICATIONS

The redesign of the teacher education programs at BRIET offers a case study of possibilities for success and challenges inherent in the promotion of school university partnerships. Now in its fifth year, the BRIET program consistently and often constructively brings together school and university personnel to confer on, negotiate, and assess the goals and processes of field experience. Some of the difficulties that traditionally accompany student teaching have been addressed. However, clinical faculty, cooperating teachers, supervisors, BRIET staff, and university faculty continue to struggle with clarification of roles and responsibilities and the purpose and operation of field teams.

What does the BRIET case suggest for other collaborative reform efforts? Most broadly, collaborative reforms in teacher education have the potential to alleviate some of the strains in student teaching. Structural changes that encourage dialogue on program planning and implementations create opportunities to clarify role expectations and expand the common ground that lies between the two worlds of the school and the university. However, as we pointed out earlier, our purpose here is to consider unresolved issues and tensions.

Traditional roles are likely to persist in the face of collaborative reform efforts. The traditions of the student teaching triad, including beliefs in the efficacy and appropriateness of the one-on-one relationship of pre-service and cooperating teacher, the tensions over authority in educational matters between classroom teachers and university representatives, and the strains that individuals experience when they are expected to cross the borders from school to university or vice versa, are unlikely to dissipate simply because new structures and goals are articulated.

We find several plausible reasons for this persistence. First, it is possible, as in the BRIET case, that when school and university personnel develop a partnership for reform, there is reluctance on both sides to appear to be determining the roles and responsibilities for other people. When individuals are trying hard to resolve issues of authority by simply avoiding stepping on each others' toes, a great deal may remain unsaid. Thus, as individuals endeavor to preserve the professional freedom of colleagues, roles are left ambiguous.

It must also be noted that most reforms, such as those at BRIET, place new time demands on individuals who already face daily if not hourly time deficits. Teacher education is not the first priority of most of the people involved. Collaboration takes time away from already busy schedules. Thus, a second possible explanation for the persistence of traditional roles is that time cannot be given to developing and implementing new roles and procedures.

Failure to fully comprehend, accept, or comply with new roles and relationships does not necessarily mean that roles are not clearly specified or individuals are too conservative, not enlightened enough, or unwilling to sacrifice their time and energy for change. Rather, a third potential reason for persistence of tradition is that statements of goals and expectations neither have been nor will be applied to individuals and groups who are "blank slates" in regard to their roles in teacher education. Such directives will be received in light of the past experiences and perceptions of the different players in their roles in teacher education. New roles statements are likely to be interpreted, reckoned with, resisted, challenged, and/or redefined by those to whom they are designed to give direction.

In order to exploit effectively the wealth of practice and to design roles in which individuals and groups will be comfortable and productive, traditions must be considered both as potential obstacles to change and as potential resources for creating viable change. Our experience suggests that individuals may fall back on traditional roles because they find little guidance for defining roles in a new way. Alternatively, persistence may suggest that there are elements of traditional roles that ought to be retained.

Research has identified authority issues as resulting in suspicion of motives, questioning of expertise, and a competitive rather than cooperative mode of operations in the field. Changing these traditions and creating a sense of parity among roles and within relationships is not as simple as making statements about "shared ownership" and soliciting input. Individuals must consider how issues of power and authority might be, if not resolved, at least brought into arenas for more open and constructive consideration.

Left unresolved, such issues distract from focusing on the real purpose of collaboration, improvement of the education of future teachers. In BRIET, for example, this happened when the issue of who conducts the assessment of student teachers took priority over such issues as what is achieved by assessment and on what criteria assessment can and should be made. More broadly, in the pursuit of comfortable, tension-free student teaching relationships, left unanswered are questions about just how collaboration can improve teacher education, what actually can and should happen in student teaching, and what role practitioner wisdom plays in teacher education.

As we consider and work with collaborative arrangements for teacher education, then, the potential benefits for student teachers must be at issue. Traditionally the player with the least power and the most precarious position, student teachers are also those who find themselves most often treading in the uncomfortable space between school and university. If there are empowerment benefits for school personnel inherent in teacher education roles that provide for autonomy and significant program input, we must seek ways to extend such benefits to student teachers, who are, in fact, what teacher education programs ought to be all about.

We believe that important work has been done through the BRIET schools partnership. The new program generated enthusiasm and recommitment to teacher education, challenged some long-held assumptions and practices in the field, and brought the voice of teachers into teacher education. Examination of the difficulties encountered is provided in hopes of furthering the "steady work" of this and the many other school-university collaborations devoted to the promise of improvement in teacher education.

NOTES

1. The terms used to name the roles in the student teaching triad vary among institutions and within institutions over time. For example, supervisors may also be called mentors; cooperating teachers have been referred to as critic teachers or master teachers; student teachers may be called prospective or pre-service teachers, trainees, or candidates. For clarity, we will use the terms supervisor, cooperating teacher, and student teacher throughout this chapter.

2. While roles and relationships may be defined by the goals, procedures, and specifics of each teacher education program, the traditional arrangement involves the cooperating teacher agreeing to have a student teacher observe and work in his or her classroom for a period of one-half to one semester. It is agreed, usually implicitly, that the cooperating teacher will use his or her years of experience to assist the student teacher in increasing competence in the classroom. The supervisor conveys the requirements of the university for successful completion of the experience and monitors their implementation and the student teacher's progress, usually through a series of visits to the school site and filing of reports with the university. The supervisor may also provide resources and support to cooperating and student teachers. The student teacher is expected to fulfill requirements set out by the university and the cooperating teacher and/or the student teaching placement school.

3. The language of this paragraph comes from the reports of various institutions' teacher education reform efforts: see Sears, Marshall, and Otis-Wilborn, 1988; University of Arizona, 1988; Wolfe, Schewel, and Bickham, 1989; Buttery, Henson, Ingram, and Smith, 1986; Ellerman and Arnn, 1989; Takacs and McArdle, 1984; Heathington, Cagle, and Blank, 1988; South Central Conference, 1989.

4. Beginning in the fall semester of 1989 and extending through June of 1992, data were collected from the primary triad players in regard to their activities, perceptions, and experiences in their roles. Each of the 13 university supervisors who served during the three years was interviewed at least twice; each of the 10 clinical faculty and 10 BRIET liaisons was interviewed at least twice; 24 student teachers were interviewed before, during, and/or at the close of their student teaching experience; each of the 17 teachers serving as coops during 1989–1990 was interviewed; the approximately 30 cooperating teachers from 1990–1992 were surveyed at the close of the student teaching period. Other data sources included fieldnotes from clinical faculty meetings, cooperating teacher seminars, supervisor staff meetings, and various documents related to the teacher education program.

5. Clinical faculty were invited to collaborate with BRIET in three major areas: research, the pilot field experience program, and teaching methods courses. Within these three broad areas, each clinical faculty member designed his or her own role.

6. Other enunciated BRIET goals included encouraging and supporting reflection and reflective practice and expanding the ability to respond constructively to student diversity among student teachers and all program participants.

REFERENCES

Arends, R. (1990). Connecting the university to the school. In B. Joyce (Ed.), *Changing school culture through staff development* (pp. 117–143). Association for Supervision and Curriculum Development Yearbook. Alexandria, VA: ASCD.

Bush, W., Moss, M., & Seiler, M. (1991). An alternative to traditional student teaching. *Mathematics Teacher*, 533–537.

Buttery, T., Henson, K., Ingram, T., & Smith, C. (1986). The teacher in residence partnership program. *Action in Teacher Education, 7*(4), 63–66.

Carnegie Forum on Education and the Economy (1986). *A nation prepared: Teachers for the 21st century*. Washington, DC: Author.

Clark, R. (1988). School-university relationships: An interpretive review. In K. Sirotnik and J. Goodlad (Eds.). *School-university partnerships in action: Concepts, cases, and concerns* (pp. 32–65). New York: Teachers College Press.

Clift, R. & Say, M. (1988). Teacher education: Collaboration or conflict? *Journal of Teacher Education, 39*(3), 2–7.

Cochran-Smith, M. (1991). Reinventing student teaching. *Journal of Teacher Education, 42*(2), 104–118.

Cornbleth, C., & Ellsworth, J. (1994). Clinical faculty in teacher education: Roles and relationships. *American Educational Research Journal, 31*(1), pp. 49–70.

Dell, D., Echols, J., Elardo, R., Fish, G., Forni, R., Minklein, S., & Reed, B. (1989). Proposal to pilot schools of professional development for elementary and secondary teacher education. Unpublished.

Doyle, W. (1986). Teacher education as part-time work. *Teacher Education Quarterly, 13*(1), 37–40.

Ellerman, G., and Arnn, J. (1989). A functional clinical faculty model. Paper presented at the Annual Conference of the National Council of the States on Inservice Education, San Antonio, TX.

Elmore, R., & McLaughlin, M. (1988). *Steady work: Policy, practice, and the reform of American education.* Rand Corporation.

Emans, R. (1983). Implementing the knowledge base: Redesigning the function of cooperating teachers and college supervisors. *Journal of Teacher Education, 34*(3), 15–19.

Feiman-Nemser, S., & Buchmann, M. (1985). Pitfalls of experience in teacher preparation. *Teachers College Record, 87*(1), 53–65.

Fields, G. (1988). A field-based approach to improving teacher supervisory skills. *Action in Teacher Education, 10*(1), 43–53.

Gore, J. (1991). Practicing what we preach: Action research and the supervision of student teachers. In R. Tabachnick and K. Zeichner (Eds.), *Issues and practices in inquiry-oriented teacher education* (pp. 253–272). New York: Falmer Press.

Guyton, E., and McIntyre, D. (1990). Student teaching and school experiences. In W. Houston, (Ed.) *Handbook of research on teacher education* (pp. 514–534). New York: Macmillan.

Heathington, B., Cagle, L., & Blank, M. (1988). Seeking excellence in teacher education: A shared responsibility, *Teacher Educator, 23*(4), 19–29.

Holmes Group. (1986). *Tomorrow's Teachers.* East Lansing, MI. Author.

James, T., Etheridge, C., & Liles, D. (1991). Student teaching delivery via clinical training sites: New linkages, structural changes and programmatic improvements. *Action in Teacher Education, 13*(2), 25–29.

McDaniel, E. (1988–89). Collaboration for what? Sharpening the focus. *Action in Teacher Education, 10*(4), 1–8.

MacNaughton, R., Johns, F., & Rogus, J. (1982). When less seems like more: Managing the expanded field experience of the 80s. *Journal of Teacher Education, 33*(5), 10–13.

Molner, L., DiStefano, P., & Kerschen, T. (1990). Promoting professional growth through a school-university partnership: The University of Colorado partners in education project. Proposal submitted for The Far West Region Holmes Group Conference, Seattle.

Niemeyer, R., & Moon, R. (1988). Supervisory sense making. *Action in Teacher Education, 10*(1), 17–23.

Nolan, J. (1985). Potential obstacles to internal reform in teacher education: Findings from a case study. *Journal of Teacher Education, 36*(4), 12–16.

Oja, S. (1988). Some promising endeavors in school-university collaboration: Collaborative research and collaborative supervision in the University of New Hampshire five-year program. Paper presented at the Holmes Group Second Annual Conference, Washington, D.C.

A progress report to the Holmes Group. (1990). College of Education, University of Oregon.

Richardson-Koehler, V. (1988). Barriers to the effective supervision of student teaching: A field study. *Journal of Teacher Education, 39*(2), 28–34.

Sears, J., Marshall, J., & Otis-Wilborn, A. (1988). Teacher education policies and programs: Implementing reform proposals of the 1980s. Paper prepared for the Southeastern Educational Improvement Laboratory.

South Central Conference features collaborations with principals, teachers. (1989). *Holmes Group Forum, IV*(1) 17–18.

Takacs, C., & McArdle, R. (1984). Partnership for excellence: The visiting instructor program. *Journal of Teacher Education, 35*(6), 11–14.

The University of Arizona Cooperating Teacher Program. Final report: Project portrayal; Program assessment report; Practice profile. (1989). Tucson: College of Education.

Wolfe, D., Schewel, and R., Bickham, E. (1989). A gateway to collaboration: Clinical faculty programs. *Action in Teacher Education, 11*(2), 66–69.

Yee, A. (1968). Interpersonal relationships in the student teaching triad. *The Journal of Teacher Education, 19*(1), 95–112.

Zeichner, K. (1980). Myths and realities: Field-based experience in preservice teacher education. *Journal of Teacher Education, 31*(6), 45–55.

Part IV

Extending the Professional Development School

Most of the existing work on professional development schools has focused on the preparation of teachers. There are, however, a number of ways in which the conception can be expanded.

Trevor Sewell, Joan Shapiro, Joseph Ducette, and Jayminn Sanford discuss in some detail the special problems involved in establishing professional development schools in urban settings. The concept of a professional development school is that of a "real" school in a real district instead of the historically insulated and isolated laboratory school connected to a college or university. In this sense, an urban professional development school is quite appropriate. Nevertheless, additional problems of resources, commitment, and leadership emerge for professional development schools in urban settings. The kinds of criteria outlined by Goodlad and Murray that emphasize learning with understanding for all children are especially challenging in the urban context that is much more accustomed to working on a deficit or remedial model.

What is good for teachers may be even better for administrators. Robert Stevenson explores the possibilities for utilizing the concepts and criteria for professional development schools for teachers as ways of exploring this innovation as also germane for the preparation of administrators. In an argument somewhat reminiscent of Labaree's, he suggests that traditional conceptions of university research may be more attuned to similarly traditional conceptions of administrative authority and power rather than to emerging themes of collaboration. Stevenson proposes that useful, collaborative inquiry into schooling based on the assumption that neither the university nor the school has a corner on expertise is more likely to develop sound educational practice than traditional models. Furthermore, collaborative preparation is, in turn, more likely to foster such collaborative inquiry.

Nor is the conception of a professional development school of interest only to universities and schools. Although Case noted that the Connecticut Department of Education was sometimes at odds with the growth of professional development schools, Lee Teitel describes a case in which a state department of education utilized the concept of professional development schools to mandate simultaneous school and university renewal around the reform of middle school education. Although the heavy-handed way in which the state department implemented the project had a number of negative effects and led to the fading out of several partnerships, it also served to get several other sites into the process of collaborating with each other, a process that they admit might never have occurred without the state's prodding. The professional development school concept can be used as an extremely important policy tool of state departments of education provided it is handled with care.

TREVOR E. SEWELL, JOAN P. SHAPIRO,
JOSEPH P. DUCETTE, and JAYMINN S. SANFORD

Chapter Eleven

Professional Development Schools
in the Inner City
POLICY IMPLICATIONS FOR
SCHOOL-UNIVERSITY COLLABORATION

Can America preserve its preeminent economic status or solve its complex social problems in the twenty-first century if educational opportunity and academic achievement continue to be primarily the province of a privileged social class or ethnic group? Perhaps the answer to this question is reflected in the grave concern of educational reformers whose vision, whether driven by economic prosperity or social tranquility, is to shape educational policies to enhance students' success irrespective of social class, ethnicity, race, gender, or other differences. It is in this context—devastating academic failure and its corollary, economic inequality of the less privileged in society, in particular, some people of color and those of the lower socioeconomic class—that the educational issues embedded in the concept and practice of Professional Development Schools (PDS) in the inner city must be framed.

From whatever perspective school reform is conceptualized, effective teaching is central to the objective of enhancing student achievement. It is axiomatic that underlying exemplary teaching, particularly in the inner city, teachers need to have an abiding belief that "all students can learn" (Gollnick & Chinn, 1994), not just that some students can learn. Pugach and Pasch (1992) stated this idea eloquently:

Indeed, given the current state of American education, particularly with respect to the education of minority students, there is likely no more ambitious conception of teaching than that of establishing and acting on the belief that all students can learn (p. 4).

SALIENT CHARACTERISTICS OF INNER-CITY SCHOOLS

If effective teaching and an abiding belief that all children can learn are central to the objective of enhancing student achievement and if teacher preparation is at the core of the PDS concept (Goodlad, 1984; Holmes Group, 1986), the salient features of inner-city schools, which unquestionably influence teacher behavior, must be given considerable attention. The need to highlight the known characteristics of inner-city schools as a prerequisite to discussion of the urban PDS is strengthened when one invokes the familiar argument that the effectiveness of sound pedagogical strategies is substantially diminished by the grim socioeconomic realities of children's lives.

The ultimate success of the current educational reform movement should be judged by the extent to which inner-city schools demonstrate improvement in academic achievement. Therefore, the inner-city PDS is arguably critical to the school reform movement in which the solutions to "troubled" urban schools have been decidedly evasive. Historically, we have failed to replicate broadly exemplary accomplishments in inner-city schools, which has resulted in considerable ambivalence about the potential to achieve generalizable success. As Englert (1993) noted, the literature on urban schools is somewhat schizophrenic in its presentations. On the one hand, low academic achievement of students (Maeroff, 1988) and "savage inequality" in resources (Kozol, 1991) are well documented and indicate that the problems in inner-city schools are insurmountable. In stark contrast, others have illustrated the successful path that some urban schools can and have taken (Comer, 1980; Edmonds, 1986).

All things considered, however, the usual picture of the inner-city school is bleak and unforgiving. There are endless statistics on the poverty, low attendance rates, and poor levels of achievement of too many inner-city students. Massive data accumulated over several generations depict the schools located in American cities as being burdened with the most complex and intractable educational problems.

Despite the many problems of urban schools, the inner-city PDS offers unique opportunities for teacher preparation, research, and exemplary practice that are often not possible in a more affluent, less diverse suburban school. The salient features of the inner-city PDS should not, however, be perceived only in the context of the distinguishing variables associated with environmental circumstances. Perhaps, most importantly, the ideological thinking attributable to social-class status, ethnicity, and lives battered by sociocultural afflictions should also be perceived as having insidious implications for curricular content and teacher behavior.

This environment of inequity in educational and economic opportunities provides a unique background for the discussion and potential resolution of many of the most enduring controversies about human ability, equality of educational opportunities, and racial segregation. It is noteworthy that inner-city schools have become a fiercely combative arena in which the debate about the socioeconomic conditions of America's disadvantaged citizens is centered. Whether we debate the social and economic progress of the disadvantaged from a meritocratic premise or from the perspective of a dysfunctional family environment, the problems associated with educational failure, violence, drug addiction, poverty, teenage pregnancy, and illiteracy are often laid at the door of the urban schoolhouse. And, because inner-city schools reflect the social class and racial composition of the city, the educational process must necessarily confront formidable political and ideological issues, such as the controversies surrounding ability testing, multicultural education, and the effects of poverty on the teaching/learning process.

Perhaps a key issue for the PDS in the inner city is how to ask the difficult questions related to school failure. When considering the life experiences of disadvantaged children in the inner city, it becomes obvious that the nature of early childhood experience is quite sufficient to explain differences in achievement and testing, whether the prejudice maintained relates to race-ethnicity or social class. The concomitant occurrence of poverty, lead poisoning, in utero exposure to alcohol, and, at times, hunger engenders learning failure in all groups of children (Sewell, Price, & Karp, 1993). For these reasons, Haberman and Dill (1993) challenged us to recognize that: "Teaching children in poverty how to learn, how to think, how to analyze and reflect is apparently not the same type of challenge as teaching these strategies to broadly advantaged children" (p. 353).

Are the social class of the neighborhood, occupation of parents, and ethnic background important correlates or predictors of educational outcome? Data on the differential impact of these environmental variables on intellectual functioning and school achievement are unambiguous. Consequently, the connection between poverty and effective parenting, as well as poverty and learning failure of the child, must be addressed with extreme caution. Sewell, Price, and Karp (1993) noted:

> When poverty coexists with social problems not directly related to poverty (child abuse, drug and alcohol abuse), the consequences to the child's ability to learn are amplified; moreover, there are effects of poverty that are directly related to learning failure: lack of parental education, poor diet, and exposure to lead in the environment. (p. 27)

Given the realities of the environment in which in the inner-city PDS exists, one might do well to ask questions such as these: What knowledge bases should inform educational practice in urban schools? Moreover, what educational practices should inform our knowledge bases? While it is taken for granted in the PDS model that a teacher should have considerable preparation within the discipline(s) that she or he will be teaching, will these knowledge bases suffice? Should we prepare teachers for the inner city by offering them knowledge in interdisciplinary and multicultural areas as well? How should PDS sites in the inner city deal with educational practices that are based on scientific research (e.g., psychological testing), that casts doubt on the ability of all children to learn?

The inner-city PDS is uniquely positioned to question contemporary educational theories and practices, especially from a practitioner's perspective. Through its innovative, collaborative partnership with the university, the PDS can expose the gap between democratic principles and the social realities reflected in the schools that constitute a microcosm of society. The partnership in inquiry between practitioners and professors has the potential not only to enhance the PDS model but also to improve the reputation of educational research, particularly in the improvement of learning in inner-city schools.

OVERVIEW OF SCHOOL-UNIVERSITY COLLABORATIONS

A historical analysis of school-university collaboration indicates that collaborative trends usually occur in direct response to a crisis in education. In the 1950s, the gap between the curricular offerings in late high school and early college led to the collaborative efforts of schools and universities. In the 1960s and early 1970s, efforts to better understand the relationships between learning and chronological age provided an impetus for such continued collaboration. In the late 1970s and early 1980s, economic concerns recreated the crisis, initiating renewed collaborative agreements (Smith, 1986). In each case, collaboration faded when the crises ceased to exist or when a misunderstanding led to disenfranchisement (Boyer, 1981; Maeroff, 1983). Nonetheless, some educators argue that each school-university collaboration leaves the participating institutions more sophisticated in subsequent efforts (Smith, 1986).

The Rise of the Professional Development School

The current crisis in education, articulated in *A Nation at Risk* (National Commission on Excellence in Education, 1983) and elaborated by numerous subsequent reports, focuses on the inability of United States schoolchildren to excel in the global economic and intellectual competition of industrialized nations. Once again, we are exploring collaborative efforts in general. Specifically, we have been led to the formation of the PDS.

In the five years since the Holmes Group (1990) published *Tomorrow's Schools*, the concept of an entity called "the Professional Development School" has become so firmly entrenched in the educational reform literature that there remains little need to defend its existence. As the recent analyses by Darling-Hammond (1994) and Petrie (1993) demonstrated, the PDS exists in a large and growing number of school districts associated with a diverse group of teacher preparation institutions. Despite the widespread acceptance of the general concept, however, the exact criteria defining a PDS still need to be stipulated. As Goodlad (1993) stated:

> Within a very short span of years, the words "professional development school" (PDS) have been attached to a wide range of concepts and practices. Most commonly, they are used to convey the idea of a school that participates quite actively in the pre-service teacher education program of a college or university. But, in both concept and practice, this participation ranges from taking on a cadre of student teachers isolated from one another in classrooms . . . to a symbiotic partnership in which school and university personnel share the decisions of operating both the school and the entire length and breadth of the teacher preparation program. (p. 25)

While Goodlad is undoubtedly correct in his contention that the term "PDS" covers a wide range of school-university collaborations, the exact definition of this innovation is less important than the philosophy underlying this reform movement. Lanier (1993) explained:

> Not simply schools that would be good places for preparing future teachers, PDSs are places for responsible, enduring innovation in education. And they are not simply places for restructuring schools: 'fixing them so we get them right this time.' Rather, they are places for ongoing invention and discovery; places where school and university faculty together carry on the applied study and demonstration of the good practice and policy the profession needs to improve learning for young students and prospective educators. (p. ix)

A strong argument can be made that the creation of the PDS was an inevitable consequence of the reform movement that began with *A Nation at Risk* (National Commission on Excellence in Education, 1983) and continued through the various tracts, polemics, and remedies of the Reagan-Bush era. If, as the literature asserts, schools are failing, in part as a result of poor teaching, and if there is at least some validity to the contention that teachers are incompetent because they have received inadequate training from the institutions of higher education certifying them, then it follows that these schools, the teachers, and their teacher preparation institutions would form a coalition—if for no other reason than self-defense. Whether any of these negative assertions is true is far less important than the fact that many of the stakeholders in public education—politicians, parents, and presidents of colleges and universities, to name a few—believe them to be true. Thus, whatever form it may take, the PDS can correctly be viewed as an overdue and critical component of the necessary reform movement in teacher education.

Historical scholarship about school-university collaboration can inform the practice of those involved in the PDS. Proponents of school-university collaboration, in general, and PDSs, in particular, emphasize the need to institutionalize reform in teacher education that is based on long-term relationships between schools and teacher preparation institutions (Carnegie Forum on Education and the Economy, 1986; Goodlad, 1990, 1993; Holmes Group, 1986, 1990). With few exceptions, however, the historical literature about school-university collaboration and more recent scholarship about the practice of collaborative teacher education view conflict and differences in the institutional cultures as problematic. Communication breakdowns and cultural clashes have short-circuited the school-university collaborative process (Case, et al., 1993; Goodlad, 1993; Maeroff, 1983; Schwartz, 1990; Tom, 1973). In fact, the short lives of some school-university collaborative efforts have been attributed to communication problems, natural exclusivity of school-university cultures, different orientations and work paces, and mistrust and turf competition (Barth, 1984; Caruso, 1981; Haberman, 1971; Maeroff, 1983; Smith, 1988; Stanfield, 1981; Tom, 1973). This less popularized literature about processes of collaboration reveals a continued need to overcome obstacles, create common languages, release control, and manage suspicion.

Learning by Example: An Inner-City School-University Collaboration

In the recent climate of educational reform, a clear trend has surfaced that focuses on the effort to ameliorate the educational problems of the inner city. To this end, the urban school has become an arena for reform. While these reform efforts are characterized by a number of distinctive problems and issues, four issues related to school-university collaborations in the inner cities have been identified: (a) the sheer size and scope of not only the urban school system but the urban university as well, (b) difficulties in dealing with ongoing reforms, (c) issues of clashes of cultures, and (d) issues of multiculturalism.

Foundations, businesses, and other agencies and organizations, including universities, have found their way to the inner city in the hope that they can bring about some changes to improve future work forces. Urban universities frequently find themselves trying out their reform ideas in an environment where they often must "piggyback" their efforts on reforms that are already under way in a given site. This is one example of the clash of cultures that characterizes the interactions between universities and school districts. Because they may mask themselves in many ways, these clashes are not always diagnosed and, as a result, are often handled inappropriately. In addition, culture clashes are not limited to schools and universities. In fact, in an inner city, multiculturalism is prevalent, existing even when there appear to be students of one color in a school. Issues of social class and national origin can make a seemingly homogeneous group of students anything but that.

A ready illustration of the special issues faced by inner-city school-university collaborations is found in the example of the School District of Philadelphia–Temple University efforts. A brief overview is provided below.

The School District of Philadelphia consists of approximately 250 public schools servicing more than 200,000 children annually in grades K–12. The district is divided into seven geographic areas, each with a regional administrative office that governs education at the preschool, elementary, and middle school levels. High schools are governed by the central administration in cooperation with each regional superintendent's office. A large and diverse group of colleges and universities place over 1,000 teacher education students in the school district's public schools each semester. The bulk of these students come from Temple University, where the College of Education prepares the majority of district personnel in metropolitan Philadelphia. The typical teacher education student at Temple, and in most of the other institutions in the region that produce teachers, is a young white woman with a middle-class background. Often, she is afraid to work in inner-city schools and views her fear as ample reason to be excused from learning to teach all of the children of the state from which she seeks certification. Some faculty support her in her expression of fear, reinforcing the idea that fear is an exonerating circumstance.

Additionally, Temple University is actively involved with city schools through a large number of other projects. Each of Temple's 14 colleges, and many of its departments, offer some formalized activity in Philadelphia public schools. These activities range from summer programs for local schoolchildren to articulation, apprenticeship, and adoption agreements. Most of these programs were developed to address needs identified as unique to inner-city schoolchildren. Each is based on a service orientation to a relationship between schools and universities that coexist in an atmosphere of educational crisis and despair.

CHALLENGES UNIQUE TO THE URBAN PROFESSIONAL DEVELOPMENT SCHOOL

While need may be greatest in inner cities, people who live and work in urban communities are often wary about accepting benevolence because it sometimes comes at a high price. Similarly, among inner-city educators, there is a certain reticence about accepting charity because a hidden cost is often extracted in terms of self-esteem, self-control, and self-worth. While the university culture defines professorial involvement in public schools as a service activity, inner-city school practitioners often resent a service-oriented approach to collaboration.

The common sense aspect of working together to improve a city's educational systems and the excitement of engaging in mutually beneficial work lead the PDS team to confront challenges as they arise and search for a sense of balance and reason amidst ambiguity, rather than retreat in frustration and misunderstanding. Nevertheless, many of the problems identified by scholars of school-university collaboration continue to plague the practical work of the inner-city PDS.

The continued low achievement levels of many urban schools have encouraged a myriad of educational reform proposals focused on urban centers. Each year, there are new ideas, new approaches, and new philanthropic interests that carry with them favored educational philosophies. Inner-city schools are beholden to the charitable spirit of those who have the power of financial backing. While teachers and parents cautiously buy into ideas that spring forth from every aspect of society, it becomes increasingly difficult for them to maintain enthusiasm for new approaches while holding the front line. Administrators become skilled in developing reform ideas that meet the parameters of funders, while leaving some latitude to explore those things that they think will really make a difference. The lack of resources often encourages thriftiness at the expense of quality for survival sake's in the same way that families often lower the thermostat to preserve precious oil for the winter months. This process serves to foster a triage approach to addressing issues particular to urban education. There is not enough to do what needs to be done. There is little way to be certain how much is forthcoming. Thus, the most tangible and pressing issues are addressed at the expense of other less threatening needs.

Issues of Size and Scope

The size and scope of urban school systems and urban universities are factors unique to the inner-city PDS. Like other educational systems, the inner-city PDS is a microcosm of the society in which we exist. Society in the inner city is more recognizable by its negative elements than by its positive attributes. The number of people necessary to represent all of the constituencies and educational interest groups in cities surpasses those ideal to group processes. The number of formal and informal networks involved in instituting and implementing a PDS between two large bureaucracies renders inner-city partnerships subject to the tradewinds of educational criticism and political fancy. The simplest idea can become a most daunting task.

Nevertheless, urban educators continue to sift through the plethora of recycled educational reform approaches, revamping and adapting them to the unique needs of the rapidly changing urban environment. Although some approaches are more practical than others, so much of what is proposed is generated outside of the urban experience—with children who have little resemblance to inner-city students, in schools that function in what seems like a different time and place. As a result, many urban educators are discouraged from wholeheartedly accepting and participating in the national educational reform agenda. The more common occurrence is for individual schools and individual teachers to consider making emotional and professional investments in approaches that grow out of their articulated needs and their personal impressions of what may have a positive impact on education in their particular settings.

Issues of Dealing with Ongoing Reform

Understanding the difficulties in dealing with ongoing reforms can best be achieved by examining the real-life example of the School District of Philadelphia–Temple University PDSs. Each of the five PDSs partnered with Temple University's College of Education was involved in their own extensive programs of school reform, revitalization, and renewal at the inception of the PDS collaboration. Each school was engaged in a process of dividing into smaller charters or houses and writing curricula that would connect academic disciplines. The elementary school and the middle school had each experienced little or sporadic success in their efforts to improve academic achievement. And the three comprehensive high schools had experienced a decrease in student enrollment and staff morale with the advent of magnet schools that drew away the top students.

Concomitantly, the city school district had adopted a five-year restructuring plan incorporating 10 points deemed by parents, teachers, and administrators to be vital to school success. Two of the 10 points, namely, "creating and sustaining partnerships" and "lifelong learning," directly supported the new relationship with the College of Education. The district's existing long-term commitment to school reform, and stated intention to encourage educators to continue to learn, rendered the development of the urban PDSs with Temple University unique. Rather than having the burden to introduce the idea of reform and convince school district personnel of its importance, the college was in a position to support and expand a developing self-initiated reform effort, adding the distinct dimensions of theoretical expertise and an opportunity to participate in the training of future teachers.

The College of Education did not enter into the partnership with preformulated plans and strategies for action that the school district personnel could accept or reject. With two related goals of concretizing the historical commitment to the urban community in which the University exists, and improving the preparation of future teachers, the college initiated a reciprocal relationship that would define itself through reflection, discussion, and negotiation. Thus, through the PDS partnership, the common agenda of educational reform was expanded to include: (a) kindergarten through graduate education, (b) the ideal of teachers and faculty as lifelong learners, and (c) the vision that teachers are empowered to impact the future of their profession by working with aspiring teachers. The College's goal of improving teacher preparation programs was theoretically and practically linked to the schools' goal of educational reform. Although these goals reflected the self-interests of the partner institutions, they were not mutually exclusive and have, in fact, increasingly become mutually dependent.

The national and local threat of deteriorating urban educational systems and the independent desire of each partner to improve academic achievement citywide united the leadership of the school district and the university to mobilize their distinct resources to address this crisis in education. A team was developed to direct and oversee the PDS partnership. Through frequent, formal communication, relationships developed that have proven to be the backbone of the PDS partnership.

In describing the partnership, a college PDS team member stressed the importance of the relationship: "We have developed a collaborative rather than an expert model with democratic decisions and equal input. We have regular meetings where trust was eventually established."

A PDS team member from the school district confirmed this idea: "As our vision develops, clearer lines of communication have been established, and trust has been built. We will continue to have conversations involving many more voices, promising many other possibilities."

Two inferences can be drawn from such comments. First, the parties involved initially distrusted one another. Second, formal channels of communication are important, if not vital, for large group interaction.

Issue of Clashes of Cultures

One cause of clashes of culture is disagreement about how to channel the limited resources available to the schools and universities for their PDS partnerships. Clashes of culture can even arise within either of the partners. For example, the need for health and social services intervention in the schooling process lends itself to the involvement of schools of medicine, dentistry, nursing, and social work in inner-city schools. Within the university at large, these constituent schools will deliver services that are too often uncoordinated or overlapping.

Cultural clashes between institutions, however, constitute the paramount concern. Discrete methods of internal power utilization within the school and university institutional cultures present a conflict between the PDS partners in developing a mutual understanding. This type of conflict is described in the historical literature about school-university collaborative programs and cited as one reason for their early demise (Case, et al., 1993; Maeroff, 1983; Smith, 1988; Tom, 1973). Both the school district and the university operate within a set of principles and relationships comprising cultural understandings that are unique to each institution.

Historically, universities operate under the premise of individual faculty empowerment. Within universities, faculty have traditionally assumed the locus of control through a number of governance bodies. However, other informal groups affect governance councils in such a way as to effectively assume a level of decision making power through political influence. In large, urban universities, conflict and cultural clashes can be utilized informally to institute change efforts. Baldridge (1971) conceptualizes change as occurring when conflict, struggle, and cooperation simultaneously exist:

> This is premised on a conflict orientation to universities . . . but it is a strategic kind of conflict in which both parties have at the same time common interests and points of conflict. . . . Conflict in the university is essentially strategic . . . the essence being negotiation and the exchange of advantages and favors . . . for interest groups in the academic community are struggling with one another and at the same time cooperating. (p. 203)

The School District of Philadelphia, on the other hand, has historically utilized a clear hierarchal format for decision making. The district's new 10-point restructuring plan, discussed earlier, emphasizes site-based management and shared decision making. Consequently, each PDS appears to be struggling with the changing relationships among teachers and school-based administrators. Principals are trying to release control of the power that they have traditionally held, while simultaneously preparing teachers to assume power. Teachers are trying to interpret and adjust to the additional power and its inherent accompanying accountability.

In returning to the example at hand, the Temple University College of Education entered the PDS partnership without preformulated objectives. As described earlier, the process was undertaken without the university having a specified set of theories and activities that could be interpreted as a package to be accepted, rejected, or sabotaged by the schools. Unaccustomed to universities assuming this open-ended stance, teachers who were members of the PDS team repeatedly asked: "What kind of program is this?" Or, "What do you want us to do?" In response, the college faculty consistently replied: "We aren't going to tell you what to do." Or, "What would you like to see happen?" (Sanford & Mahar, 1993).

Theoretically, although the partners agreed that the objectives should be allowed to emerge spontaneously, the historical relationship between schools and universities seemed to encourage the continued expectation that the university would provide unilateral direction for the partnership in this time of crisis. Similarly, some in the university seemed to subscribe to this service-oriented, singularly directed approach. During PDS team meetings, public school teachers continued to expect the university's focused response to their requests for specific services. University faculty, in turn, were not as clear about the specific ways in which school personnel could affect the programs but were hesitant to respond exclusively to the specific school-focused issues (Sanford & Mahar, 1993). Part of the urban PDS team process appears to be a mutual resistance of the inclination toward a university-directed collaboration in crisis.

A school district administrator described her idea of cultural conflict between the groups specific to this collaboration in a paper presented at the national conference of the American Association of Colleges for Teacher Education:

> Within our profession, we use language which is divisive rather than cohesive in bringing us together to share strengths. Teachers in schools speak of academia as residing in an ivory tower, which describes a fairy tale existence to college work and one which is unrealistic to the preparation of teachers. Early childhood and elementary teachers are referred to as "cutesy" by their colleagues who teach in middle and senior high schools. Teacher educators who want to actively participate in the school community find themselves ostracized by the professional culture which exists in the university. Often, inference is made by university staff that there is a lack of academic scholarship in the schools. (Scott, 1993, p. 1)

Likewise, a PDS teacher described cultural conflict within groups from her perspective during a year-end evaluation of PDS activities: "It has been difficult helping teachers to accept and understand that this is a collaborative effort and assuring teachers that they have meaningful information about effective teaching—and others want to hear their ideas and concerns."

Issues of Multiculturalism

People often think of inner-city schools as offering a unique environment of multiculturalism and diversity. While, at first glance, many inner-city schools may appear to be monocultural, a closer analysis of urban demographics indicates that many disenfranchised international and American ethnic groups move through urban areas en route to the American dream. While there, they send their children to neighborhood public schools. Therefore, predominately black schools often see people of African ancestry who have immigrated from southern cities, the Americas, and the Caribbean; African nationals; and a variety of Latino and Asian national and ethnic groups. The cultural exchanges of these ethnic groups are as rich in their diversity as that found in multiracial schools. The fact that most inner-city schools have large numbers of students of color is a sociopolitical reality that educators may utilize to help prospective teachers who represent majority cultures to find their place in a multicultural world.

Such problematic cultural exchanges are inherent in school-university collaboration, in general, and the urban PDS practice, in particular. These problems directly parallel and mirror cultural clashes that exist among and within educational institutions on all levels. They are both an impetus for and a product of inferences flavored by society's sporadic hysteria about educational results.

Everyone's future depends, to some extent, on all of today's school-children. Perhaps it is this dependency that contributes to the tendency to cling to outdated policies and practices that threaten the goal of mutual reform. The array of interest groups and how and where they enter into the dialogue about educational issues thrusts the field of education into a perpetual state of conflict and cacophony. Conflict in this sense can be viewed as a positive occurrence in that it denotes a level of forethought, communication, and commitment and reflects emerging clarity. Such conflict defies lethargy.

POSSIBILITIES OF INNER-CITY PARTNERSHIPS

And yet, all of these seemingly problem areas of the inner city can be precisely the opposite, opening a wealth of possibilities. For example, the scope and size of inner-city schools and urban universities demonstrate that there are possible sites that can be appropriate for one group of students and other sites that can be better for others. There is ample room for experimentation and for comparisons over time. Given their typically large size, urban universities can offer a wealth of expertise and services through their many colleges and schools. One university administrator stated:

> And if we are going to think of children as having nutritional needs, health needs and these major problems that need more than teaching input, then the collaboration with other colleges and schools in the university is invaluable and will enable our teachers in preparation to understand the child as a whole. We need to understand how to deal with the child from the perspective of his or her social environment as well as from a medical perspective. So that collaboration will help us sufficiently to strengthen our teacher education program. (Sanford, 1993)

Although it may seem as if there are too many institutions and agencies all knocking down the inner-city schoolhouse doors, these different groups can actually lead to broadening partnerships. For example, one of the most interesting of the collaborations between the School District of Philadelphia and Temple University's College of Education is a corporate partnership. This triumvirate has had a powerful effect on both an elementary school and a middle school in the city. These kinds of collaborations could not exist unless many groups had an interest in providing the opportunity for all children to learn—and creating a work force of literate, intelligent individuals.

Clashes of cultures do, in fact, exist within the urban PDS. But sometimes these clashes can be diminished and even lead to real understanding. For example, in the corporate partnership described previously, the leaders of the three groups—the principals of the schools, the dean of the College of Education, and the director of corporate giving—initially had very different expectations for their organizations. The principal wanted extras for her children: more assistance in the classroom through student teachers, books for the library, and trips beyond the school walls. The dean wanted to assist the children in improving their achievement, while also hoping for an excellent site to prepare future teachers. And the director of corporate giving wanted to see real improvement of standardized test scores. Over time, however, these leaders realized that they had a great deal in common not only professionally but personally as well. Instead of focusing on different goals, as they had initially, they began to share stories and develop trust, forming an alliance of understanding with a real desire to assist inner-city youth in ways that were meaningful to each of them. This partnership has grown over the past three years; to a large extent, the initial clashes and misunderstandings are no longer obstacles.

Issues of multiculturalism can be exceedingly positive. They can enable children from different social classes to learn from each other. They can enable children from different cultures to appreciate each others' backgrounds. Above all, they can create a learning environment and respect for difference. Additionally, the predominantly white, female, middle-class teachers can learn more about difference firsthand during their preparation program. Through the students, their parents, and the community, new teachers have the opportunity to grow and learn in ways that could never be attained in a suburban classroom.

CONCLUSION: THE PLACE OF THE INNER-CITY PROFESSIONAL DEVELOPMENT SCHOOL IN THE PREPARATION OF TEACHERS

In concluding a discussion of the inner-city PDS, it is necessary to restate an early assertion. Specifically, our experiences with the five PDS sites associated with Temple University have led to the belief that the inner-city PDS is critical, not only to our own success as an institution preparing teachers but ultimately to the success of the current educational reform movement. From the perspective of those institutions that have developed similar collaborations with more affluent school districts, Temple's collaboration with a large, urban school district attempting to educate more than 200,000 children each year, many of whom live in poverty, must seem an enormous disadvantage. Our experience has been exactly the opposite. Both because of what they are and what they can become, the inner-city PDS is necessary for the adequate preparation of teachers for the twenty-first century. In fact, if there were no inner-city PDS sites, we would have to invent them. Two advantages of the inner-city PDS are now described.

Preparing Future Teachers to Value Diversity

It is well known that the current teacher corps is composed primarily of white, upwardly mobile women and that the present cohort of administrators consists largely of white, middle-class men (Apple, 1986; De Lyon & Woddowson Migniuolo, 1989; Sleeter, 1992). While the literature argues strongly for the recruitment of more diverse teacher and administrator groups, and while we agree strongly with this movement, the evidence indicates that this is not currently happening. In fact, it seems as if the teachers and administrators who are currently in the pipeline are even less diverse than those trained during the 1980s. This is especially unfortunate in light of the strong trend toward greater diversity in the student populations who will attend school in the near future.

The clear issue for teacher preparation institutions is to somehow find a way to prepare the teachers of tomorrow not only to exist in a diverse environment but to value diversity for what it brings to their teaching (Ducette, Shapiro & Sewell, in press). This goal would be challenging under any circumstance, but it becomes frighteningly difficult with teachers who will, under the most likely scenario, be as white, female, and middle class as those in the current teacher corps.

Consequently, the inner-city PDS has, as one of its prime functions, to serve as the major building block in educating future teachers to understand, utilize, and value student diversity. This rationale for the inner-city PDS has been put forth in a clear and convincing manner by Pugach and Pasch (1992), who stated:

> In light of the disparity between the demographics of the school age population and those of the teaching force, it is crucial that the reform of teacher education consider how to address issues of diversity forthrightly, honestly and in a sustained manner. The experience garnered to date . . . has led us to conclude that the challenge of facing one's own biases in the process of becoming a teacher is best accomplished in the context of schools whose teachers deal with diversity on a daily basis. . . . Urban professional development schools provide an important source of potential to address this problem and may help novices, as well as experienced teachers, understand their own personal patterns of beliefs around the issue of working with students who differ from themselves. (p. 4)

In the context of diversity, the inner-city PDS plays a vital role in the reform movement in teacher education.

Fulfilling the Promise That All Children Can Learn

The primary reason why the inner-city PDS is vital in the preparation of teachers focuses on the premise that, as educators, we must not only believe but also be able to demonstrate that all children can learn. Like so many educational truisms, the assertion that "all children can learn" is as widely held as it is broadly violated. The discrepancy between this belief and the reality of too many inner-city schools touches on one of the central paradoxes of the American dream.

Our society is built on a number of cherished beliefs. One of these is that all people are created equal, thereby leading to the assumption that everyone possesses the same inherent right to achieve. Another is that only the best and the brightest will succeed, and that this principle of meritocracy will, and should, determine who will win and who will lose. When applied to success in school, these aspects of the American belief system underlie many of our attributions about educational achievement. Numerous publications (see Weiner, 1979, for a review) have demonstrated that a lack of effort and a lack of ability are the two reasons most often cited by teachers, administrators, and parents for school failure. Poverty, inadequate resources to support learning, unstable homes, and the host of other inner-city realities mentioned at the beginning of this chapter seldom make the list of reasons for school failure. Put in more colloquial terms, the common belief is that children fail because they are lazy or stupid or both. To use another common metaphor, the academic playing field is not level. Nowhere is this better demonstrated than in an inner-city school.

In far too many inner-city schools, the American dream of equality of educational opportunity is shown daily to be false. This continual reinforcement of disillusionment raises a series of difficult questions. How, for example, can a society that says it believes in equality of opportunity allow large numbers of its children to attend schools where failure is the expected outcome and where resources, facilities, and philosophies make achievement difficult, if not impossible? How can we continue to state in our public documents that we believe all children are capable of learning, when large numbers of our children in the inner city are forced to live in environments where the barriers to learning are too often insurmountable? The answers to these questions are both obvious and disturbing. In fact, the American promise of an equal opportunity to a quality education is hollow and barren.

The issue for an institution preparing teachers is that the inner-city school just described cannot and should not be a site for practicum or student teaching. Such a school almost inevitably produces in the pre-service teacher a series of perceptions that are exactly the opposite of everything in which we believe. If Haberman and Dill (1993) are correct that teaching children in poverty is not the same challenge as teaching children from advantaged backgrounds, those who will be teaching in inner-city schools must undergo a supervised experience in inner-city schools. It is our belief that the PDS concept is an ideal model to provide this preparation.

It is clear that the only appropriate site for preparing teachers is one where all participants (teachers, administrators, parents, and the children themselves) believe that all children can learn and where this belief has at least some basis in reality. While a PDS is not the only inner-city school where these conditions can occur, it is arguably the best option that currently exists.

The establishment of an inner-city PDS site, where a university focuses its resources, creates an environment where achievement is possible for all students. Although it is true that this model is not widely replicable (for no university has the resources to accommodate every school in a large urban district), and it does not produce success for every student, and that some of the collaborations between school districts and universities do not succeed, each of these factors is less important than the simple fact that such an environment is possible and necessary. Our student teachers have a right to be prepared in such an environment, and teacher preparation institutions have an obligation to create it.

REFERENCES

Apple, M. W. (1986). *Teachers and texts: A political economy of class and gender relations in education*. New York: Routledge & Kegan Paul.

Baldridge, V. (1971). *Power and conflict in the university*. New York: John Wiley and Sons.

Barth, R. (1984, November 24). Can we make a match of schools and universities? *Education Week*.

Boyer, E. (1981, April). Schools and universities need each other. *Educational Leadership, 38*(7), 556.

Carnegie Forum on Education and the Economy. (1986). *A nation prepared: Teachers for the 21st century* (Report of the Task Force on Teaching as a Profession). New York: Author.

Caruso, J. (1981, April). Collaboration of school, college, and community: Bridge to progress. *Educational Leadership, 38*(7), 558–562.

Case, C., Norlander, K. A., & Reagan, T. G. (1993). Cultural transformation in an urban professional development center: Policy implications for school-university collaborations. *Educational Policy, 7*(1), 40–60.

Comer, J. (1980). *School power: Implications of an intervention project*. New York: The Free Press.

Darling-Hammond, L. (Ed.) (1994). *Professional development schools.* New York: Teachers College Press.

De Lyon, H., & Woddowson Migniuolo, F. (Eds.) (1989). *Women teachers: Issues and experiences.* Philadelphia: Open University Press.

Ducette, J.P., Shapiro, J. P., & Sewell, T. E. (in press). Diversity in education: Problems and possibilities. In F. Murray (Ed.), *A knowledge base for teacher educators.* American Association for Colleges of Teacher Education.

Edmonds, R. (1986). Characteristics of effective schools. In U. Neisser (Ed.), *The school achievement of minority children.* Hillsdale, NJ: Lawrence Erlbaum Associates.

Englert, R. M. (1993). Understanding the urban context and conditions of practice of school administration. In P. Forsyth & M. Tallerico (Eds.), *City schools: Leading the way.* Newbury Park, CA: Corwin Press.

Gollnick, D. M., & Chinn, P. C. (1994). *Multicultural education in a pluralistic society.* Columbus, OH: Merrill.

Goodlad, J. I. (1984). *A place called school.* New York: McGraw-Hill.

Goodlad, J. I. (1990). *Places where teachers are taught.* San Francisco: Jossey-Bass.

Goodlad, J. I. (1993). School-university partnerships and partner schools. *Educational Policy, 7*(1), 24–39.

Haberman, M. (1971, Summer). Twenty-three reasons universities can't educate teachers. *Journal of Teacher Education, 22,* 133–140.

Haberman, M., & Dill, V. (1993). The knowledge base on retention vs. teacher ideology: Implications for teacher preparation. *Journal of Teacher Education, 44*(5), 352–356.

Holmes Group. (1986). *Tomorrow's teachers: A report of the Holmes Group.* East Lansing, MI: Author.

Holmes Group. (1990). *Tomorrow's schools: A report of the Holmes Group.* East Lansing, MI: Author.

Kozol, J. (1991). *Savage inequalities.* New York: Crown Publishers.

Lanier, J. T. (1993). Forward to *Professional development schools,* L. Darling-Hammond (Ed.). New York: Teachers College Press.

Maeroff, G. I. (1983). *School and college: Partnerships in action.* Princeton, NJ: Princeton University Press.

Maeroff, G. I. (1988). Withered hopes, stillborn dreams: The dismal panorama of urban schools. *Phi Delta Kappan, 69*(9), 633–638.

National Commission on Excellence in Education. (1983). *A nation at risk: The imperative for educational reform.* Washington, DC: Superintendent of Documents, U.S. Government Printing Office.

Petrie, H. G. (1993). Professional development schools. *Educational Policy, 7*(1), 3–4.

Pugach, M., & Pasch, S. (1992). The challenge of creating professional development schools. Paper presented at the annual meeting of the American Educational Research Association, San Francisco.

Sanford, J. S. (1993). School/university collaboration: Conflict and collaboration in teacher education reform. Unpublished dissertation. Harvard University Graduate School of Education.

Sanford, J., & Mahar, B. (1993). A five-year program of teacher education: Implementation in the context of valid resistance. Paper presented at the annual conference of the American Association of Colleges for Teacher Education, San Diego.

Schwartz, H. (Ed.). (1990). *Collaboration: Building common agendas* (Teacher Education Monograph No. 10). Washington, DC: ERIC Clearinghouse on Teacher Education.

Scott, L. (1993). School-university partnership: An urban school district perspective. Paper presented at the annual conference of the American Association of Colleges for Teacher Education, San Diego, CA.

Sewell, T., Price, V., & Karp, R. (1993). The ecology of poverty, undernutrition and learning failure. In R. Karp (Ed.), *Malnourished children in the United States: Caught in the cycle of poverty.* New York: Springer Publishing.

Sleeter, C. E. (1992) Resisting racial awareness: How teachers understand the social order from their racial, gender and social class locations. *Educational Foundations, 6*(2), 7–32.

Smith, R. (1986). Toward redefining the school-college connection: A review of the literature. Unpublished paper. Harvard University Graduate School of Education.

Smith, R. (1988). *School-college collaboration: A case study of Lilly Endowment linkage grants in Indiana.* Unpublished dissertation, Harvard University Graduate School of Education, Cambridge, MA.

Stanfield, R. (1981). Teamwork for high schools and colleges. *Educational Record, 62*(2), 45–47.

Tom, A. (1973, September). Three dilemmas: School-university ventures. *The Clearinghouse, 48*(1), 7–10.

Weiner, B. (1979). A theory of motivation for some classroom experiences. *Journal of Educational Psychology, 71,* 3–25.

ROBERT B. STEVENSON

Chapter Twelve

Critically Reflective Inquiry and Administrator Preparation
PROBLEMS AND POSSIBILITIES

Discussions concerning the preparation of educational administrators frequently focus on such issues as the appropriate length of internships or clinical experiences, the extent to which practicing administrators should be involved in the program, and the number of courses in different areas of educational administration that students should be required to complete. Although these issues of the means of preparing administrators are important, more fundamental questions about the goals and ideological assumptions underlying preparation programs are often neglected. Assumptions about the relationship between theory and practice and how knowledge of educational practice is acquired profoundly influence the particular approach to the education of school administrators. In advocating the concept of professional development schools, the Holmes Group (1990) not only proposed different sites and means for the preparation of educational professionals but also challenged conventional assumptions about the source and acquisition of knowledge of educational practice.

The intent of this article is to examine these different assumptions and their implications for reconceptualizing the roles and relationships of those

Original was first published in *Educational Policy, 7*(1), March, 1993, © Corwin Press, Inc. Reprinted here by permission of Corwin Press, a Sage Publications Company.

involved in administrator preparation in a professional development school
(PDS) model.[1] Three orientations to the preparation of school administrators
are first described for the purpose of comparing different views of the role of
students and practitioners in the production and verification of knowledge.
When compared with the purposes and assumptions of PDSs, only the reflective inquiry orientation emerges as consistent. A central premise of these proposed schools is that school-district administrators and university faculty
should collaboratively participate in systematic inquiry into problems of practice. By drawing on case studies of problem-based administrative preparation
and inquiry-oriented teacher education programs, two dilemmas or tensions
involved in creating this kind of collaboration are analyzed. These dilemmas
involve the integration of theory and practice and the reconfiguration of roles
and relationships among students, cooperating administrators in schools, and
university faculty. Finally, a way of addressing these dilemmas is proposed.

ORIENTATIONS TO THE EDUCATION
OF SCHOOL ADMINISTRATORS

> The practice of administrators, managers, and policy analysts is irreducibly
> value-laden, being routinely concerned with questions of what ought to be
> done or what is the right course of action to advise or follow. (Evers &
> Lakomski, 1991, p. vii).

The practice of university faculty involved in preparing educational
administrators, managers, and policy analysts is similarly value-laden.
Decisions about programmatic goals and actions involve consideration of
moral and ethical principles that define our ideals or sense of what we should
strive to achieve. Differences among faculty in these principles or ideals are
likely to account for different orientations to administrator preparation and for
much of the intellectual debate surrounding this preparation. However, a person usually argues about the strategies for educating practitioners (be it teachers or administrators) within the parameters of a single orientation (Zeichner,
1983). When individuals with different orientations discuss preparation programs, the debate is often unsatisfactory and irresolvable because they fail to
address the set of common assumptions about the goals of education that
underlie a particular orientation. By explicating these different sets of assumptions and their associated orientations, I hope not only to further the general
debate about administrator preparation but also to specifically stimulate consideration of the role that PDSs might play in that preparation. For this purpose, three broad orientations to professional preparation are identified: craft,
traditional scientific, and reflective inquiry. Although these dominant orientations to education exist in many professional fields, the assumptions underlying each are discussed in relation to the preparation of school administrators.

The Craft Orientation to Administrator Preparation

Historically, the education of school administrators was based on the notion of administration as a craft in which prospective administrators were viewed as novices needing to participate in a kind of apprenticeship with an expert or master "craftsperson," namely, an experienced and competent administrator. The assumption underlying this orientation is that knowledge about administrative practice is acquired largely by a process of trial and error and that the practical wisdom of the experienced administrator can be used to reduce the amount of "on the job" learning and the number of mistakes that the novice must endure to become a skilled administrator.

The role of most craft-oriented preparation programs is to transmit to the student the knowledge of good practice acquired by experienced administrators. Thus, the student is treated essentially as a passive recipient of the knowledge of others. This knowledge is conveyed by faculty recruited largely on the basis of their extensive administrative experience in schools, by adjunct or clinical faculty members who are still practicing administrators, and, to a lesser extent, through internships and field experiences that place students in direct contact with practitioners. In each case, the expertise of practitioners is highly valued and has a prominent place in the preparation program. This approach to administrator preparation is still common in many state colleges and small private institutions, although often not because of an explicit philosophical commitment but for reasons of economic expediency accorded by the part-time employment of adjunct practicing administrators.

An alternative craft-oriented approach is to regard the preparation program, at least the formal course work, as providing knowledge about administration and not about how to be an administrator (Blumberg, 1989). The focus of the administration courses is on developing a basic understanding of administration and a perspective or way of thinking about administrative work. Knowledge about being an administrator is seen as learned on the job, beginning with the administrative internship.

Although mastery of a repertoire of discrete administrative skills is seen as important, the emphasis in this orientation is on the holistic development of the person's abilities as an administrator. These abilities are usually viewed as tacitly recognizable rather than amenable to explicit specification. So, acceptable performance is usually measured not against explicit prespecified criteria but on the basis of the student's overall capacity to think and act like an administrator as presently defined implicitly in the field.

Traditional Scientific Administrator Preparation

The dominant orientation to the education of school administrators, especially in research universities, is the traditional scientific (or "theory") movement, which has origins first in scientific management and later in behavioral science (Evers & Lakomski, 1991). It is exemplified by competency-based approaches to preparing individuals for administrative roles and focuses on the development of specific and observable skills that are believed to be possessed by any effective administrator. Underlying this focus are the assumptions that specific behaviors of administrators can be directly linked to organizational effectiveness and that those behaviors are generalizable across different contexts.

As in the craft orientation, the prospective administrator is not generally viewed as an active agent in determining the objectives or content of his or her program. The source of professional knowledge for the program's content, instead of residing in the practical wisdom of practitioners as in the craft orientation, lies in the research base on management and behavioral science and administrator effectiveness. This empirically tested knowledge is seen as having a direct application to practice. So, the task of the preparation program is to help students understand general principles about administrative behavior, which provide rules that they can follow in their future roles. The knowledge and skills to be developed are usually prespecified, and performance is measured by the level of mastery of that knowledge and skills.

The goals of administrative practice receive limited attention, being treated not as a matter of debate but of general consensus. With goals accepted as given rather than as problematic, the primary concern is the development of students' technical efficiency in performing administrative tasks as defined by the current role of administrators. Thus this orientation emphasizes the preparation of educational leaders who will be equipped to effectively carry out existing practices and to question and improve those practices with respect to their efficiency. On the other hand, graduates are unlikely to have been prepared to question the relationship of existing practices to educational purposes and the possible need to transform structures that might be constraining the attainment of desired ends.

Reflective Inquiry in Administrator Preparation

Criticisms of the lack of attention to "real" problems of practice in the theory-driven or scientific approach to administrator preparation (Bridges, 1977) have contributed in part to efforts to develop more integrated approaches to the study of theory and practice. A common response has centered on the notion of reflective practitioners who engage in a continual process of inquiry into their own professional practices (Schon, 1983, 1987). In this orientation, prospective professionals are cast as active agents in their own education. Rather than being viewed as passive recipients and implementers of knowledge created in universities, they are encouraged to generate knowledge through a process of systematic inquiry. The focus of the preparation program is on developing practitioners who will be able to make informed, reflective, and self-critical judgments about their professional practice.

In contrast to the other orientations, reflective inquiry emphasizes more than inquiring into questions of means and the technical skills of being an administrator. There is a concern for examining the ends (what ought to be?) as well as the means (how can we do it?) of educational practice. In other words, both intentions and actions are viewed as important subjects of inquiry, with attention paid to the congruency between the two.

Educational practice, however, as Tabachnick and Zeichner (1991) pointed out, is not necessarily improved merely by practitioners being reflective and more deliberate and intentional in their actions because "in some cases, this greater intentionality may help solidify and justify teaching practices that are harmful to students" (p. 2). In preparation programs, they argue, we need to address the subject, purposes, and quality of reflection that should be encouraged. After identifying five traditions of reflective practice in teacher education that have differing emphases with respect to these issues, they argue for a "social reconstructionist" tradition that encourages teachers to reflect on the contribution of their actions toward greater equality and social justice in both schools and the larger society.

University courses emphasizing reflective inquiries, however, only involve isolated individuals located in different schools and do not provide a systemic means of addressing the cultural and structural conditions in schools that are necessary to support the continuous participation of administrators and teachers in reflective inquiry. These conditions are only likely to be created when reflection and inquiry are accepted as a central focus of professional practice in schools. Such a principle has been advocated as an organizing feature of professional development schools.

PROFESSIONAL DEVELOPMENT SCHOOLS

Professional development schools were proposed by the Holmes Group (1990) in its report, *Tomorrow's Schools*, as sites for the preparation of school professionals, including administrators. These schools are seen as embodying a commitment to a spirit of experimentation and a continual process of thoughtful inquiry and reflection. This experimentation and inquiry is envisaged as a collaborative effort between university faculty and school professionals in which the latter are not simply the receivers and implementers of the products of educational research but active participants in setting and carrying out a research agenda for improving school practices and enhancing the knowledge base of educational activity. Collaboration is also extended to the provision of practical experiences for prospective teachers and administrators (and other professional school personnel). But instead of simply serving as a clinical setting, the PDS is viewed as a center of collaborative and systematic inquiry in which the school's own critical questions of practice become the focus of professional preparation, school research, and the professional development of practitioners.

The Holmes Group also argues that PDSs must be concerned with more than the technical question of improving the efficiency of instruction. Not only must the PDS "engage in the struggle to better its students' present and future lives" but it also must participate in "social and political action to acquire additional resources and press the claims for justice on the larger society" (p. 33). Thus, the Holmes Group implicitly advocates a social reconstructionist view of reflective inquiry by stressing the need for a commitment among school and university faculty to the social ideals of equity and social justice.

As evident from the discussion, the goals and principles of PDSs are highly compatible with the reflective inquiry orientation to the preparation of school administrators. These goals and principles, however, require fundamental changes in the traditional roles of, and relationships between, university and school faculty and in the traditional relationship between research and practice (Holmes Group, 1990). We need, therefore, to develop new ways of conceptualizing the work of both university and school faculty who might be involved in the preparation of future administrators. The few documented case studies of courses and programs that have been designed to promote the development of reflective practitioners provide some insights into how new roles and relationships and the integration of research, theory and practice might take shape in a preparation program within professional development schools.

THE PROBLEM-BASED APPROACH
TO REFLECTIVE INQUIRY

Reflective inquiry is a relatively recent orientation to the preparation of educators, and few systematic efforts have been made to implement this approach. Even with the aid of researchers who have been engaged in national studies of administrative preparation programs (M. Milstein, personal communication, 1992; Murphy, personal communication, 1992), no documented examples could be identified of a reflective inquiry-oriented program for educational administrators that focuses on actual problems of practice in a school setting. However, a recent case study of a pilot seminar on the principalship describes an effort to nurture reflective practice by engaging the participants in analyzing fictionalized case problems of administrative practice and developing written action plans for their resolution (Hart, Naylor, & Sorensen, 1992). In this university-based course, expert practitioners attended four seminar sessions "to coach students through the process of thinking about problem definition and problem-solving as they developed plans for action" (Hart et al., 1992, p. 7).

This approach, which has been termed the problem-based approach and is being actively promoted by the National Policy Board for Educational Administration (1989) and the Danforth Foundation, emphasizes the development of problem solving, decision making, and conflict resolution skills that will enable school administrators to "cope with real people in real schools" (Schmuck, 1988). For example, in the seminar described above, the coaching sessions, the debriefing sessions with the instructor, and an evaluation panel of professors, superintendents, and principals to which students presented their action plans all focused on students' problem-solving skills, including their ability to reflect on and apply theoretical and experiential knowledge. The assumption is that these skills will equip administrators to better solve the many problems they encounter daily in their schools. Unlike the traditional scientific tradition, however, the skills are not necessarily viewed as being able to be prespecified in advance but instead are treated as emerging from intensive study of case problems.

This view of knowledge and skills emerging from the process of inquiring into a problem creates a different role for students, cooperating school administrators, and university faculty. Significantly, difficulties were reported in the seminar on the principalship among both some students and experienced administrators in adjusting to their respective roles of active problem solver and facilitating coach. Students sometimes sought the direct advice of their coaches on appropriate actions; coaches often succumbed to this pressure and reported experiencing more difficulty in posing appropriate questions than in offering suggestions (Hart et al., 1992). Ironically, students indicated that the least helpful coaching was "the most directive about what should be done" (Hart et al., 1992, p. 13).

The problem-based approach is intended, in part, to respond to the disjuncture between the calm and analytic thinking on selected issues emphasized in the university settings in which administrator preparation takes place and the instantaneous thinking and decision making on multiple, disjointed issues demanded in the often chaotic and reactive situations in which school administrators function. Whereas this approach has arisen within the context of proposals for restructuring the organization of schooling and the role of teachers and administrators (particularly with respect to decision-making authority), there is an assumption that university preparation must be tied more closely to the present job demands of school administrators. The focus is on preparing prospective administrators to cope with these demands rather than to address how school and larger social structures might be creating the demands and limiting their actions.

The conception of reflective inquiry in the problem-based approach and the seminar on the principalship differs from that underlying the Holmes Group's notion in professional development schools. Besides reflecting on hypothetical rather than actual problems being faced in schools, the assumption of this kind of reflection is that educational actions are improved by being more intentional and deliberate. No explicit consideration is given to whether proposed actions contribute to such goals as equity and social justice or whether actions need to be directed toward altering the conditions or structures in which educators work.

PERSISTENT DILEMMAS IN
INQUIRY-BASED EDUCATION

To examine the use of reflective inquiries into real problems of practice in professional preparation that are more aligned with the notion proposed by the Holmes Group, the teacher education literature was searched. Six documented case studies (from four countries) of inquiry-based approaches were identified as addressing the integration of theory and practice and the redefinition of roles and relationships. Although these were common themes, an analysis of the six cases revealed differing approaches to the two issues.

A common theme in the case studies was the need for reconceptualizing the role of school faculty in the preparation program, including their relationship with university faculty. For example, instead of the traditional arrangement of one student with one cooperating teacher, with its implied mentor-intern relationship, collaborative field teams were established in several programs (Altrichter, 1988; Ellsworth & Albers, 1991; Robottom, 1988). These teams did not have designated leaders but were intended to be collectively led, although, predictably, at different sites individuals in different roles often assumed leadership. The intent in each case was to foster collaborative inquiry and support among those actively involved at the school or "a more collegial and democratized system of planning, mentoring and evaluation" (Ellsworth & Albers, 1991, p. 7). The field teams also had formal connections to the university, usually through the traditional involvement and role of supervising teachers (i.e., university graduate students) who had responsibility for facilitating communications between the school and university and for assessing the student teachers.

Despite their attention to reconceptualizing the roles of key players, the case studies revealed a tendency for people to retreat into the traditional roles to which they had been accustomed. For example, whereas some cooperating teachers were reported as seeing the value of working as part of a field team and showing signs of acceptance of an extended role of being teacher educators rather than only providers of placements for prospective teachers, others rejected this arrangement, perceiving team meetings as an "invasion" of their one-on-one relationship with their prospective teacher (Ellsworth & Albers,

1991). Similarly, although there was some evidence of the emergence of a more collegial view of their induction into teaching among the prospective teachers, they "did not appear to perceive themselves as playing an active or definable role in the program" (Ellsworth & Albers, 1991, p. 23) but maintained the traditional role of student as passive recipient.

The meetings of some of the field teams in one of the teacher education programs were also viewed as typical mentoring sessions in which the cooperating teachers functioned as experienced, particularistic problem solvers rather than as posers of broader issues of teaching, learning, and schooling. This exemplifies a second persistent problem, namely, a focus on technical or instrumental concerns to the extent of neglecting broader issues and contexts that affect educational practice. The failure to address broader issues and contexts was reported in several programs despite their explicit attention to these issues in courses or seminars. A dominant concern for techniques and effectiveness was evident, for example, in student teachers' action research projects (Robottom, 1988). Although some students "made the social conditions of schooling problematic and considered the moral and ethical implications of their work" (Robottom, 1988, p. 82), the majority of projects focused on such technical issues as discipline and classroom management divorced from any connection to matters of curriculum and instruction (Gore & Zeichner, 1991).

Another persistent dilemma was manifested in the question of evaluation of the prospective teachers, with cooperating teachers continually asking "Who has the final say in the decision of a final grade' (Ellsworth & Albers, 1991, p. 28). This question apparently created tensions in the relationship between university and school personnel in some programs, in part because it revealed the underlying issue of who should have the authority to make judgments about the quality of teaching. A related concern—and a very important one in inquiry-based approaches to practitioner preparation—was the extent to which visiting university personnel felt free to critique "both specific classroom practices and more general aspects of the cooperating teacher's approach to teaching" (Ellsworth & Albers, 1991, p. 29). Both of these tensions may reflect a concern for what kind of knowledge about educational practice should be valued. Practitioners tend to argue that their craft or experiential knowledge should be privileged, whereas the theoretical knowledge of university people should be distrusted when dealing with actual practices in schools. Academicians, on the other hand, often claim that practitioner knowledge is deficient with respect to providing a broader understanding of the purposes and processes of teacher education.

This argument over whose knowledge should be privileged raises the issue of the integration of theory and practice. A variety of approaches were developed in the teacher preparation programs to better integrate practical experiences in schools with the study of theory in university-based course work (Ellsworth & Albers, 1991; Gore & Zeichner, 1991; Robottom, 1988). In one program, assignments of "tasks" required students to try out different strategies in their placements and then reflect critically on their teaching after explicating "their own theories in relation to theories advanced in the literature of the field and their own practical teaching experiences" (Robottom, 1988, p. 109). Another strategy involved focusing university seminars on the students' school-based inquiries or action research projects, including preparation for conducting them and relating them to assigned readings (Gore & Zeichner, 1991; Zeichner & Liston, 1987). In another case, an attempt to integrate theory and practice involved cooperating teachers meeting with methods course professors from the university (Ellsworth & Albers, 1991). Underlying these efforts was a concern not for demonstrating the direct application of theory to practice but for theory and practice to inform one another. In other words, students were encouraged to reflect on practice by reference to scholarship and to reflect on theories by reference to actual practices (Robottom, 1988).

In contrast, in analyzing hypothesized problems of administrative practice, students in the principalship seminar were expected to directly apply knowledge derived either from theory or practice to their action plans (Hart et al., 1992). In this case, students, of course, did not have the opportunity to observe the effects of their proposed actions and hence were unable to use their own experiences of administrative actions to reflect on theory. Nevertheless, the relationship between theory and practical actions appeared to be conceptualized as a unidirectional rather than an iterative process.

Each of the above problems (i.e., the tendencies to retreat into traditional roles, to focus on instrumental rather than broader concerns, and to dismiss the value of forms of knowing not traditionally associated with one's role) can be attributed in part to individual and institutional factors that serve to maintain the dominance of certain beliefs and dispositions over the competing views and values of an inquiry-oriented preparation program. Before analyzing these factors, we need first to examine how the role of school administrators might differ from that of teachers and the implications of this difference for an inquiry-oriented administrator preparation program.

THE COMPETING ROLES OF SCHOOL ADMINISTRATORS

Over the past century, the role of the school administrator has changed from "principal" teacher to manager of an increasingly complex organization. In such organizations, the central task of the administrator has been described as reconciling the personal interests of the individual with the collective interests of the organization (Hodgkinson, 1991). Stated somewhat differently, the special concern of the school administrator is "nurturing a school from a collection of individual students and teachers into a learning community" (Holmes Group, 1990, p. 52). Whether viewed in terms of conflict resolution or the development of a community of learners (or both), the task is complicated in education by the lack of clarity of the collective purpose or goals of schools (not to mention the means). The challenge for the educational leader is to articulate the organizational values and goals and then to motivate people and mobilize resources to realize those goals (Hodgkinson, 1991). This demands considerable time and attention in identifying and constantly articulating the school's instructional goals and priorities and working with teachers to try to ensure that their curriculum and instructional beliefs and practices are consistent with, and effectively contribute to, the school's goals.

Yet numerous studies have indicated that most administrators spend the majority of their time attending to bureaucratic concerns, despite their stated preference for addressing curriculum and instructional issues (Cuban, 1988). This conflict between demands and desires has been heightened by the effective schools literature, which has emphasized that the "effective" principal is an instructional leader as well as an administrative manager (Jacobson, 1990). The pressure to perform these competing roles has created considerable tension for principals in trying to clarify and balance these different functions.

This situation of goal ambiguity and role conflict for school administrators adds a dimension to administrator preparation that has not been salient to teacher preparation because a teacher's role is clearly to teach, although recent restructuring reforms intended to increase teachers' involvement in school decision making could likely contribute to creating greater role stress for teachers (Bacharach, Bamberger, & Mitchell, 1990). One way in which this additional concern can be addressed in an inquiry-oriented administrator preparation program is for the role of school administrators to become a subject of inquiry. In other words, aspiring school leaders might engage with their experienced administrator mentors in reflective inquiry into leadership roles by examining how their mentor's practices resolve the dilemma of role conflict.

Action research, which provides a method by which practitioners (both individually and collectively) can systematically inquire into and critically reflect on their own educational practices and situations, could be used to investigate the nature and extent of attention to administrative and instructional leadership roles. The purposes of action research have been described as the threefold improvement of one's practices, one's understanding of those practices, and the situations in which those practices are carried out (Kemmis & McTaggart, 1988). In this "emancipatory" conception of action research, critical reflection includes the articulation and reasoned justification of educational intentions (to create more defensible reasons for actions) and the examination of the relationship between those intentions and the consequences of one's actions. In other words, administrators could use the process for clarifying their organizational goals and for questioning the congruency between these and their administrative actions. Furthermore, inquiry and reflection in action research are directed both internally (to the practitioner's own educational practices) and externally at both the institutional characteristics of schools and the social and political influences that circumscribe those practices. Therefore, the contextual influences on the definition and enactment of administrator roles are appropriate subjects for action research inquiries. By participating in such inquiries into their own practices, administrators would be modeling reflective practice and thereby be encouraging their teachers to also engage in reflective practice.

ROLES, RELATIONSHIPS, AND KNOWLEDGE GENERATION IN ADMINISTRATOR PREPARATION

Given this role ambiguity and conflict faced by school administrators, how might the three problems encountered in the mainly teacher education programs be manifested in an inquiry-oriented administrator preparation program? The role of school administrators in a traditional scientific administrator education program is to provide practical knowledge to balance the theory that is seen as being the province of university faculty. In an inquiry-oriented preparation program, however, the role of cooperating or clinical administrators needs to become more of a collaborator in helping the prospective administrator inquire into problems of practice. In conjunction with university faculty, such a role might entail assistance in identifying problems or concerns of significance to the school and to the student, planning possible actions to resolve identified problems, collecting data on the consequences of selected actions, and interpreting the effects of the prospective administrator's actions based on the analysis of the data. The reported experiences of the practitioner coaches in the reflective seminar on the principalship (as well as from the teacher education programs) indicate that in providing this kind of assistance many school administrators are likely to encounter difficulty in resisting the inclination, especially when pressured by students, to provide their own "answers" to the problems that are the subject of aspiring administrators' inquiries. However, if the focus of an inquiry is a genuine dilemma that the cooperating practicing administrator is experiencing, then this tendency might be reduced. Even if their solutions are not offered, if the dialogue between the practicing administrator and student administrator is framed exclusively in terms of a search for techniques, then broader contextual influences on the problems of practice are unlikely to be considered.

The traditional role of university faculty in a scientifically oriented program is first to delineate to students the questions that need to be asked. The expected source of knowledge for students to answer the questions is usually scholarship, that is, the published ideas and evidence produced by university (and occasionally practitioner) writers and researchers. This reliance on scholarship or the experience of authorities creates a dependence on only one type of knowing and excludes the practical knowledge of those who work in the situation to which the problem applies (Stevenson, 1991). In an inquiry-oriented preparation program, the contextualized knowledge of both the practicing and aspiring administrator should receive equal recognition with the decontextualized knowledge of scholarship in the sense that understanding should be grounded in both experience and practical issues, on the one hand, and in texts and theoretical issues, on the other. If university faculty continue to demand that prospective administrators rely on academic knowledge in their courses, then the dichotomy between theory and practice and the schism between school and university faculty will probably be maintained. Broader social and political issues might be addressed, but how these issues might inform the actual work of, and problems encountered by, a school administrator is unlikely to be explored. Thus theory is likely to remain privileged in educational administration courses in the university setting, and practical wisdom is likely to continue to guide administrators' practice in schools.

RECONCEPTUALIZING THE ROLES AND CONCEPTIONS OF THE WORK OF SCHOOL AND UNIVERSITY FACULTY IN ADMINISTRATOR PREPARATION

As discussed earlier, the persistence of traditional roles and relationships and of traditional conceptions of the dichotomy between research and practice emerged as strong themes in the teacher education studies. This persistence has been attributed in part to the educational histories and predispositions of teachers and students toward their roles (Stevenson, 1991). Even when considerable time was spent working closely with cooperating teachers (and students) in justifying and explaining reflective inquiry, the traditional conception of student teaching predominated (Zeichner & Liston, 1987). In other words, the dominant view of student teaching as an apprenticeship in which experienced teachers pass on their tips and solutions to practical problems undermined efforts to engage students in inquiry and reflection.

One explanation for the persistence of these prior beliefs and dispositions is that school and university personnel remain situated in separate institutions and therefore bring "to their role perspectives and traditions which reflect the culture of that institution" (Cornbleth & Ellsworth, 1994). The research-oriented university culture values commitments to carefully crafted theoretical analysis and scientifically generated knowledge that is intended for an academic audience, whereas schools prize knowledge that is concrete and has immediate relevance and practical application to the specific problems with which they are confronted (Cuban, 1992). The reward systems in each institution reflect these different values, with university faculty members being promoted on the basis of their individual productivity in a specialized area of research, whereas practitioners are evaluated on their practical contribution to students and the school in which they work.

Cuban (1992) argued that these different cultures can be united by focusing on the practical and moral dilemmas inherent in teaching:

> Serious scholarly examination of the uncertainties, ambiguities and moral dilemmas of teaching students at different levels of formal schooling is precisely one basis for assembling intellectual communities among educators. Such collaborative inquiry into core teaching activities common to all levels of schooling invigorated by respect of professors for wise practitioners and of practitioners for thoughtful professors could forge coherent communities of researchers, professional educators, and practitioners (p. 9).

Yet the nature of this "scholarly examination," as suggested by the language, locates intellectual control in the hands and minds of university faculty members. An emphasis on examining irresolvable contradictions common to different educational contexts for the apparent purpose of furthering our knowledge of teaching is in the traditional domain of scholarly inquiry conducted by professors. Practitioners' orientation is to specific problems or concerns and the actions necessary to address those problems. Put simply, university faculty are inquiry-oriented and school faculty are action-oriented.

If the interests and traditions of the two groups are to be united in a collaborative form of inquiry, then both groups must bring to the collaborative inquiry a feeling of their own cognitive authority and an openness to the potential contribution of the other group. This condition can be established if two criteria are satisfied. First, the problems selected as the subjects for inquiry should be of genuine concern and interest to the school. These problems also need to be deemed suitable for providing sufficient scope to enable the objectives of the preparation program to be met. In this way the interests of administrator preparation can be united with the interests of school improvement (and presumably the interests of administrators in their own professional development). The second criterion is that school and university faculty recognize that they share a common involvement in inquiry. Outstanding teachers and administrators engage in an informal form of inquiry in making rational pedagogical and administrative decisions. They consider a range of alternative actions for achieving their goals and purposes, make judgments about an appropriate course of action based on available knowledge and relevant values, informally observe the consequences of the action that is taken, and then reflect on and assess the overall effects of the action. This process, which professionals use in their everyday activities, differs only in function, time frame, and rigor from the systematic inquiry of the scholar.

The function of informal inquiry is to provide answers to inform actions that need to be taken, whereas the function of the more formal scholarly inquiry is to produce reliable knowledge about perplexing questions (Short, 1991). The former is governed by the exigencies of practice, and the latter is governed by the methods and procedures developed by the community of scholars associated with the particular kind of formal inquiry. In educational practice, "problems are primarily related to doing something rather than knowing something," and while the "doing is best accomplished in the presence of knowing . . . it is the taking of action that is the fundamental characteristic" of educational activity (Short, 1991, p. 11). The more trustworthy the state of knowing in which practitioners make decisions about appropriate actions, the better informed their actions are likely to be.

In a collaborative inquiry into real problems of practice in schools, university faculty can provide their time, their methodological understanding of the requirements of systematic inquiry for developing reliable conclusions, and their substantive understanding of research and theory that may help inform the problems or questions under study. School administrators can contribute a contextual understanding of the practical issues involved, their own practical theories of teaching and administration, and a sense of the extent to which inquiry can be formalized without disrupting educational practice. Prospective administrators, who are usually teachers, bring the same understanding but with a focus on teaching and learning. They, therefore, can contribute their understanding of classroom issues at the same time as having the opportunity to develop an understanding of both administrative practice and how such practice can be informed by inquiry.

The quality of educational practice is dependent on the quality of sustained inquiry because educational actions should be continually informed by the most reliable and relevant knowledge. Furthermore, the quality of practical inquiry is dependent on the expertise with which it is conducted. The best expertise resides in neither school nor university faculty alone but in the combined knowledge they can generate collaboratively. Creating the conditions for collaborative inquiry to happen will not be easy, given the individualistic traditions in both institutions, but it is difficult to argue that there are any more promising possibilities for improving schools, schools of education, and the preparation of educational administrators.

NOTE

1. I wish to thank Cheryl Albers, Stephen Jacobson, and Hugh Petrie for their helpful comments and suggestions during the development of this chapter.

REFERENCES

Altrichter, H. (1988). Enquiry-based learning in initial teacher education. In J. Nias & S. Groundwater-Smith (Eds.), *The enquiring teacher: Supporting and sustaining teacher research* (pp. 121–134). London: Falmer.

Bacharach, S., Bamberger, R., & Mitchell, S. (1990). Work redesign, role conflict, and role ambiguity: The case of elementary and secondary schools. *Educational Evaluation and Policy Analysis 12*(4), 415–432.

Blumberg, A. (1989). *School administration as a craft.* Boston: Allyn & Bacon.

Bridges, E. M. (1977). The nature of leadership. In L. L. Cunningham, W. G. Hack, & R. O. Nystrand (Eds.), *Educational administration* (pp. 202–230). Berkeley: McCutchan.

Cornbleth. C., & Ellsworth, J. (1994). Teachers in teacher education: Clinical faculty roles and relationships. *American Educational Research Journal, 31*(1), 49–70.

Cuban, L. (1988). *The managerial imperative and the practice of leadership in schools.* Albany: State University of New York Press.

Cuban, L. (1992). Managing dilemmas while building professional communities. *Educational Researcher 21*(1), 4–11.

Ellsworth, J., & Albers, C. M. (1991). *Roles and relationships in the field team.* Unpublished monograph, Buffalo (New York) Research Institute on Education for Teaching.

Evers, C. W., & Lakomski, G. (1991). *Knowing educational administration: Contemporary methodological controversies in educational administration research.* Oxford: Pergamon.

Gore, J., & Zeichner, K. M. (1991). Action research and reflective teaching in preservice teacher education: A case study from the United States. In R. Stevenson & S. Noffke (Eds.), *Action research and teacher education: International perspectives* (pp. 51–99). Buffalo, NY: Buffalo Research Institute on Education for Teaching.

Hart, A. W., Naylor, K., & Sorensen, N. B. (1992). Learning to lead: Reflective practice in preservice preparation. In F. C. Wendel (Ed.), *Applications of reflective practice* (UCEA Monograph Series) (pp. 5–22). University Park, PA: University Council of Educational Administration.

Hodgkinson, C. (1991). *Educational leadership: The moral art.* Albany: State University of New York Press.

Holmes Group. (1990). *Tomorrow's schools: Principles for the design of professional development schools.* East Lansing, MI: Author.

Jacobson, S. L. (1990). Reflections on the third wave of reform: Rethinking administrator preparation. In S. L. Jacobson & J. A. Conway (Eds.), *Educational leadership in an age of reform* (pp. 30–44). New York: Longman.

Kemmis, S., & McTaggart, R. (1988). *The action research planner*, (3rd ed.). Geelong, Victoria: Deakin University Press.

Murphy, J. (1992). Personal communication.

National Policy Board for Educational Administration. (1989). *Improving the preparation of school administrators: An agenda for reform.* Charlottesville, VA: Author.

Robottom, I. M. (1988). A research-based course in science education. In J. Nias & S. Groundwater-Smith (Eds.), *The enquiring teacher: Supporting and sustaining teacher research* (pp. 106–120). London: Falmer.

Schmuck, R. (1988). Beyond academics in the preparation of educational leaders. *OSSC Report 28*(3), 1–11.

Schon, D. A. (1983). *The reflective practitioner.* New York: Basic Books.

Schon, D. A. (1987). *Educating the reflective practitioner.* San Francisco: Jossey-Bass.

Short, E. (1991). Introduction: Understanding curriculum inquiry. In E. Short (Ed.), *Forms of curriculum inquiry* (pp. 1–25). Albany: State University of New York Press.

Stevenson, R. B. (1991). Action research as professional development: A U.S. case study of inquiry-oriented inservice education. *Journal of Education for Teaching (17)*3, 277–292.

Tabachnick, R., & Zeichner, K. M. (1991, April). The reflective practitioner in teaching and teacher education: A social reconstructionist perspective. Paper presented at the annual meeting of the American Educational Research Association, Chicago.

Zeichner, K. M. *(1983).* Alternative paradigms of teacher education. *Journal of Teacher Education 34,* 3–9.

Zeichner, K. M., & Liston, D. P. (1987). Teaching student teachers to reflect. *Harvard Educational Review 57*(1), 1–22.

LEE TEITEL

Chapter Thirteen

The State Role in Jump-Starting School-University Collaboration
A CASE STUDY

With school-university collaboration considered one of the most promising concepts of the 1990s, described by many (Goodlad, 1988; Holmes Group, 1990) as a key to the "simultaneous renewal" of schooling and teacher preparation, what can a state department of education do to promote it? This chapter describes and analyzes an ambitious state project in which one department of education (DOE) instigated, facilitated, and, in effect, "jump-started" the formation of partnerships between middle schools and teacher preparation institutions. The case is offered not because it necessarily describes the best way to promote collaboration but, rather, as a contribution to the discussion about the policy options available to state departments of education in this important arena.

The project brought together six urban middle schools and four colleges and universities with the twin goals of restructuring the middle schools (changing them from traditional junior high schools) and developing or improving middle school teacher preparation programs at the colleges. The middle schools involved had anywhere from zero to three years of restructuring experience (and no experience with collaboration). Only one of the colleges or uni-

Original was first published in *Educational Policy, 7*(1), March, 1993, © Corwin Press, Inc. Reprinted here by permission of Corwin Press, a Sage Publications Company.

versities had a middle school teacher preparation program, and only one had much experience in collaborations of this nature. None of the institutions in the partnerships created by the DOE had any significant history with one another; in many cases, they had never heard of one another.

The case is of particular interest because the DOE maintained an extremely high profile in this project. It selected and then invited each institution to participate, created the matches, required and observed joint monthly planning meetings, provided several days of partnership training, and intervened in collaborations that did not appear to be working well. At the end of a planning year (1990–1991), the DOE evaluated the collaborations to decide which had made sufficient progress to receive funds for two additional years of implementation money. To place this high-profile approach in perspective, this chapter, after a note on methodology and a brief chronology and summary of events, explores the options available to a state department of education. Three questions are raised: What can a third party (like a state DOE) do to promote collaboration? How might it proceed strategically? How should such an effort be evaluated? After briefly addressing each question with the data from the case, the second half of the article uses several different perspectives from the literature on interorganizational relations to assess the relative success of this particular project.

RESEARCH METHODOLOGY

The research is qualitative in its approach, using multiple perspectives on the events that are described and analyzed. Data were collected through observation at the several "institutes"—daylong training and discussion sessions held by the DOE for participants. In addition, written materials were examined (DOE memoranda to the participating institutions, their reports to the DOE, etc.). These sources were supplemented by semistructured interviews with one or two key figures from each of the collaborating institutions and from the coordinators and staff at the department of education. Three rounds of interviews were conducted: the first in December 1990 or January 1991, the second in May 1991, and the third in March 1992.

CASE SUMMARY AND CHRONOLOGY

Spring 1990

The department of education contacts selected schools, colleges, and universities to invite their participation. The DOE tells them that it is seeking funding from a national foundation to provide schools and teacher preparation institutions with support and some limited funds (about $3,000 to $6,000) for one year of collaborative planning and, furthermore, that the DOE anticipates applying for second- and third-year implementation funding at a slightly higher level per year per school. The participants are told that if their partnership comes up with a plan deemed workable, they have a good chance of continued funding. All the administrators at the invited institutions agree to participate.

August 1990

During the summer, participants are informed that the state has received the foundation planning grant. In late August, the DOE convenes meetings in several locales around the state to bring the partners together for the first time. Each institution is asked to bring a planning team to this meeting. Being asked to attend this meeting is the first time that most of the participating institution's staff hear about the project. In most cases, this is the first contact ever between the schools and the partnering teacher preparation institution.

September to December 1990

Two all-day institutes are offered by the DOE for all participants in October and November, providing workshops on restructuring middle schools and on clinical site models, respectively. In addition, each partnership holds monthly joint planning meetings, which are usually attended by DOE staff. This period is characterized by considerable confusion as participants get to know each other as people and as institutions and try to sort out what the roles and expectations of each other and of the DOE are. Many raise concerns with the DOE about their partners—how ready they are for the project or how committed they appear to be, or complain that the representatives on their partner's planning team keep shifting. Staff from the DOE intervene in four of the six partnerships, pressuring institutions to enlarge or stabilize their planning team and to follow up on commitments and, in some cases, suggesting that an institution should consider withdrawing from the program.

January 1991

The DOE issues guidelines for the implementation proposals that partners will need to submit jointly by May to be eligible for implementation money. Participants are told that this is the last "gate;" that if their proposals pass this DOE evaluation they will be in the program for the next two years (assuming the DOE receives the foundation support for continuation). Guidelines are very specific and prompt some participants to express the wish that the DOE had been this clear about what it wanted earlier. By this point, most of the earlier turmoil is settled. No one has dropped out, and by now a key liaison at each institution has been identified, facilitating the growth of personal relationships between partners. During a round of confidential interviews this month, participants express their excitement and enthusiasm about what kinds of joint activities they will conduct; many indicate that they have privately pledged to one another to continue regardless of DOE funding.

February to May 1991

The DOE conducts one institute day in March, dealing with team building and school change. Most of the activity and energy during this period is focused on joint discussion and writing of the proposals, which identify what, if funded, the partners would do for the subsequent two years. In most cases, one or two people from each institution work on this with their counterparts, thereby cementing the close personal connections established over the winter. Proposed activities include development or enhancement at the middle school of adviser-advisee programs, cooperative learning, curriculum integration, parental involvement, and community service projects for students. At the college or university, courses are proposed that focus on urban middle school issues and on mentoring to help prepare middle school faculty for the placement of student teachers.

June 1991

All six projects receive conditional approval, pending clarification of some of their language and subject to having the state receive the continuation grant.

September 1991

The department of education receives the two-year implementation grant, and the projects get the official "go ahead" to move into their implementation activities.

October 1991 to June 1992

The DOE conducts two all-day institutes, one in October featuring a panel of school and college teachers and administrators describing several different models of school-college partnerships, and one in May to share progress reports on how each site has managed to overcome the various obstacles to successful collaboration. Progress during this period is quite uneven. Two institutions face staff turnover issues, so the bonding and planning from the previous year gets renegotiated or put on hold; most of the other partnerships are able to implement much of the agenda they planned. Most of the partnership activities for this year center around a course or series of in-service workshops, presented by college faculty (sometimes co-taught by middle school teachers) and planned, in most cases, by teachers, school administrators, and college personnel collaboratively. The scale of these activities varies from one-shot in-service workshops to weekly credit-bearing courses delivered on site. Other models include having college faculty meet regularly with one or more middle school clusters to focus on a particular topic, such as cooperative learning or interdisciplinary units. Also going on during this period at one site is a "directed study" class where college students are observing and tutoring in the middle school. The courses and workshops are generally viewed very positively by all participants and, in two middle schools, are complemented by internal "commitment teams" or study groups focusing on specific aspects of middle school restructuring. Teachers in two schools participate in mentoring courses in preparation for student teacher placements in 1992-1993.

ANALYSIS

In this section, three questions concerning the role of a state department of education in promoting collaboration are explored. Each is then followed by a brief description of what the DOE described in this case study did. A subsequent section of this chapter includes a more thorough discussion of the implications of the DOE's approach.

What Can a Third Party Do to Promote Collaboration?

One of the college administrators involved in the project responded to a question about the role of the DOE in the project with the comment, "The Department needs to be mindful of the fact that there are two entities in this collaboration and not three." Although his comment reflects his unhappiness with the interventionist role the DOE took with his college, he raises a legitimate question about what the appropriate role of a third party is in promoting partnerships. Indeed, most of the school-university collaborations reported in the literature have developed quite independently of any state role or the involvement of third parties (Clark, 1986; Frazier, 1988). Although some have received support from outside entities, such as the National Network for Education Renewal or the Coalition of Essential Schools, most grew out of the interest of the local individuals or organizations. But as a policy issue, what can state departments of education do to promote it?

Because this is a relatively new line of inquiry, it helps to look to other areas for guidance. Theorists on interorganizational relations in the nonprofit and private sectors note the important role that third parties, such as trade organizations for business groups or state hospital associations for hospitals, can play in promoting partnership formation among their members (Aldrich & Herker, 1977; Pfeffer & Salancik, 1978). Schermerhorn (1981) summarized these findings about third-party contributions:

> They may facilitate interorganizational communication and awareness by bringing representatives of the various organizations into contact with one another. They may also directly promulgate cooperation as a positive value.

Finally, they may provide slack resources useful in overcoming resource constraints that inhibit members from exploring possible benefits of cooperation.
(p. 87)

In this case, the DOE played all the roles described for third parties in the
literature and, in some ways, went well beyond the facilitating roles of bringing people into contact with one another, promoting collaboration as a positive
value, and providing resource incentives to overcome inhibiting factors. For
instance, as a convener, the DOE did not just provide a neutral forum for
potential collaborators to meet and connect. It made the matches, secured commitments, and then provided a place where people could learn about each other
and about collaboration and could work out their problems. During institute
days, the department provided team-building activities, using ropes and other
Outward Bound techniques, as well as structuring other joint tasks, like the
production of a common mission statement for each partnership.

The department did not simply promote the concept of collaboration "as
a positive value" but made it a requirement of participation. DOE staff
attended most of the collaborative team meetings and made clear their expectation that proposals for continued funding had to meet standards for collaboration both in their content (what joint activities were planned) and in their
process (how collaboratively the planning was done).

The DOE also played a fourth role that is less commonly done by third
parties in partnership formation. In all but two of the relationships, DOE staff
intervened to address an institution's concern about the commitment or readiness of its partner. In one case, the department pressured an institution into
providing a larger and more consistent planning team; in another it threatened
to drop a school if it failed to show evidence of "readiness" to go forward.
These actions have played to mixed reviews. Eight months later, the administrator quoted at the beginning of this section still resents the pressure. On the
other hand, the beneficiaries of the interventions describe them as essential: "I
couldn't press [partner] more than I did. A third party could. If the state hadn't
played the 'heavy'—saying 'you do this or get out'—we might not have gotten
past [our initial difficulties]."

Choice Points That Influence Strategy

The levers of influence described above provide a starting point for a
third party planning to promote collaboration. But once it decides to try to
manipulate these levers, a state department of education still has a wide range
of choices to make. It might hold a conference on school-university collaboration and educational reform, encourage (or require) the formation of partnerships through the regulatory process, offer a grant program as an incentive to
those who form partnerships, or offer staff support and technical assistance to

interested schools and colleges. This partial list just hints at the spectrum of choices available. Decisions would undoubtedly be influenced by factors like the amount of money available, the expertise of the department staff, the history of school-university collaboration in the state, the degree of centralization, and the level of proactivity the department wishes to pursue. And even if a state department of education opts for an interventionist pilot program, such as the one described in this case, there still remain important decisions about how to implement the program that will undoubtedly affect its outcome. Some of these are now listed, followed by the choices made by the DOE in this case.

Strategic choice points include how the schools and teacher preparation institutions are selected. Is it a competitive process? Do institutions have to give evidence of being ready for the project, or of having widespread staff commitment to it? How should matches be made? Should prospective partners apply together, or should the state be involved with the match?

Once selections and matches are made, who should be worked with in the schools and colleges and how? Should widespread staff and administration involvement be required, or should it be more "top down," or more "bottom up?" How much should the department insist on collaboration and how active should it be in promoting it? Should it serve as a resource and guide, or as a taskmaster? If partnerships are failing to thrive or are unbalanced (e.g., dominated by one party), should the department intervene?

What levels of support should be provided, and how much discretion should participating institutions have over their funds? What activities and resources should be organized to benefit all the partners, and what should be targeted for individual needs? What mix of funding and services is appropriate? Should participants be evaluated for continuation of support, and if so, how?

The department of education described in this case started the project in a centralized, high-intervention, top-down fashion, although that approach has changed significantly over the two years. Schools were initially selected by the department of education, largely because of their track record in other DOE school improvement grants. Universities were asked because of their proximity, background, and/or interest in developing middle school teacher preparation programs. The matches were made by the department and, when problems arose, the DOE intervened to maintain them.

The project was started in a top-down fashion, with initial commitments made by deans and principals. After funding was secured, the department quickly moved to expand to involve a wider group of staff at each institution. The DOE required each institution to send a team of three to five individuals to the institutes and to the monthly partnership meetings. Throughout most of the first year, the pace and the requirements for continued participation were centralized—handed down from the department. Participants needed to write joint mission statements in the fall (whether they felt ready to or not) and produce a joint proposal for continued funding in the spring. By the end of the planning year, however, the DOE staff was noticeably more open to suggestions and more flexible in the requirements put forward.

The choices that the DOE made in how it promoted collaboration in this project have had profound effects. These are more fully explored in the second half of the chapter, after a brief discussion about how to measure the success of a project like this one.

What are Appropriate Measures of Success?

Real partnerships are those that can lead to substantial school and university change. Yet the words partnership or collaboration are used to apply to a wide range of ventures. Interorganizational relations (IOR) theorists make a useful distinction between partnership activities that are mostly cooperative and usually informal, involving relatively little threat to autonomy, no real pooling of goals, and relatively few resources, and those that are more coordinated or collaborative—generally more formalized, involving greater levels of joint goal setting and decision making, higher-ranking members, and greater resources (Rogers & Whetten, 1982; Su, 1990). Activities that increase the mutual interdependence of partners and move closer toward collaboration have a greater potential to change the collaborating organizations, but they also may lead to conflict over issues of "turf" or quality control. To explore the extent to which a project like this one has been successful in promoting collaboration, four possible sets of questions are listed below, followed by a discussion of how various aspects of this project measured up:

1. What actual changes have been made that can be attributed to participation in the project?
2. What are the types of joint activities planned and implemented by the partners, and to what degree do they represent coordinated or collaborative activities?
3. To what extent have the partnerships become institutionalized? Are they still dependent on personal contacts and relationships to sustain them?
4. How much progress have they made to some preset ideal for a school-university partnership? What pace of change is reasonable?

One way to assess progress is by looking at the changes that appear to be consequences of the project. These range dramatically on an institution-by-institution basis. At one school, involvement in the project has centered on having a college faculty member conduct a series of sessions on cooperative learning with one cluster. Although this has been of clear value to a few teachers, it is of minor impact in the overall dynamics of the school. Similarly, coteaching a course with the college partner on middle school issues, which has been the focal point of another partnership, has been innovative and important for the two middle school teachers involved, but has not led to any real change at the school or the college. (Interestingly enough, both the schools where little change can be attributed to the project are dynamic places where substantial restructuring is going on as part of other funded initiatives. The monies from this project pale in comparison to the other initiatives, so it is perhaps understandable that project-inspired change is minimal at these sites.) At the other end of the spectrum, two schools have established "commitment teams" or team-based study groups to explore specific topics—for instance, setting up adviser-advisee programs or using interdisciplinary approaches to cooperative learning. This has been a particularly powerful approach to school change when it has been coupled with enrollment in a college-sponsored course, especially when one third to one half of the staff members are involved. The course not only provides a weekly forum for discussion and an infusion of research-based articles on middle school topics but, as one principal put it, "You have all these people going around the school trying to develop action plans" for the course, which adds greatly to the energy and effort for school improvement. Another school has begun to implement interdisciplinary approaches in two of its clusters as a result of college faculty in-service workshops. The sixth school has experienced the "breath of fresh air" of having college students in the building as tutors and observers. Several middle school teachers have guest lectured at the college and have been involved in joint curriculum development for the college's proposed new certification program.

At three of the colleges and universities, measurable gains have to do with moves toward establishing a middle school teacher training program; at the fourth, the focus has been on developing urban connections for an already well-established middle school program. One college has started the internal approval process for a new middle school certification program (developed collaboratively with its school partner); the college has already shown its support by posting as its number one hiring priority a position of middle school expert. (The position was filled during the summer of 1992.) Another teacher preparation institution with a strong secondary school orientation has piloted a middle schools issues course offered at the school site. The coordinator reported that it has paved the way to subtle but important shifts in faculty attitudes about the possibilities of mounting a middle schools program:

> My faculty is interested and has moved from the 'Go ahead and you do it' stage to the 'it's a good idea and we should do it' stage. . . . Persistence has paid off. People knew we needed to do it but didn't know if it could be done. Now they are seeing that it is working fine.

The college with a previously existing middle school program has expanded its urban orientation through the project. The fourth institution, which co-taught a middle schools issues course with teachers from its partner school, has announced its "commitment" to middle school teacher preparation. Its plans, however, to search for a middle school specialist faculty member have been delayed due to funding shortages.

Overall, these activities of the first two years of the project have been largely cooperative, with only a minimal threat to turf issues or autonomy. The delivery of courses or other in-service workshops, even if the content is customized and the courses delivered on site, does not require high levels of joint goal setting. However, when middle school teachers have important input into shaping courses that get institutionalized (as they are at one college as part of a new certification program), then the mutual interdependence increases. Other activities closer to the collaborative end of the spectrum have not yet been implemented on other than a minuscule scale—activities such as the placing and supervising of student teachers or the use of middle school teachers as college faculty. These activities required a greater interdependence than others and may have more potential "sticky issues" than there would be in the offering of a course. A truly collaborative approach to student teaching placement and support, for instance, requires much more interaction and judgment and can play to the worst fears of both "sides." Questions of quality control can cut both ways. Some school people worry about the caliber of the student teachers or express concerns earlier in the year that they would be "flooded" with more students than they could comfortably handle. College faculty and administrators, on the other hand, worry about the "readiness" of their partnering schools to provide an excellent quality middle school placement for their students.

A third method of assessing the relative success of a project like this is its degree of institutionalization. These partnerships are still based largely on personal and individual connections, making year-to-year transitions difficult due to staff turnover. One school had a particularly hard time starting the planning year because the principal who had agreed to participate in spring 1990 was on leave the following September. Much of the planning year was spent sorting out how to proceed and then developing some plans with the college partner, only to have the awkward transition process repeated the following year when the principal returned. A few institutions are experiencing turnover of their liaisons as they go into the third year. It will be interesting to see if their transitions are smoother, indicating a higher degree of institutionalization of the relationship.

A final consideration takes into account the time required for broadbased change. What is reasonable to expect after one year or after two? Meaningful change takes time, but how much? The DOE had hoped for collaborative ventures like joint action research, joint professional development, collegial supervision of student teachers, swapping and co-teaching of courses, peer coaching (mixing faculty at both levels), portfolio assessment, and others. As the previous paragraphs describing school achievement indicate, most of these are not in place at the end of the second year; only a few more are likely during the coming year. The following question then remains: What pace is reasonable and what can be expected at this point?

A closely related question is how much should the department push to see these kinds of activities or other more highly collaborative ventures take place. Most participants in the project express the sense that DOE staff members are disappointed in them and want more—faster movement, more change. A college faculty member captured this spirit:

> I always feel apologetic when I talk to the DOE [about our progress] even though we are doing the best we can. . . . The irony is that we are on our own timetable which will probably meet their goals, even though they may be unhappy with us about it."

A principal who is very enthusiastic about the project described how he and his college partner have evolved a comfortable pace of progress with one another, but he added,

> It is interesting that it is not the pace that the department would like to see. I can't help feel that folks at the DOE who are living this full-time have never grasped that this is a part of our lives and there is a shifting around of priorities at different times. [The project] is not always the most important thing. There has been the expectation that we're giving this the same effort all the time. We know and [our partner] knows we downshift at times, rev up at times. . . . I think the DOE wants us to move faster. Yet I am thrilled that we've been able to keep it as high a priority [as we have] for so long.

The tension over how concrete and how high the DOE's expectations should be was reflected at an April 1992 meeting with DOE staff and the higher education deans. When the DOE program coordinator circulated a list of expectation benchmarks for the 1991–1992 and 1992–1993 school years, participants protested about the timing (getting it halfway into the project), about the lack of consultation with them before establishing standards, about several of the specific benchmarks, and about the whole notion of a formal and apparently inflexible list of expectations that had to be met. The DOE staff quickly softened the "requirements" aspect and have continued to work at finding a balance point that provides leadership and a clear vision of goals with reasonable expectations.

THE IMPACT OF THE DEPARTMENT OF EDUCATION'S ACTIVIST ROLE

This section continues to draw on the IOR literature as well as the perspectives of the structural, human resources, political, and symbolic frames (Bolman & Deal, 1984) to assess the impact this particular approach has had.

The first part looks at the ways that elements of the DOE's approach hindered partnership formation; the second explores the more positive aspects.

Hindrances to Partnership Formation

The many roles played by the DOE—funding conduit, visionary, regulator, and policymaker (regarding teacher preparation requirements), facilitator, intervener, and ultimately evaluator of which partnerships were permitted to continue—occasionally have come into conflict with one another, causing a variety of structural problems. For instance, some participants reported feeling that they could not always be totally forthright with department staff. If they expressed a problem during the planning year, they worried that it might have reduced their chances of receiving funding for the implementation years. Conversely, some reported fear that if they appeared too enthusiastic about a particular collaborative activity they thought they *might* do, it would be codified into regulation by the department and they would *have* to do it.

The confusion over the many roles played by the DOE was sometimes exacerbated by the involvement of different subunits of the department in the project. Occasionally, especially in the early stages, participants received conflicting information from different departmental sources. Historically divided into units that worked with school improvement programs and those involved with certification of teacher preparation institutions, the department was required by the project to develop an unprecedented level of *internal* collaboration. Like the schools and the colleges, these units within the DOE have needed to learn about each other, sort out turf issues, and overcome different cultures and modes of supervision to create and disseminate a unified vision. Like the schools and colleges, they have had to do this on a hurried timetable, short-handed in a time of diminishing resources, and with little previous planning time. By the end of the planning year, the DOE, in recognition of the way these structural problems were slowing down the project, had reorganized and developed structures to enhance its ability to project a clear and consistent message to the schools and colleges. During the second year, regular monthly project team meetings improved communication and successfully engaged staff from the different subunits into ownership of the project.

Other structural problems have surfaced in the formation of partnerships between the individual schools and colleges due to the top-down and accelerated approach of the DOE. This has affected several aspects of the participants' interorganizational collaboration—their decisions to collaborate, their stages of partnership formation, and the extent and depth of their institutional involvement.

The Decision to Collaborate. Researchers and theorists who have studied interorganizational collaboration have noted a number of decisions and evaluations that each institution must make as prerequisites for developing and sustaining collaborations:

> It is necessary first of all for administrators to have a positive attitude toward interorganizational coordination. Otherwise they will define their organizational problems in such a way that coordination does not appear to be a useful solution. Next, they must recognize an organizational need for coordination that is salient enough to justify absorbing the costs inherent in coordination. Once the need has been articulated then the search for potential coordination partners is initiated. After the pool of candidates has been assembled the members are evaluated in terms of their desirability and compatibility. Finally, after deciding to coordinate, the participating organizations must assess their capacity to adequately manage the on-going coordination process. (Whetten, 1981, pp. 14–16)

Because of the accelerated timetable and prearranged partnerships established by the DOE, partners have skipped or minimized each of these steps. Participants made the first two of Whetten's (1981) decisions quickly and casually. When asked to join by the DOE, all agreed to participate, but none went through the thoughtful cost-benefit analysis that Whetten's second step suggests. In fact, most participants retained a primary interest in the internal growth that might come out of the project. With little history or experience, few participants had a clear understanding of exactly what the collaborative process would entail. One middle school leader recounted her understanding about the project when she committed to it back in June 1990:

> Collaboration with the university was secondary. I understood the focus to be on internal change—discussing it, mapping it out. . . . I knew that [teacher preparation institution] would be developing a team, but I understood that we would be working in parallel. I pictured a process that rather than move together step by step we would work independently and tie in later. That kind of process seemed safe to me. I am very protective of the time and energy of my staff. I wouldn't have wanted to commit otherwise.

As the project unfolded, she realized that collaboration was as much on the agenda as restructuring and that the department was more interested in it: "They always come to the meetings with [teacher preparation institution], but know little about all the things that go on here in-between. Collaboration gets more attention although restructuring is more important internally." For most of the institutions, the realization that this project was about collaboration as much as it was about internal reform came several months into the planning year, precluding the possibility of a thoughtful evaluation of the costs and benefits of involvement.

Similarly, the two steps related to establishing a pool and then choosing a partner were totally bypassed. These relationships were all arranged by the

DOE. None of the partners had any significant working history; some had never heard of the other institution or did not know where it was. Although only one or two have openly complained about their partners (and several have praised the DOE's choice), most participants say they wish they had a voice in the selection. Although no one has asked to quit or to get a new partner, the consequences of the disempowerment over selection have shown up within the partnership dynamics in concerns over how "ready" or "committed" the other party was. This effect was very powerful (in two thirds of the partnerships, participants asked the DOE to intervene with their partners) but relatively short-lived. By the second half of the planning year, relationships had progressed so that only one institution registered a complaint about a partner with the DOE, and even there, the partners expressed a preference for dealing with it themselves.

Finally, Whetten's fifth step—a thoughtful assessment of one's own institutional ability to commit to the partnership—not only did not happen before the start-up in most cases, but in some settings, the process does not appear to have taken place at any point in the first two years.

The Stages of Partnership Development. The accelerated pace of the project also had an impact on the stages that partners would normally go through in developing a collaboration. Schermerhorn (1979) cited nine steps of interorganizational development, including recognition and awareness of one another, establishment of mutual trust, common interest identification, recurring intra- and interorganizational cost-benefit analyses, and program implementation and institutionalization. These stages, while they may be repeated, have a logic and a sequence to them. But because the decision to participate in this project preceded any contact between the partners, any logical flow to partnership development had been disrupted. Consequently, most of the first half of the planning year was a jumble of Schermerhorn's steps, with a number of critical activities going on in parallel. No one had an opportunity, for instance, to identify what interests they had in common or to hold preliminary discussions about what each might offer and expect of the other in a clinical training site. When those conversations finally had taken place, they were in the context of a committed relationship, changing dramatically the flavor of any negotiations. Furthermore, those discussions had to take place even as the partners have been trying to understand how the other institution is organized, to make connections with appropriate counterparts, to develop trust, and to plan a proposal for grant continuation.

The Depth of Institutional Involvement. A final consequence of the accelerated process is the increased difficulty that most institutions have had in engaging more than a handful of people in the project. Although it is quite common for collaborations to start with just a few key individuals from each organization (Schermerhorn, 1979), for any lasting institutional change to be made, support and involvement in the partnership must be more widespread (Gold & Charner, 1986). But one reason why this has been difficult is the way the top-down approach used in the beginning ignored the human resource needs of the people who would be affected by the project. The hurried and somewhat casual way in which schools, colleges, and universities committed to the project tended to limit broader institutional involvement. Almost all the decisions to join the project were made quickly and unilaterally by principals, deans, or coordinators. In most cases, little was done to involve the rest of the staffs until late August, when teams had to be—often hastily—put together for the meetings convened by the DOE. In some cases, August, a particularly diffi-cult time of the year for school systems, was the first attempt at recruitment, and it was hard: Sometimes, teachers or university faculty were indifferent or unenthusiastic or concerned about whether the payoffs to their institution were worth the time investment. One college administrator describes what it was like at the first meeting with teachers who had only just learned about the part-nership: "They were hostile. They asked us what we were doing there [at the school] and what we would do for them. I can't blame them; they had no prepa-ration for this." Because of this top-down start, many leaders have struggled throughout the first year and much of the second to include more than just a handful of staff members in the project.

A problem from the political perspective has been the perceived conflict between the priorities of the collaboration and the internal needs of each insti-tution. As one principal summed it up, "When the crunch comes, our minds are on our internal issues and so are theirs—so we don't always come as prepared [to joint planning meetings] as we should be." Institutions that are involved in serious internal upheaval and change have had a particularly hard time bring-ing time and attention to bear on collaboration issues. For instance, most of the principals see involvement in teacher preparation as separate from, and sec-ondary to, the internal restructuring process they are overseeing. As one put it, "We haven't been able to mesh the two. It would be better if we did more on restructuring and then, after a year, worked more with [partner]." This short-age of time and energy has been exacerbated during the constant cutbacks, lay-offs, and reductions that have characterized the educational scene in the state. The economic climate has made it especially difficult to use scarce resources to put together a planning team to work on what may be seen as an optional activity.

Perspectives on Successful Aspects of the Project

Those institutions that have been more successful in transcending these structural and human resource problems have done so by drawing on the sym-bolic and political approaches to it. Some have looked at the *costs* of collaboration and somehow manage to reframe these into *benefits* by emphasizing how the resources provided by the grant can address important internal needs. One participant summed this up in allegorical terms, giving an example of the psychological boost that these resources have provided in difficult economic times:

> Number one on my private list [of reasons for getting and staying involved with the project] was to keep an educational "campfire" going all year, defending us against the encroachment of wild animals. I knew the potential was there for terrible morale this year. It has been that for us—an educational campfire, so we were doing more than hanging in and holding on. [The project] forced us to come up with concrete goals—and to carve out time to meet and talk. Otherwise, this would have been a first-aid year. We found ourselves saying "We can't believe we are building in innovation in this time of trouble." We learned that it is not impossible to do good things in difficult times.

Another principal noted the importance of recognition as a resource. In her view, the validation associated with the grant far exceeded the monetary value in helping bring about change in her school. A similar symbolic connection is found in the views of a principal that involvement with the project indicates "to my staff that they are a part of something important beyond the scope of the classroom and school. They can feel plugged into education [innovation] in America. It sounds corny, but often people don't see beyond the classroom."

Some school and college leaders have obtained broader buy-in and involvement by managing to mesh, in a more political way, the goals of the collaboration with their internal goals. In those schools further on the path to restructuring, school people can make a case for a connection between collaboration, teacher preparation, and the improvement of the school. One principal characterized her ultimate goal as "developing an excellent middle school. But the way we will continue to be an excellent middle school is by working to help teachers get prepared." Similarly, in those colleges or universities where supporters of the project have been able to convince colleagues that this collaboration is helping them move forward on their own agenda (e.g., developing middle school teacher preparation programs or promoting an urban focus), there are increased signs of broader involvement. Finally, small as the amounts of funding were, the grants provided school and college leaders with critical "slack resources" (Pfeffer, 1981). In a climate full of cutbacks and reductions, the money represented the only uncommitted funds available in some institutions for faculty development.

In addition to helping mesh with the *internal* political needs of the schools, partners have helped each other in operating in the *external* political system as well, by serving as outside advocates for one another. For example, in lobbying to get the college to hire a middle school specialist, college staff jointly planned with their middle school partner to approach the college president. Although it turned out to be unnecessary, it illustrates an important form of support. The college reciprocated by joining (with DOE staff as well) to successfully petition a superintendent to allow the middle school to have greater autonomy over planning for its in-service days. Another middle school, in danger of being closed due to fiscal cutbacks, knew that its involvement with a cutting-edge partnership model for middle school development was a powerful plus in helping keep the building open.

On the broader political and symbolic scene, political considerations may be seen as encouraging participants to stay with the project. In spite of a pace that has whipped them through or bypassed what theorists see as critical prerequisites to collaboration, no institution has been willing, even under pressure, to withdraw from the program. This persistence can be attributed to a number of factors. Most participants retain an extraordinarily high level of commitment and enthusiasm. Some are excited about the prospects of simultaneously improving middle schools and teacher preparation; others see the project helping them move their institutions in new directions; others simply express a dogged determination "not to be seen as the one who did not make it work." At one point, an administrator, frustrated with the paperwork, the small amount of money, and the large DOE expectations, described "feeling trapped," not wanting to quit because of how it would look at his own central office or how it might affect future dealings with the state DOE. In a somewhat more positive framing of the sense of being committed, one university professor put it this way:

> For better or worse, we are going to have some collaboration. Maybe I sound cynical in tone, but I will try like hell to make it work. Divorce is not an option here—we have been given an opportunity.

Another antidote to the confusing and stressful process of partnership formation has been the strong interpersonal relationships that have grown between key individuals at each partnering institution. As one participant noted, "We need[ed] to be 'people' to one another before moving forward on details of the project." This spirit is typified by one principal who commented that it was not until January, halfway through the planning year, that she could define what she wished from her university partner and what her school could offer. She added that this understanding evolved only after a personal connection was made:

> In the beginning, we spent a lot of time on goal setting and mission statement. Both [the college coordinator] and I were frustrated by that. Then, in

November, he came over for a conversation—just the two of us—and we hit it
off, and we have been able to start to move to the specifics.

For some, this crucial "getting acquainted" process has had to take place
in informal ways—at barbecues in someone's backyard or over meals on a
joint field trip to look at a restructured middle school. Many of the participants
expressed frustration with the pace and the formality of the DOE-sponsored
institutes that pushed them, as one quipped, "to talk about our joint mission
together when we haven't even had our first date."

By the spring of the planning year, these one-to-one relationships had
been solidified within each partnership, although some of these were upset by
turnover in the second year. Underlining the importance of these human and
structural links, institutions that had not yet done so by the end of the first year
appointed a specific liaison to coordinate the collaboration. Partners who
knew, liked, and understood one another have been able to move to a different
stage in their relationships. In the second round of interviews (May 1991), participants were able to describe quite frankly the strengths and weaknesses of
their partners but did so with much more sympathy than they had shown earlier. What had looked in the fall like evidence of their partner's lack of commitment, by spring appeared as an example of how large or unwieldy an
institution their partners come from or how hard it is for their partner's institution to commit resources in a time of fiscal uncertainty. After making the personal connections and learning more about each other's institution, they have a
clearer idea of what each brings to the mix and have developed an understanding of the frustrations and challenges facing their partners. For instance, a middle school teacher noted that "if I decide to try something on Monday, we can
have it up and running by Wednesday." After months of wondering why the
college moved so slowly, she now has a better understanding of the long-range
planning and governance process her college counterpart must undertake.

As the relationships have developed, participants have run into some
surprises. College people, spending more time in their partnering school, have
discovered that their partner's "restructured" middle school does not look very
different from a conventional junior high school; similarly, school people have
noticed that their college partners still have a long way to go in developing or
improving their middle school teacher preparation programs. But because of
the strong interpersonal connections that have evolved, these reassessments
have not led to any expressed desires to pull out of the project or to find another
partner. One participant, when pressed by the interviewer about some
expressed misgivings about the institution's partner, illustrated this by saying,
quite simply and with great concern, "But if we pulled out now. what would
happen to them?"

CONCLUSION

The Department of Education has played an activist role in this collaboration initiative and has, in effect, jump-started the whole process. This
approach has bypassed steps that interorganizational theorists view as critical
to relationship building and has made for a challenging year as partners have
scrambled to go through several stages simultaneously. It has left people out
and made it harder to build internal consensus about collaboration. On the
other hand, it has also helped the institutions move quickly from a point of having no connections to one where most are in committed relationships and are
enthusiastically working on a collaborative agenda that has the potential for
improvement of both sets of institutions. The project has put the issues of middle school education and teacher preparation squarely on the agenda for the
state and for key schools within it. Two comments made at the end of the first
year sum up this positive aspect:

> This isn't just about money or funding or recognition. It has to be able to
> meet the needs of the school. We're a different school as a result of this project.
> We'll carry on. We've grown through it. The department has pushed us to
> examine ourselves, set some goals for ourselves. With or without the $5,000
> [of continuation money], we'll be doing them. We'll try to fund them in some
> other way. (a middle school principal)
>
> We went from zero—never thinking of middle schools—to getting a
> release time position for [a faculty member to coordinate]. We're so excited by
> this. Middle school teacher preparation is clearly on the agenda now, and it's
> all because of this grant. (a college administrator)

It is clearly too soon to try to make any final assessments about this
ongoing project. Any interim evaluation will hinge on what criteria are used:
the degree of mutual interdependence, levels of institutionalization, amount of
measurable change, or the movement that partners have made toward a preset
ideal standard. Each of these criteria will have to be judged with the subjective
question of what might be considered reasonable progress toward meeting it.
Despite the inability to make a final judgment, there are several important
lessons in the case.

The first requires separating the *concept* of state department of education
involvement in promoting collaboration from the *mechanics* of how it was
done in this case. The case study clearly demonstrates that a state department
of education can be effective in promoting school university collaboration. At
the same time it illustrates the second lesson: *how* a department of education
proceeds is critical to the progress of the endeavor. This lesson in process has
not been wasted on the department of education in the case under study—the
DOE staff have actually shown a remarkable ability to change and adapt their
approach to improve the project's management.

During spring and summer 1992, the DOE added four new partnerships as part of a planned second round of expansion. In drawing up their new procedures for this second round, the DOE staff included changes that reflected what they thought they had learned. They decided not to "create forced marriages" but to have institutions find partners and apply together. To avoid uneven levels of commitment to the project, they used a competitive bid process requiring evidence of institutional commitment. Frustrated by the particularly slow pace of change in the colleges and universities, they sought to ensure that higher education institutions were as willing as the middle schools to engage in systemic change. Finally, they pledged to provide "consistent on-site technical assistance" to all participating institutions and to do so through a well-coordinated team that drew on staff from the appropriate subunits of the DOE. It remains to be seen whether the four new partnerships will have an easier and smoother start-up year than did the first six, but the new procedures provide evidence of a DOE staff willing to examine and learn from its experience.

A final consideration concerns the underlying philosophy of simultaneous renewal—the assumption that it makes sense to try to link schools and teacher preparation institutions together for the improvement of both. Some of the tensions described in this case are inherent in the "simultaneous renewal" aspect of the project: By teaming teacher preparation institutions with schools in the process of restructuring, by definition, student teacher placements will not be in "finished," established middle schools, nor will student teachers be coming from perfect middle school preparation programs. Yet the rhetoric of the ongoing national discourse on school improvement has produced a clear set of beliefs: Renewing and improving schools, teaching, and teacher preparation cannot be done in isolation but will require schools and universities to forge new partnership paradigms (Goodlad, 1988; Holmes Group, 1990). If this is true, and I believe it is, then the kinds of connections begun in this project must be made a hundred- and a thousandfold across the country—not just between exemplary institutions but between ordinary schools and colleges or universities. The project described in this case will be an interesting one to watch to see if these institutions, most of which were not particularly ready or looking for collaboration, can, over the coming years, go forward to turn the rhetoric of educational reform and simultaneous renewal into a reality.

REFERENCES

Aldrich, J., & Herker, D. (1977). Boundary spanning roles and organization structure. *Academy of Management Review 2*, 217–230.

Bolman, L., & Deal, T. (1984). *Modern approaches to organizations.* San Francisco: Jossey-Bass.

Clark, R. (1986). School/university relations: Partnerships and networks (Occasional Paper No. 2). Seattle, WA: Center for Educational Renewal.

Frazier, C. (1988). An analysis of a social experiment: School/university partnerships in 1988 (Occasional Paper No. 6). Seattle, WA: Center for Educational Renewal.

Gold, G., & Charner, I. (1986). *Higher education partnerships: Practices, policies, and problems.* Washington DC: National Center for Work and Learning.

Goodlad, J. (1988). School-university partnerships for educational renewal: Rationale and concepts. In K. Sirotnik & J. Goodlad (Eds.), *School-university partnerships in action: Concepts, cases and concerns* (pp. 3–31). New York: Teachers College Press.

Holmes Group. (1990). *Tomorrow's schools: Principles for the design of professional development schools.* East Lansing, MI: Author.

Pfeffer, J. (1981). *Power in organizations.* Cambridge, MA: Ballinger.

Pfeffer, J., & Salancik, G. R. (1978). *The external control of organizations.* New York: Harper.

Rogers, D., & Whetten, D. (1982). *Inter-organizational coordination: Theory, research and implementation.* Ames: Iowa State University Press.

Schermerhorn, J. (1979). Inter-organizational development. *Journal of Management, 5(1),* 21–38.

Schermerhorn, J. (1981). Open questions limiting the practice of interorganizational development. *Group and Organizational Studies, 6*(1), 83–95.

Su, Z. (1990). *School/university partnerships: Ideas and experiments, 1986–1990* (Occasional Paper No. 12). Seattle, WA: Center for Educational Renewal.

Whetten, D. (1981). Inter-organizational relations: A review of the field. *Journal of Higher Education, 52*(1), 1–28.

Part V

Critique

Although the preceding chapters have explored the problems of professionalization, partnership, and power in professional development schools, the
overall picture is still one of general commitment and belief in them as a major
component of educational reform. But is that belief necessarily justified? What
critiques can be offered of the movement?

Roy Creek speaks to us quite forcefully of the tremendous practical difficulties of implementing and sustaining professional development schools.
Like Trevor Sewell and his colleagues he reminds us of the special problems
attendant to the school clientele of urban America. The fact that schools are
run by highly politicized boards and deal with highly political teacher and
administrator unions provides a sobering reminder of the difficulty of sustaining professional development schools in the face of changing political whims.
Creek is also not sanguine about the likelihood of significant change in the university, despite the numerous recent calls for reform. Finally, despite their differences, there are also similarities among professional development schools
and the all but vanished laboratory schools. In particular, the difficulties of
continued funding and the differing cultures among laboratory school teachers
and university professors would seem to be equally problematic for professional development school initiatives as they were for laboratory schools. In
short, real reform is real hard.

Margaret Wilder brings us up short with her reminder that far and away
the largest pool for prospective teachers is still the suburban, white middle
class, and most of those teacher candidates are women. Her own studies and
the experiences of others provide little optimism that such prospective teachers
will have the ability to deal with the pressing needs of an increasingly diverse
student population. Nor is it obvious, despite claims to be committed to multi-

culturalism, that schools of education have the knowledge, skill, and commitment to prepare professionals for a truly multicultural, multiethnic, and multiracial society. Schools have typically reflected society rather than led it. Is there any reason to believe that professional development schools will be any different?

Gender issues have also been a major factor in any discussion of the history of school reform. Joan Burstyn points out that schooling has long been a "profession" in which the leaders have been men and the workers have been women. The conceptions of professionalism that inform most educational reform proposals pay scant attention to gender equity and notions of caring. They are still largely technical in nature and rely implicitly on being able to discover laws of teaching and learning that can then be implemented by male administrators telling women teachers what to do. They pay little attention whatsoever to emerging conceptions of gender equity, caring, and women's ways of knowing.

Whatever the promise of professional development schools, these critiques give us pause. There are practical, social, racial, cultural, and gender concerns that must be addressed if this reform is to have any kind of effective staying power.

ROY J. CREEK

Chapter Fourteen

The Professional Development School
TOMORROW'S SCHOOL OR
TODAY'S FANTASY

The professional development school (PDS) is conceived to be a new kind of educational institution that will be a partnership between public schools and universities. The partnership would be characterized by mutual governance arrangements, enduring budget allocations, new positions that span institutional boundaries, an integration of school and university faculties, new incentive structures in the university, and both school and university faculty who are committed to the collaboration. Given the present state of American education, "tis a consummation devoutly to be wished." The most detailed elaboration of the rationale for professional development schools appears in a report of the Holmes Group titled *Tomorrow's Schools* (1990).

An alternative perspective is that the call for PDSs reveals a tacit awareness that many universities made serious mistakes when they abolished their campus laboratory schools, and that those decisions have contributed significantly to the decline of both teacher education and basic education in America (Bayne, et al., 1991). But the question ought not to be whether we should have university based schools *or* special-purpose public schools. The questions should be, can existing campus laboratory schools be maintained and are professional development schools a realistic supplement in the movement toward educational reform?

The message that PDSs will not have an impact upon the reform of American education unless significant policy changes are made will be neither

241

reassuring nor inspiring to those who are already convinced that the PDS is the
key to the restructuring of our system. That reform is needed is not disputable.
The issues generated by the spate of reports that interpenetrated the eighties
have been often reiterated and require no further discussion here. Even Bracey,
who contends that the sum of the allegations that education has become sub-
standard constitutes "a big lie" (Bracey, 1991), concedes that "there are plenty
of problems that we ought to be working on." Everyone seems to have a
scheme for resuscitating the system. Options range from school assignments
based on family income (Schmidt, 1991) to schools of choice (Raywid, 1991;
Willie, 1991). The Holmes Group's belief that PDSs, spread across the nation,
will produce a more responsible way of introducing worthy new ideas into all
schools is not unlike the U.S. Department of Education's sourcebook, *America
2000*. Each outlines some of the problems facing American education and sets
an ambitious agenda for their resolution. For the vision of *Tomorrow's Schools*
to materialize, groups with vested interests will have to make a number of con-
cessions, and existing policies and practices will need to undergo major trans-
formations. Consequently, the broad-based implementation of professional
development schools across the country faces a number of obstacles. When
significant changes are anticipated in schools, at least four major constituencies must have their concerns addressed. They include the public school clientele, the school administration, the teachers, and the university participants.

PUBLIC SCHOOL CLIENTELE

The school clientele includes the children in attendance and their parents. If the PDS is located in an area that services some segment of the 23 percent of American children who live in poverty, (Hodgkinson, 1991), our most
imaginative inventions may be little more than wishful thinking. The latest
results from the National Assessment of Educational Progress (NAEP) reveal
that, nationwide, students from disadvantaged urban areas and extremely rural
areas have the lowest average reading proficiencies (*Education Week*,
September 22, 1993). The parents of these children are perceived to have neither the time nor the inclination to participate in the business of the school.
Although the educational literature is replete with site-based management
models that purport to involve parents in shared decision making (Brandt,
1992; Davis, 1989; Kessler, 1992; Lueder, 1989; Seely, 1989; Solkov-
Brecher, 1992), one of the only two clear recommendations relative to parent
involvement coming out of the Arizona At-Risk Pilot Project was *not* to initially require high levels of commitment or participation from parents
(Vandergrift & Greene, 1992). The challenge to educate such clients to the
idea of the PDS by describing the educational scheme in detail and spelling out

the benefits that their children will derive involves answering all of the questions related to children being taught by interns, student teachers, and other abecedarians, the orchestration of personnel assignments, and the rationalization for the school's assumption of responsibilities that heretofore were the domain of the university. Since the PDS will not necessarily be a "school of choice," overwhelming parental support for all of the PDS initiatives cannot be guaranteed and ought not to be taken for granted.

However, it is possible that the idea of garnering parental support might be temporarily disregarded. There is a reasonably high probability that the parents of children from disadvantaged homes do not have pleasant memories of their own educational experiences. Although that reality is unfortunate, it is also a basis for discouraging much parent input during early planning stages and unveiling the PDS as an educational model that is dramatically different from the unproductive schools that these parents remember. But such a possibility presupposes equally dramatic changes in the conventional orientation of many educators. A Harris poll revealed that about 90 percent of new teachers believe that children come to school with so many problems that it is difficult for them to be good students (Metropolitan Life Survey, 1991). Those teachers will have to cease their lamenting about poorly prepared pupils; administrators will need to give less heed to the plaints of faculty who denigrate the value of children because of their family backgrounds; and child development experts will have to ponder the possibility that the parental involvement of drug addicts, alcoholics, and child abusers may not be in a child's best interests. None of this is to suggest that parents' concerns about their children's schooling can be or should be summarily dismissed. Rather, it is more likely that their judgment of the value of education will be enhanced when they see a school that does not remind them of their own bad educational experiences.

ADMINISTRATION

The levels of administration that need to be considered in any dealings with public schools include a school board that is responsible for establishing the system's philosophy and budget, a central administration that interprets policy for the district, and the building administrators who are responsible for the on-site implementation of district policy. The first and most influential of these is the school board. School boards are political entities. They are susceptible to change. They are responsible to a citizenry where only one quarter of the households have children in public schools (Hodgkinson, 1991) and where educators compete with police and firefighters for municipal tax dollars.

At a time when more than half of the states, including nine of the ten largest, are coping with severe budget shortfalls (Education Commission of the States, 1991), funding sources are likely to be scant. If a substantial portion of the permanent budget allocation sought by the Holmes Group to provide "institutional support and staying power" is to come from underfunded school boards and overburdened taxpayers, that particular aspiration for the PDS is overly optimistic. The Holmes Report acknowledges that some of the components in a PDS will require "startup funds or venture capital not available to other schools." The notion that the soft money that was used to inaugurate a PDS can be expected to endure as a line item in a public school district's budget is arguable, and a perpetual quest for external monies hardly constitutes a predictable and enduring source of funds.

The central administration of a school district has the responsibility for implementing an established philosophy and the corresponding authority to stipulate educational practice. The extent to which variety is tolerable across schools in a particular district will dictate whether the existence of a PDS is viable. Where site-based management is in practice, prospects may be more auspicious; however, a successful professional development school is expected to be "richer in resources than many other schools in the same district (Holmes Group, 1990). When there are legal challenges to school funding formulas in 19 states (Toch, 1991) because of perceived inequities *across* districts, the superintendent who is willing to accept such differential allocations as a permanent condition *within* a district will have to find the idea of a professional development school to be particularly compelling.

The bulk of the literature on effective schools supports the importance of the role of the building principal (Brookover, 1981; Edmonds, 1979), despite contrary perspectives (Gersten, Carnine, & Green, 1982). The most successful of these administrators are those who make teachers simultaneously empowered and accountable. They engage their faculty in an ongoing pedagogical conversation that is the impetus for instruction and enable teachers to participate in decisions pertaining to school organization, curriculum, and management. Less effective principals employ a "top down" management style and tend to be building managers rather than transformational leaders. Since it is a tenet of the Holmes Group that they will locate schools in communities "now poorly served by public education," they will, by definition, be entering into many partnerships with ineffective schools that are led by less effective principals. The idea that an evolving partnership will somehow revitalize these administrators to the extent that they will enthusiastically join the university faculty in teaching and mentoring activities may be one of the more quixotic ideas perpetrated by the Holmes Group. If building level administrators have not shared leadership and responsibility with their own faculties, the incentive to share anything with university personnel is apt to be fragile and short-lived.

PUBLIC SCHOOL TEACHERS

Perhaps the most vital component of the idealized PDS is the school faculty that is as committed to teacher education as it is to the education of the children who are its primary responsibility. But as Howey (1990) warned, "Unless and until major inroads are made with teachers and teacher unions, the improvements in teacher education and socialization envisioned by many are but a pipe dream." In the 1990s, unionized school teachers' salaries are comparable to or better than those of their counterparts in schools of education. They may, with good reason, choose to snub the paltry stipends that institutions of higher learning have been used to paying them for their services. Nevertheless, they will expect to be paid for additional work. Supervising novice teachers, teaching university classes, developing curricula, and engaging in a pedagogical dialogue with university types are all activities that fall into the "extra work" category. The price tag for this extra labor could be significant. Even those highly motivated individuals who are intrigued by new challenges will have to work with their unionized colleagues; and that includes the building union representative. They will not have the option of "volunteering" their energies and initiatives. The expectation that the excitement of the intellectual quest defined by the Holmes Group will, in and of itself, be a psychological magnet is to ascribe motives that may not exist. Moreover, schemes for designating professional development schools as "regulatory free zones," and seeking rule by rule waivers from explicit regulations are not likely to find support in the teachers' unions.

UNIVERSITY PARTICIPANTS

And how will the university faculties perceive this opportunity? In his criticism of the lack of progress that the Holmes Group has made, Howey (1990) cites "faculty closing ranks and looking solely to themselves for renewal" as being a large part of the problem. The meetings that have crucial impacts upon the lives and careers of university faculty take place on campus, not in some elementary or secondary school located several miles away. For half a century, academic success or failure has been measured using prevailing scholarly criteria. Will even the most altruistic college educators who have any sense of history immerse themselves in otiose off-campus activities at their own professional peril?

Ernest Boyer wishes that things were different. In his appeal to the academy, *Scholarship Reconsidered* (1990), he espoused "a broader and more capacious meaning" of scholarship. The traditional functions would be replaced by the scholarships of discovery, integration, application, and teaching. He is impressed by "field-based" programs in education (and other disciplines) that involve students in clinical experience and apprenticeships. In virtually every chapter of his treatise, Boyer urges institutional changes that would significantly enhance the evolution of PDSs. Endorsements for his position come from such notables as former Stanford University president, Donald Kennedy; former Harvard University president, Derek Bok; and Russell Edgerton, president of the American Association for Higher Education.

These leaders contend that numerous supporters of higher education believe that teaching loads in colleges and universities have declined precipitously. These same supporters also perceive that faculty perform research that is not relevant to societal needs, and that there is a decline in academic citizenship. Along with the authors of *An American Imperative: Higher Expectations for Higher Education* (1994), they are calling upon universities and colleges to redirect attention to undergraduate teaching, and to focus on pressing social needs, such as the reform of kindergarten through grade 12 education.

Unfortunately, both these perspectives and Boyer's text are filled with irony. The doctorate-granting institutions that embrace the research model and aspire to high academic rankings even when research dollars are in short supply are often members of the Holmes Group. It would be incongruous to expect that the disparate importance given to the essential functions of research, teaching, and service will be substantially mitigated by the research universities in the Holmes Group, where faculty hierarchies and academic snobbery prevail. In these milieus, the big rewards accrue to scholars and grant-seekers, not teacher trainers, and certainly not teachers of children. Thus far, there is no evidence that the new incentive structures in the university envisioned by the Holmes Group and hoped for by Boyer and Edgerton have materialized anywhere. It is not clear when or if they ever will.

PROFESSIONAL DEVELOPMENT SCHOOLS AND CAMPUS LABORATORY SCHOOLS

Given so many substantial impediments, it is no surprise that "although every single practice within the ideal package is in successful operation in some form, somewhere, no single professional development school . . . *actually exists*" (Holmes Group, 1990). Howey (1990) attributed much of the consortium's stagnation to an "elitist and exclusionary posture. Nowhere is this attitude more obvious than in the organization's efforts to dissociate the PDS from the campus laboratory school. The fear that the PDS might be misconstrued as some kind of a parthenogenetic clone of the traditional laboratory school permeates Holmes Group literature.

In its major treatise, *Tomorrow's Schools*, the Holmes Group (1990) stresses that professional development schools are not laboratory schools for university research nor demonstration schools, although it acknowledges that "the professional development school . . . resembles the laboratory school movement in some respects." If the differences between laboratory schools and PDSs seems obscure, it is because what should distinguish one kind of school from another are the functions in which each engages. A cursory exploration of the respective functions of laboratory schools (Goodlad, 1980) and professional development schools (Tomorrow's Schools, 1990) does not reveal any substantive differences.

Laboratory schools speak of the education of the children enrolled in programs and the development of new and innovative practices within a context of experimentation. PDSs promote high quality learning for diverse students.

Laboratory schools talk of research, inquiry and the development of theory pertaining to the conduct of education. PDSs refer to research projects that concern all educators' knowledge about how to make schools more productive.

Laboratory schools speak of preparation of new teachers. PDSs speak of practical, thought-provoking preparation for novice teachers.

Laboratory schools speak of inservice education of experienced teachers through demonstration and discussion of the principles underlying observed practices. PDSs are concerned with new understandings and professional responsibilities for experienced educators.

The functions are not only similar, they are presented in an order that would make any first-year graduate student a candidate for accusations of rank plagiarism. This is not an inference that would be reached from a reading of the analects of *Tomorrow's Schools*. What, then, is the source of the fervor on the part of the Holmes Group to distance itself from what appear to be like-minded educators? Why has the laboratory school taken on the form of a dysphemism for the PDS? Is it merely elitist arrogance? Or are there other reasons?

An obvious consideration is the reluctance on the part of all self-styled innovators to acknowledge the origins of their newly postulated ideas. Another is that the laboratory schools' impotence in university politics resulted in a decline in numbers, from 212 in 1964 (Kelly, 1964) to a reported 76 in 1975 (Hendrick, 1980). To associate with such an effete movement would be tantamount to condemning the PDS to its own protracted irrelevance.

The Holmes Group knows some of the history of the laboratory school and recognizes the futility of even attempting to have twenty-first century university dollars earmarked for the support of a children's school, irrespective of its codicillary occupations. It is also possible that the Holmes Group's strategic plan must be not only distinctive but also mutable enough to be adapted to the requests for proposals coming from the foundation community and that will be the source of the enduring budget allocations coveted by the consortium. But a project designed to restructure the schools of America should be less self-serving. The matter of whether the PDS is a novel idea or merely a different version of the university laboratory school would be irrelevant if the need for educational reform were not so considerable and the ways that laboratory schools and PDSs are not fungible were not so trivial. Arguments that laboratory schools are different because they cater to select populations would hold more water if the plethora of self-proclaimed PDSs from obviously well-to-do neighborhoods represented at Holmes Group meetings were not so manifest and if there were not so many public laboratory schools that educate needy children.

In any event, locales where laboratory schools have been discontinued, almost always because of financial exigencies, are not likely to be fertile ground for PDS conversions. A review of the contretemps that occurred at the College Learning Laboratory (CLL) at State University of New York College at Buffalo (SUC-Buffalo) is instructive. The CLL was a research and demonstration school operated at SUC-Buffalo under an agreement between the college and the public school district. It was staffed by a faculty that was comprised of public school teachers and SUC-Buffalo faculty members. The student body, admitted by lottery, was racially integrated and included a substantial number of special needs children. Clinical teaching, research, curriculum development, and demonstration were described as vital to the school's mission. It was "committed to being a significant center for new programs, innovative teaching techniques, dynamic and forward-looking curriculum development, and effective integration of technology into the mainstream of educational reform and revitalization (Buck & Tosto, 1990). The school appeared to have all of the elements sought in a PDS: partnership between the college and the public schools, mutual governance, the integration of faculties, and tax dollars to support the budget. But by the beginning of the 1991–1992 school year the collaboration had been dissolved. It would be paradoxical for the dissolution of the CLL partnership to be coeval with the creation of a PDS in Buffalo, and the issue would not be terribly relevant unless the Buffalo experience reflects what might happen elsewhere. Can anyone believe that the CLL would still exist if SUC-Buffalo were a major research institution and a member of the Holmes Group? Whether the casuistry of parsimony and indifference that resulted in the summary termination of the CLL was the result of insufficient funding or bureaucratic hyperorthodoxy is irrelevant. What is important is that under the same circumstances the existence of any similarly constituted school is so fragile that its role in the restructuring of American education is a sham.

At a glance, the existence of all of these impediments appear to imply that the conceptualization of the professional development school is so fraught with difficulties that it cannot succeed. But improving schools is a complicated problem. After America was shocked out of its educational torpor by the orbiting of the Russian Sputnik in 1957, we should have learned that stylized curricula and quick-fix instructional models do not work and do not last. After the publication of *A Nation at Risk* (1983), we should have learned that the publication of reports, sourcebooks, and similar screeds do not constitute fundamental educational change. And after the publication of *Tomorrow's Schools*, we ought to be cautious about disregarding the history of campus laboratory schools and overestimating the efficacy of PDSs. The PDS envisioned by the authors of *Tomorrow's Schools* may be realized, but only when serious systemic changes are made.

CENTER OF INQUIRY

The Holmes Group believes that schools should be places for reflection and inquiry. It defines inquiry as the common task of both university and school faculty. It also acknowledges that the PDS needs to seek ways to involve parents in school activities. Tutoring, storytelling, and modeling are suggested parental roles (Holmes Group, 1990). This limited interpretation of what a center of inquiry should be is far too anemic. In a true center of inquiry, teachers, teacher trainees, administrators, parents, children, and university personnel *all* engage in a continuing dialogue that is the impetus for what is learned, why it is learned, and how it is learned (Creek & McDonald, 1990). Inquiry is everyone's task. The agenda is to generate new knowledge, promote intellectual growth, and cultivate an inquiring attitude in every participant. Only when the PDS is a true center of inquiry that allows for the legitimate intellectual participation of all of its constituents will it engender the necessary parent and public support to become an enduring reality.

PROFESSIONAL TEACHERS

A blurring of the work roles of university professors and classroom teachers is endemic to a PDS. Because every classroom teacher may not possess the ability or inclination to perform certain professorial responsibilities, and because not every university professor will be able to cope with children in a classroom, it is more important to consider the composition of instructional teams than it is to isolate the characteristics desired in a single PDS teacher. Just as competitive athletic teams are comprised of people with different skills, effective teaching teams need to be carefully constructed if the continuing ped- agogical conversation is to endure. Furthermore, as long as classroom teachers are paid under contracts that stipulate the numbers of days, hours, and prepara- tions that they are responsible for, a disproportionate number of them will retain a "clock watcher's" mentality. Under this circumstance, sincere initia- tives to engage classroom teachers in new roles and assignments will be frus- trated. Teachers in PDSs need to be paid a substantial annual salary for *all* of their professional activities. Fairly remunerated professionals will be far more likely to contribute to the success of a PDS.

CONCLUSION

The problems facing American education did not happen overnight. Embarrassing international test comparisons have been publicized for a decade and the decline in SAT scores is more than 20 years old (Ferrero & Creek, 1981). Consequently, lasting reform will probably have to to be sys- tematic and incremental. Because it is conceived to be an entity whose priori- ties are longevity and inquiry, the properly constituted PDS could become a key to educational reform if specific attitudinal and policy changes are made. The attitudinal changes are most needed in the university community where needs for funding and recognition serve to subvert initiatives for legitimate reform. The policy changes are needed in teacher unions and administrative structures that restrict the activities and imaginations of classroom teachers.

REFERENCES

Bayne, M., Creek, R. J., Hechtman, J., Buck, C. L., Johnson, J. R., Tosto, B., Ulm, G., & King, A. R. (1991). Laboratory schools of the future. In *Laboratory schools of the future*, (pp. 158–171). Honolulu, HI: National Association of Laboratory Schools.

Boyer, E. (1990). *Scholarship reconsidered: Priorities of the professoriate.* Princeton, NJ: Foundation for the Advancement of Teaching.

Bracey, G. W. (1991). Why can't they be like we were? *Phi Delta Kappan, 2,* 104–117.

Brandt, R. (1992). On building learning communities: A conversation with Hank Levin. *Educational Leadership, 50*(1), 19–23.

Brookover, W. (1981). Review of why do some urban schools succeed? The Phi Delta Kappa study of exceptional urban elementary schools. *Harvard Educational Review, 51,* 439–440.

Buck, C. & Tosto, B. A. (1990). The college learning laboratory. *National Association of Laboratory Schools Journal, 14*(2), 1–13.

Creek, R. J., & McDonald, W. C. (1990). The Falk laboratory school: A center of inquiry. *National Association of Laboratory Schools Journal, 15*(1), 1–11.

Davis, B. C. (1989). A successful parent involvement program. *Educational Leadership, 47*(2), 21–23.

Edmonds, R. (1979). Effective schools for the urban poor. *Educational Leadership, 37,* 15–24.

Education Commission of the States. (1991, Fall). States of crisis. *Agenda, 1*(2), 35.

Ferrero, G. W., & Creek, R. J. (1982). The relationship of school related variables to functional economic competency. *Journal of Educational Research, 74*(3), 170–173.

Gersten, R., Carnine, D., & Green, S. (1982). The principal as instructional leader: A second look. *Educational Leadership, 40*(3), 47–50.

Goodlad, J. I. (1980). How laboratory schools go awry. *UCLA Educator, 21*(2), 47–53.

Hendrick, I. G. (1980). University controlled laboratory schools in historical perspective. *UCLA Educator, 21*(2), 54–59.

Hodgkinson, H. (1991). Reform versus reality. *Phi Delta Kappan, 73*(1), 9–16.

Holmes Group (1990). *Tomorrow's schools: Principles for the design of professional development schools.* East Lansing, MI: Author.

Howey, K. R. (1990). Changes in teacher education: Needed leaderships and new networks. *Journal of Teacher Education, 41*(1), 3–9.

Johnson Foundation. (1994). *An American imperative: Higher expectations for higher education.* Racine, WI: Author.

Kelly, E. H. (1964). *College-controlled laboratory schools in the United States.* (64-66060). The American Association of Colleges for Teacher Education.

Kessler, R. (1992). Shared decision making works. *Educational Leadership, 50*(1), 36–38.

Lueder, D. C. (1989) Tennessee parents were invited to participate—and they did. *Educational Leadership, 47*(2), 15–17.

Metropolitan Life survey. (1991). *The American teacher, 1991.* Louis Harris and Associates, Inc.

Raywid, M. A. (1991). Is there a case for choice? *Educational Leadership, 48*(4), 4–12.

Schmidt, P. (1991). District proposes assigning pupils based on income. *Education Week, 11*(9), 1, 13.

Seely, D. S. (1989). A new paradigm for parent involvement. *Educational Leadership, 47*(2), 46–48.

Solkov-Brecher, J. I. (1992). A successful model for school based planning. *Educational Leadership, 50*(1), 52–54.

Toch, T. (1991). Separate but not equal. *Agenda, 1*(1), 14–17.

The National Commission on Excellence in Education. (1983). A nation at risk: The imperative for educational reform. *Chronicle of Higher Education, 26*(10), 11–16.

Vandergrift, J. A., & Greene, A. L. (1992). Rethinking parent involvement. *Educational Leadership, 50*(1), 57–59.

Willie, C. V., (1991). Controlled choice avoids the pitfalls of choice plans. *Educational Leadership, 48*(4), 62–64.

Chapter Fifteen

Professional Development Schools

RESTRUCTURING TEACHER EDUCATION PROGRAMS AND HIERARCHIES

There is renewed interest among administrators and faculty in colleges of education, as well as administrators in elementary and secondary schools, in developing more creative approaches for classroom teaching.[1] Likewise, the Holmes Group's report, *Tomorrow's Schools* (1990) "call for action," bespeaks a problem in the ways teachers are being prepared.

The professional development school (PDS), as conceived by the Holmes Group, is designed to do what the traditional "lab school" was unable to do: expose pre-service teachers to the complexities of classroom life. The university-operated lab school, according to Kennedy (1992), prepared teachers in an ivory tower environment with plenty of resources. Moreover, according to Kennedy, these lab schools did not prepare pre-service teachers to understand the learning styles of children not represented in the lab schools. In this case, it appears as though culturally relevant ways of teaching and learning that are embedded in race, culture and class predispositions were largely unaddressed in lab school settings.

Culturally relevant teaching challenges what Ladson-Billings and King (1992) referred to as the "assimilationist approach to teaching (p. 314)." Ladson-Billings argues that the assimilationist approach "sees fitting students into the existing social and economic order as its primary responsibility." On the other hand, culturally relevant teaching, according to Ladson-Billings (1992):

is the kind of teaching that is designed not merely to *fit* the school culture to the students' culture but also to *use* student culture as the basis for helping students understand themselves and others, structure social interactions, and conceptualize knowledge (p. 314).

The PDS proposes an agenda for collaboration between colleges of education and elementary and secondary schools. Unlike the training received in the lab school, pre-service teachers[2] will be placed in a "real school" environment that is operated by its community.

My discussion rests on the presupposition that PDSs, as they are currently conceived, promote an illusion of change. The PDS literature does not explain why teacher education programs need to be restructured. Moreover, the literature does not discuss why more creative teaching approaches are needed. What is mentioned in the PDS literature are proposals to broaden the liberal arts program and for strengthening the subject matter preparation of pre-service students (Case, et al., 1993). What is not mentioned in the general PDS literature, especially concerning the curriculum, are discussions of a revised teacher education curriculum that includes multicultural education. How then will PDS trained teachers learn to incorporate matters of race, class, and culture issues into their classroom curriculum? The absence of this theoretical and practical connection is the central question raised in this chapter.

Generally speaking, curriculum changes are common features of program restructuring. For instance, improved concepts for mastering the canon in liberal arts, as well as the skill-based competencies needed to teach math and science are givens. Yet, how to offer more culturally relevant ways to upgrade the skills of pre-service teachers, teacher education professors and cooperating teachers[3] that enable them to connect their own lives and experiences to teaching practices has not been addressed in the PDS discussions.

In this chapter, I question why PDS reform efforts are not being restructured and critiqued in more culturally relevant ways. In the first section, I draw upon an experience I had as an instructor in an education department. I then cite two educators who noted their experiences when applying culturally relevant teaching approaches. I use these three teaching case studies to highlight how multicultural education and culturally relevant teaching approaches are interconnected.

In the second section, I suggest that the PDS literature is currently situated in a managerial context devoid of how race, class, and cultural relations connect to desired PDS goals. I argue in this section that the managerial focus alone is insufficient for creating change in teacher preparation without a discussion detailing the specific theoretical and practical problems such structural changes are designed to correct. I also suggest that the managerial language is broad and appears unsure about desired PDS learning outcomes. Thereafter, I look at who is being trained for PDS placement and the communities within which PDS sites are currently situated. I provide demographics that profile the current pool of teachers and I relate why it is especially important for them to learn to adopt more culturally relevant ways of knowing as a standard for teaching diverse populations. I suggest that additional hierarchies are certain to emerge if PDS site selection and training is not more equitably distributed. In the concluding section, I raise additional questions that I think will contribute to a more equitable PDS model.

CONCEPTUAL FRAMEWORK

The core ideas that guide and focus my work in teacher preparation and development evolve specifically from my interest in the underrepresentation of African-American teachers in America's schools and how this shapes the schooling experiences of African-American students.[4] Educational theory and research suggest that in many learning environments, African-American teachers successfully connect the lives of African-American students to what is learned inside and outside of school (Hope-King, 1993; Foster, 1993; Murrell Jr., 1991; Meier, et al., 1989). This atmosphere of "connectedness" is perceived by African-American students as a form of caring and belief in their abilities to succeed in school (Wilder, 1993; Foster, 1993). Moreover, the presence of African-American teachers offers greater opportunities for all students to be exposed to teachers who bring different experiences and teaching approaches to the classroom.

The experience of schooling, the school infrastructure, and the relationship between students and their teachers are factors that help to shape students' and teachers' perceptions. Critical studies of schooling have shown that teachers have been known to treat their students differently as a consequence of class status, race, gender and cultural styles (Farkas, et al., 1990; Irvine, 1988; Beady & Hansell, 1981; Adair, 1984). Since class, race, and gender are often bases for inequities in the distribution of knowledge, students' futures are created and recreated differently due to patterns of socialization they learn inside and outside of school. In order to prepare tomorrow's teachers, traditional assimilationist teaching approaches like those defined by Ladson-Billings and King and often employed by those who train pre-service teachers must be discontinued. Recognizing the importance of relating learning to self should be prominently emphasized in the academic discourse (Murrell, Jr., 1991) for preparing pre-service teachers to teach their students in a multicultural society. A culturally relevant teaching approach provides a starting point.

TEACHING FOR A MULTICULTURAL SOCIETY

I was invited to teach a required undergraduate-level course, Foundations of Education, at a private, coeducational liberal arts college. The college is located in a township adjacent to a medium-sized city in the Northeast. The student population was comprised mainly of individuals of middle- to upper-middle-class backgrounds. My cursory observations of the demographic makeup of the student, faculty, and administrative personnel led me to conclude that the college was mainly populated by Euro-Americans. There was only one African-American woman, who was not tenured, teaching at the college on a full-time basis.

I entered a classroom of 25 pre-service teachers who were one course away from embarking upon their student teaching experience. That one course was the one I was hired to teach. When I entered the classroom, some students appeared (by their facial expressions) very surprised to see me. There was one African-American student in the class and there were a slightly larger number of females than males. After I introduced myself, I asked two questions. The first question was: "Please raise your hand if you are planning to teach in the public school system located in the nearby city (approximately two miles away)? One hand was raised, that of the African-American female. My second question was: "How many of you have ever had an African-American teacher on any school level?" Again, only one hand was raised, by the African-American student.

I was disappointed in my students' responses to my questions. Confronted with the underrepresentation of African-American students in my class, the reality of the African-American teacher shortage was apparent. I stood before pre-service teachers who were one semester away from entering into the teaching field, and only one of them planned to teach in the public schools located in the nearby city. I speculated that their lack of interest in teaching in the urban public school system was related to the widely publicized financial and social problems tied to public schools in the United States. I also speculated that their lack of experience with African-American scholars, and scholars of color in general, merely equipped them to acquire a monocultural understanding of a complex and competing multicultural society. I reasoned that as a result of their limited interaction with both scholars of color and a multicultural curriculum, they had likely acquired a monoculturally based teaching perspective and if so, this would render them underprepared to teach from a culturally relevant perspective. Since one of the characteristics of urban public schools is its high enrollment of African-American children and youth,[5] I did not rule out that their decision to avoid teaching in the public schools was developed from their predispositions and stereotypes about those who attend such schools.

Shortly into the semester my speculations were confirmed. My students had never been introduced to the current literature in multicultural education.[6] Nor had they been taught to reflect and interpret their own ideas about society as a whole and its relations to schooling, learning, and teaching as a consequence of their race, class, and cultural locations. The professor who previously taught the course for approximately 15 years told me he never used a text or supplemental readings. His former students revealed to me that he had never lectured on topics such as the history of women's education, the education of African-Americans, or civil rights. This information helped me to better understand the forms of resistance shown by a few students in response to some of the class readings and lectures. I remember vividly how a few students were uncomfortable during class discussions about civil rights issues and other equity issues surrounding school inequality. However, some students informed me that the course helped them to broaden their awareness of equity issues and the complexities of racism in society and how these tie into teaching practices.

I am reminded of one Euro-American student who approached me during an exam to ask me: "Who are these people?" while pointing to an exam question. The educators were Frederick Douglass, Mary McLeod Bethune, and Booker T. Washington. A question on the exam asked students to briefly discuss the educational ideals of the persons listed. Also on the list were Horace Mann and William Holmes McGuffey. The student did not have a problem identifying the Euro-American educators listed. I reminded the student that we had discussed these educators in class and that all the names on the list were drawn from the same chapter. The student replied that she didn't remember reading about the African-American educators in the assigned chapter and walked back to her seat.

Explanations concerned with why this particular student had a problem with the question is not the focus here, but suffice it to say that knowledge is cumulative and stratified. It has power when it is continuously presented and built upon. As an occasional topic, the educational ideals and the histories of non-Europeans appear unimportant and unrelated to knowledge in general and in this case becoming a teacher.

A student I interviewed for my doctoral research provides an interesting account of how school knowledge is stratified and assigned its relevance. An African-American college freshman named Sarah, who attended a prominent private Catholic high school in the same city, talks here about her high school experience:

MW: How would you describe your high school?
Sarah: I felt really extremely out of place.
MW: Why did you feel that way?

Sarah: Because it . . . I was coming from a predominantly black school, co-ed, in a Black neighborhood, to this all girls, all-white elite school. And it was like, it was really hard for me. I felt like it was gonna take a long time for me to fit in, but it really didn't. I . . . like about a month into school I decided I was going to run for the class vice president, and I ended up winning.

MW: To what do you attribute your success?

Sarah: My wonderful personality. I'm vibrant.

MW: So your experience at Winston Academy was positive?

Sarah: It was . . . I mean, I fit in pretty well after that. So, it wasn't the fact of fitting in, because I have a sense of myself. I started the Black Awareness Club at Winston. Because when my sister graduated, she was the only black senior. And the year after, one other girl . . . yea, one black senior after that. And then five seniors graduated with me. The class of 1992 . . . this past June. So, the experience was wonderful. I started the Black Awareness Club in my junior year . . . not just for black people, but to promote and to make the white community aware of my people, because I felt that we were underrepresented. We had the best assemblies, you know, after that.

MW: What do you mean, "We had the best assemblies?"

Sarah: We had the most . . . we had the most participation, the most enthusiasm. All the kids, the seniors didn't really skip out, they came to the Black Awareness assemblies, because we had the African-American Drum Troop come and African dancers. And they [classmates, teachers] really loved it. And it was just like really cultural, because they really hadn't been exposed to that kind of activity.

MW: Why did you start the club? How did it come about?

Sarah: Because junior year . . . it must've been the first week of school. I was sitting in an American Literature class. Was it that? . . . No, American government. And, um, my teacher, Mrs. Petrelli, the one who was our adviser . . . she said something, and it just like triggered my mind. It was like . . . I felt like blacks or African-Americans have contributed so much to our society, you know, as a whole and that it was just like shameful that we're sitting here and no one even . . . I just felt like that at that moment. So, that day I went to the principal and I said, "I want to start a club here." And she said, "Okay." She gave us the money that we needed and within about two weeks. . . .

MW: You had a club.

Sarah: Uh-huh, the Black Awareness Club.

MW: What about the curriculum, did you suggest additional readings about African-Americans?

Sarah: Um, no, not too many I didn't read, cause I was so bogged down with other things. I really didn't have time to do that. Our meetings were strictly . . . we had discussions and things like that, you know.

MW: Would you say that you didn't read about African-Americans while attending Winston Academy?

Sarah: African Amer . . . no, I didn't. I didn't. I just didn't. I didn't have the time to do that, cause that school . . . the school I went to was very demanding. I got a regent's [academic] diploma. A very rigid curriculum. Strict. (April, 1993)

According to Boateng, (1990) the curriculum is the primary resource that is used to "deculturize" African-American students. Boateng wrote that when African-American students cannot see themselves in the curriculum they experience the process of deculturalization. Boateng defined the process: "[D]eculturalization does not mean a loss of a group's culture, but rather failure to acknowledge the existence of their culture and the role it plays in their behavior" (p. 73).

Sarah knew that there was a gap in the school knowledge she was learning in her class. Sarah recognized the deculturalization process happening to her through the curriculum being used and from her teacher. She knew that only one view was being taught, and it did not represent her African-American culture. Sarah needed to have a "Black Awareness" connection and as a high school junior, she felt that her white peers and teachers needed to see and learn about such a connection as well. Sarah's teacher obviously did not teach outside of her trained area of specialization, and this area was not framed within a multicultural context. A limited exposure to multiple perspectives, the limited presence of teachers of color, and a monocultural curriculum all encourage students to question the relevance of multicultural education. How could it possibly be important to an academic diploma? Will such knowledge be included in the SATs? Thus reading about African-Americans is viewed by Sarah as additional work added to an already "very rigid curriculum."

Sarah informed me later in the interview that she is not interested in pursuing a career in teaching. Given her pioneering effort to bring a "Black Awareness" perspective to her high school peers and teachers, I would venture to say that if she were to become a teacher, she would probably bring a similar awareness to her students. Students who have not been exposed to teachers of color or a multicultural curriculum context and who choose careers in teaching (like my students and those in the proceeding discussion) pose a more pressing concern.

In California, King (1991) noted her students' reactions when she employed more culturally relevant ways of learning. King taught her course on the Social Foundations of Education at an elite Jesuit university and found that her pre-service teachers showed signs of anxiety about being able to "deal with all the diversity in the classroom." King relates that her students felt that their own identity, status, and security were at stake. King discovered that the cultural beliefs held by her students about why inequity persists for African-Americans "take Euro-American norms and privilege as givens" (p. 133). King suggests that students, and particularly future teachers, must learn to think critically and reconstruct their social knowledge and self-identities to become conscious of oppression.

Ladson-Billings (1991) noted that her students in California come from the "best schools and the most privileged backgrounds." She conducted an experiment in her class comprised of pre-service teachers and non-pre-service teachers. Ladson-Billings distributed a list with 15 terms associated with issues of civil-rights and multicultural education. Students were given 20 minutes to list anything they knew about the terms. Her overall findings revealed that students had not been exposed to the themes, issues, and historical significance of multicultural issues.

Are the students in my class and King's and Ladson-Billings' typical of the pre-service teachers currently being prepared to educate tomorrow's children? If yes, then will it be enough for pre-service teachers to enter a new location, such as a real school setting in a PDS site, without being reeducated from a real life curriculum? A multicultural curriculum should enable teachers to develop, as Freire (1971) and others suggested, an intellectual understanding of schooling and inequity in ways that are self-reflective, transformative, and liberatory (King, 1991; Gordon, 1993). It should also help teachers to teach in more culturally relevant ways. Rather than address the implications of this, PDS reformers are focused on managerial initiatives for strengthening the collaborative venture. What has been discussed in the PDS literature are general curricula changes and managerial approaches to program restructuring.

THE MANAGERIAL PARADOX

Conceptually, the PDS agenda has the potential to provide exposure to the realities of school life. However, the actual process by which PDSs seek to strengthen the quality of teaching, teachers, learning. and schooling is critically underdeveloped in its early stages of formation. Also missing in the PDS literature are specific educational outcomes desired from PDS-trained teachers. In other words, what will the PDS teacher do differently from pre-service teachers who are not PDS trained?

Most of the information about the collaborative venture of university-school partnerships is detailed within a managerial framework that also highlights policy issues (Case, et al., 1993; Murray; 1993; Stoddart, 1993, Teitel, 1993). The literature primarily addresses the administrative procedures that have taken place or the mechanics of how the university-school partnership was formed (Stoddart, 1993; Case, et al., 1993; Miller & Silvernail, 1994; Grossman, 1994; Whitford, 1994; Lemlech et al., 1994). The relationship between classroom teachers and university professors is highlighted as are the tensions that can accompany their collaborations. Stoddart (1993) shed light on the tensions between classroom teachers and university professors during the co-teaching process in PDSs in Utah. Case (1993) offered a discussion on how the University of Connecticut encourages the motivation for collaboration to come from school-based personnel rather than university faculty. According to Case, this approach is taken to reduce the "skepticism" among teachers and administrators about the university's intention. Teitel (1993) expanded the managerial role and brought into focus a university-school partnership that was "jump-started" by a state governing agency.

In general, the PDS interests elaborated in the literature include strategic planning initiatives emphasizing quality control by restructuring teacher preparation programs. Quality control initiatives include administrative and bureaucratic hurdles entailed in establishing new admission criteria, setting new standards for earning credits and degrees, setting new requirements for certification or licensure, recruitment criteria for administrators to facilitate PDS collaborations, and collaborating with state education departments (Case, et al., 1993; Murray, 1993; Teitel, 1993; Miller & Silvernail, 1994). Included also in the PDS literature are details and rationales for adding a "fifth year" to teacher education programs (Case, et al., 1993; Miller & Silvernail, 1994).

The PDS literature does not acknowledge if multicultural education is to become part of the PDS curriculum. With few exceptions (Case, et al., 1993; Snyder, 1994; Lemlech, et al., 1994), the PDS literature does not address whether there are PDS initiatives that recognize the need to prepare pre-service teachers to better serve students of color. While Case, et al. (1993) acknowledged the importance of including an "urban" focus to the PDS experience of pre-service teachers in Connecticut, neither he nor other PDS planners acknowledged that this same focus is needed in the PDS curriculum. Thus, the importance of having an urban focus is muddled in the broadness of the language used to describe it.

For instance, what does the "urban school" district in Connecticut look like (Case et al., 1993)? Is the "urban place" a monolith? Does the word itself inform research about school culture, student demographics, class status, and schooling practices?

While the definition of the word "urban" connotes city life, how this life becomes translated in ways that construct reality in relation to class, race, gender, and cultural norms is a question that compels discussion. To lump all city dwellers into one discrete category or social location devalues those who have socially constructed diverse identities and cultures. Educators cannot speak about urban school locations as though they are multicultural or diverse sites. It cannot be taken for granted that urban locations are not places where upper-middle-class Euro-Americans attend (urban) schools that primarily serve upper-middle-class Euro-Americans. Should we not distinguish the public school that is also a magnet school and the poorly financed public school, since both reside in the urban metropolitan area? These points of clarification are important for establishing a broader PDS purpose. Within this context, clarity of additional PDS initiatives beyond the university-school partnership venture can be related to some of the compelling social and educational problems that underpin the need for the partnership venture.

TOMORROW'S PDS TEACHERS AND PDS SITES

The National Educational Association's (NEA) "Status Report on Public School Teachers" (1990) indicates that the racial categories of teachers in America show African-Americans represent 8 percent of the teaching force, Hispanics comprise 3 percent, Native Americans comprised nine tenths of 1 percent, and Euro-American teachers comprise 87.6 percent. The enrollment of students of color has increased in 44 states between 1987 and 1992 (Hope-King, 1993), and according to the National Center for Education Statistics (NCES), half of the students in public inner-city schools are African-American and Latino (Hope-King, 1993; NCES, 1992). By 2020, it is projected that 46 percent of all children in public schools will be students of color (Hope-King, 1993; NCES, 1991).

Confronted with this reality, educators concerned with the African-American teacher shortage need not again ask the question "Who will teach tomorrow's students of color?" By now, the answer is clear. The current profile of today's teachers and those in training to become tomorrow's teaching force are comprised mainly of Euro-Americans.

The PDS literature informs us that PDS sites currently in operation are primarily located in white working- and middle-class school districts (Miller & Silvernail, 1994; Grossman, 1994; Whitford, 1994; Snyder, 1994).[7] Since PDSs appear to be preparing teachers to train in working- and middle-class school environments, it is likely that schools located in low-income neighborhoods where many students of color attend will continue to be taught from learning models developed and tested on working- and middle-class students.

Since most PDS sites are being established in working- and middle-class school districts, this reduces the opportunity of the predominant Euro-American pool of pre-service teachers to acquire the necessary social and intellectual exposure that is crucial for them to "connect" with students from backgrounds unlike their own. The lack of exposure, coupled with the fact that the PDS model has only a few sites in development, will generate a very small number of pre-service teachers who will have access to PDS sites. At this rate of progress, it will take a long time to spread PDS practices and applications to all school districts. As a result of the unevenness in PDS site selections, does this not stratify schools more than they already are?

What does it mean to be a PDS school site? Are they to be recognized as "better schools?" Will PDS pre-service teachers be viewed as "better prepared" than pre-service teachers who do not receive PDS training? Will there be different credentials or professional rewards associated with PDS training? These issues will certainly be challenged as PDSs mature. In their present design, therefore, PDSs are certain to create additional hierarchies among teacher education programs and pre-service teachers as a whole. Thus, it goes without saying that the spread of PDS practice must become more evenly dispersed.

What is not at issue here is the assumption that a Euro-American teaching force cannot teach students of color. What is at issue here is the distorted social reality (Witty, 1982) that all children develop when they do not see classrooms filled with teachers and students of different racial and cultural backgrounds. What is also at issue here is the "quality" of learning that will be imparted if students cannot connect with school knowledge. If Euro-American teachers are to teach African-American students, then Murrell's (1991) question is appropriate. He asked:

> Without a reflection upon, and interpretation of, the experiences and lives of diverse peoples, upon what will teacher education programmers draw to 'infuse' this knowledge of diversity (p. 207)?

The problem facing educational establishments, according to Murrell, is how to provide this knowledge about things not experienced. In other words, can cooperating teachers and teacher education professors from working- and middle-class backgrounds teach a predominantly Euro-American pre-service teaching force how to relate to and teach students of color?

How will PDS settings that are situated in affluent school districts inform theory and practice about improved teaching strategies that connect school knowledge to the lives of students of color? If PDS reformers are committed to this critical concern then it needs to be seen in PDS site selections and literature.

Kennedy (1992) and others (Boe & Gilford, 1992; Stevenson, 1993) pointed out that teachers acquire their teaching habits and styles from their own experiences as students and from their former teachers and these imprints are difficult to shake. This impulse, according to Kennedy, will remain strong unless teachers are offered equally strong and compelling new approaches to teaching.

Who then will help teach a predominantly Euro-American pool of pre-service teachers how to adopt new learning skills necessary to teach the children of color inside America's schools? Will they be the current pool of cooperating teachers and teacher education professors? Are pre-service teachers the only group of practitioners in need of learning new and better ways to acknowledge students of color and how to incorporate culturally specific approaches to pedagogical practice? Such a limited view is an illusion of change on how teacher education programs ought to be reformed.

CONCLUSION

I do not argue against the necessity of a managerial process for building a foundation upon which the PDS model can emerge. The success of the PDS project relies on managerial expertise for administering organizational strategies for restructuring and redesign processes. However, equally important is the need for PDS managers to more clearly define the PDS goals in ways beyond a university-school collaborative venture.

It is not enough for pre-service teachers to be exposed to or "be seen in" classrooms filled with children from diverse backgrounds. This does not capture the nature of multicultural education. Nor does it capture the complexity of multicultural knowledge and teaching. Multicultural education and effective teaching practices challenge educators to "guarantee teacher-pupil connections across lines of unequal power, language differences, and cultural expression" (Murrell, 1991, p. 207). Tomorrow's teachers must learn how to communicate knowledge cross-culturally and in meaningful ways.

If colleges of education and PDS planners are committed to reforming teacher preparation programs, they must begin by reeducating cooperating teachers and teacher education professors, as well as pre-service teachers to become, as Darling-Hammond (1994) suggested, more "infinitely skilled." According to Darling-Hammond, they are

> teachers who understand learning as well as teaching, who can address students' needs as well as the demands of their disciplines, and who can create bridges between students' experiences and curriculum goals (p. 5).

The questions that are in need of a more critical examination are: How will PDS trained teachers recreate ways that children come to understand knowledge? How will PDSs help prepare pre-service teachers to meet this challenge? It is important for pre-service teachers to, as Gordon (1993) posited (in a different context), "acquire multiple lenses through which to critique societal reality and work toward social change (pg. 449)." There must also be an opportunity for pre-service teachers to subsequently work toward greater acceptance of cultural diversity that exist within their own lives and among those they will ultimately teach.

NOTES

1. I wish to thank Mwalimu Shujaa, Bram Hamovitch, and Hugh Petrie for their helpful comments and suggestions during the development of this chapter.

2. Pre-service teachers connote students enrolled in teacher education programs. I also refer to them as PDS-trained teachers.

3. I use the term "cooperating teachers" to describe teachers who are already certified and who are employed as elementary or secondary school teachers. They represent those who assist in guiding the practical experience component of teacher training to pre-service teachers. Teacher education professors are referred to in this context as those who primarily function within university- and college-based teacher education programs and who teach college core courses.

4. While I am concerned about the underrepresentation of teachers of color generally, the specific details of my work thus far have been related to African-American teachers.

5. Ninety-five percent of all African-Americans are enrolled in public elementary schools, while 4.9 percent are enrolled in private elementary schools. Also, 96.7 percent of all African-Americans are enrolled in public high schools, while 3.3 percent are enrolled in private high schools (U.S. Department of Commerce, Bureau of the Census, 1992).

6. I support Banks' conceptualization of multiculturalism. A multicultural curriculum referred to in this chapter is curricular content that is inclusive of multiple voices. It is knowledge that is transformative in that it challenges the assumption that there is only one interpretation for understanding knowledge. Multiculturalism encourages students to question, apply experiences as they themselves live them, and become more literate to many points of view available for consideration.

7. Snyder (1994) reports that Teachers College has a second PDS site in a school that is predominantly populated by African-American students. While Snyder sheds light on the tension that is created when "outsiders" enter a school, the tension he describes is more bureaucratic in nature. More information concerning how PDS teachers relate to their students would provide more qualitative ways of assessing the effectiveness of PDS-trained pre-service teachers.

REFERENCES

Adair, A. V. (1984). *Desegregation: The illusion of black progress.* Lanham, MD: University Press of America.

Banks, J. A. (1991). Multicultural literacy and curriculum reform. *Educational Horizons, 69*(3), 135–140.

Banks, J.A. (1993). The canon debate, knowledge construction, and multicultural education. *Educational Researcher, 22*(5), 4–14.

Beady, C. H., & Hansell, S. (1981). Teacher race and expectations for student achievement. *American Educational Research Journal, 18*, 191–206.

Boateng, F. (1990). Combatting deculturalization of the African-American child in the public school system: A multicultural approach. In K. Lomotey (Ed.), *Going to school* (pp. 73–84). Albany: State University of New York Press.

Boe, E. E. & Gilford, D. M. (1992). Summary of conference proceedings. In E. E. Boe and D. A. Gilford (Eds.), *Teacher supply, demand, and quality: Policy issues, models, and data bases* (pp. 21–62). Washington, DC: National Academy Press.

Case, C. W., Norlander, K. A., & Reagan, T. G. (1993). Cultural transformation in an urban professional development center: Policy implications for school-university collaboration. *Educational Policy, 7*(1), 40–60.

Darling-Hammond, L. (1994). Developing professional development schools: Early lessons, challenge, and promise. In L. Darling-Hammond (Ed.), *Professional development schools: Schools for developing a profession,* (pp. 1–26). New York: Teachers College Press.

Farkas, G., Sheehan, D., Grobe, R. P., & Shuan, Y. (1990). Cultural resources and school success: Gender, ethnicity, and poverty groups within an urban school district. *American Sociological Review, 55*, 127–142.

Foster, M. (1993). Educating for competence in community and culture: Exploring the views of exemplary African-American teachers. *Urban Education, 27*(4), 370–394.

Freire, P. (1971). *Pedagogy of the oppressed.* New York: Harper & Row.

Gordon, B. M. (1993). African-American cultural knowledge and liberatory education. *Urban Education, 27*(4), 448–470.

Grossman, P. L. (1994). In pursuit of a dual agenda: Creating a middle level professional development school. In L. Darling-Hammond (Ed.), *Professional development schools: Schools for developing a profession,* (pp. 50–73). New York: Teachers College Press.

Holmes Group. (1990). *Tomorrow's schools: Principles for the design of professional development schools.* East Lansing, MI: Author.

Hope-King, S. (1993). The limited presence of African-American teachers. *Review of Educational Research, 63*(2), 115–149.

Irvine, J. J. (1988). An analysis of the problem of disappearing black educators. *The Elementary School Journal, 88*(5), 503–513.

Kennedy, M. M. (1992). The problem of improving teacher quality while balancing supply and demand. In E. E. Boe and D. A. Gilford (Eds.), *Teacher supply, demand, and quality: Policy issues, models, and data bases,* (pp. 65–108). Washington DC: National Academy Press.

King, J. E. (1991). Dysconscious racism: Ideology, identity, and the miseducation of teachers. *Journal of Negro Education, 60*(2), 133–146.

Ladson-Billings, G. (1991). Beyond multicultural illiteracy. *Journal of Negro Education 60*(2), 147–157.

Ladson-Billings, G. (1992). Reading between the lines and beyond the pages: A culturally relevant approach to literacy teaching. *Theory Into Practice, 31*(4), 312–320.

Lemlech, J. K., Hertzog-Foliart, H., & Hackl, A. (1994). The Los Angeles professional practice school: A study of mutual impact. In L. Darling-Hammond (Ed.), *Professional development schools: Schools for developing a profession,* (pp. 156–175). New York: Teachers College Press.

Meier, K. J., Stewart J., Jr., & England, R. E. (1989). *Race, class, and education.* Madison: University of Wisconsin Press.

Miller, L. & Silvernail, D. L. (1994). Wells Junior High School: Evolution of a professional development school. In L. Darling-Hammond (Ed.), *Professional development schools: Schools for developing a profession,* (pp. 28–49). New York: Teachers College Press.

Murray, F.B. (1993). "All or None" criteria for professional development schools. *Educational Policy, 7*(1), 61–73.

Murrell, P. C, Jr. (1991). Cultural politics in teacher education: What is missing in the preparation of minority teachers? In M. Foster (Ed.), *Readings on equal education: Qualitative investigations into schools and schooling,* (Vol. 2, pp. 205–225). New York: AMS Press.

National Center for Education Statistics. (1991). *Projection of education statistics to 2002* (NCES 91-490). Washington, DC: U.S. Department of Education, Office of Educational Research and Improvement.

National Center for Educational Statistics. (1992). *The condition of education, 1992* (CS 92-096). Washington, DC: U.S. Department of Education, Office of Educational Research and Improvement.

National Education Association. (1991). *Status of the American public school teacher 1990–1991*. Washington, DC: Author.

Snyder, J. (1994). Perils and potentials: A tale of two professional development schools. In L. Darling-Hammond (Ed.), *Professional development schools: Schools for developing a profession*, (pp. 98–125). New York: Teachers College Press.

Stevenson, R. B. (1993). Critically reflective inquiry and administrator preparation: Problems and possibilities. *Educational Policy, 7*(1), 96–113.

Stoddart, T. (1993). The professional development school: Building bridges between cultures. *Educational Policy, 7*(1), 5–23.

Teitel, L. (1993). The state role in jump-starting school-university collaboration: A case study. *Educational Policy, 7*(1), 74–95.

U.S. Department of Commerce, Bureau of The Census. (1992). *School Enrollment: Social and Economic Characteristics of Students (P20-474)*. Washington, DC: U.S. Government Printing Office.

Wilder, M.A. (1993). [*Students' relations with teachers and teaching*: In-depth Interviews]. Unpublished raw data.

Witty, E. (1982). *Prospects for Black teachers: Preparation, certification and employment*. Washington, DC: U.S. Department of Education, National Institute of Education. (ERIC Document Reproduction Service No. ED 213 659).

Whitford, B. L. (1994). Permission, persistence, and resistance: Linking high school restructuring with teacher education reform. In L. Darling-Hammond (Ed.), *Professional development schools: Schools for developing a profession,* (pp. 74–97). New York: Teachers College Press.

Chapter Sixteen

Transforming the Discourse

GENDER EQUITY AND PROFESSIONAL
DEVELOPMENT SCHOOLS

INTRODUCTION: ASSUMPTIONS ABOUT THE NEED
FOR GENDER EQUITY

Professional development schools promise a new collaboration between schools and universities, a collaboration as enticing to teachers and professors as it is problematic. Critiques have already focused on the problems of integrating two cultures, school and university, and on the failure of supporters to identify the values upon which professional development schools are based. In this chapter, I use gender as a category of analysis for two purposes: to critique the literature on professional development schools; and to suggest ways of amending the concept to place the values of care and equity at its core.[1]

Why have I chosen gender as a category of analysis? In a critique of the Holmes Group's first report, *Tomorrow's Teachers*, Soder (1986) chided the authors for

> telling us, as did rhetoricians of another time, that the major issues are settled, with major conclusions uncontroverted. The nature of the good society, the nature of good education, and the role of the teacher in enhancing both . . . are all to be taken as commonly understood and agreed upon. (p. 3)

I believe that neither the nature of the good society nor the nature of good education is settled. Yet each of us, strives, whether consciously or unconsciously, to make our practice congruent with our personal values. Hence, each participant in a professional development school holds some values, hidden or revealed, concerning the good life and good education. The kernel of these values lies in one's understanding of what it means, in terms of rights and responsibilities, to be a human being with membership in a society. In the United States, the literature on civic learning is extensive and reaches back to the first days of the Republic. Nevertheless, because we now focus in schools on the skills needed by individuals to compete for jobs, because violence among individuals appears worse than it used to be, because we now live in a "global village," and because the lifestyle we have labeled desirable endangers the environment, the discourse about ways to educate people for citizenship has changed. We have a growing literature on ways to teach mediation, negotiation, and conflict resolution. This literature assumes that an individual needs to learn skills of peaceable interpersonal communication to become a valuable member of society (Cheatham, 1989; de Bono, 1985; Fisher & Ury, 1986; Keltner, 1987; Kreidler, 1984; Prutzman, et al., 1988).

Noddings, in *Caring* (1984) and *The Challenge to Care in Schools* (1993), suggested a new focus for learning, predicated upon the values of care and equity. Only by translating those two values into behaviors within all our institutions—our homes, schools, hospitals, businesses, universities, and governments—can we work toward the good society. Noddings is only one of several scholars in different fields who urge educators to place a renewed emphasis on the individual-in-community. I endorse this renewed emphasis. Discussions of professional development are hollow shells unless they address the purpose for which the professionals are developing themselves: to establish an equitable and caring society.

A growing volume of literature analyzes the ways gender inequity pervades American society and the economic and social price we pay for such inequity (AAUW, 1992; Goldin, 1990; Wrigley, 1992). "In subtle and not so subtle ways [traditional assumptions about gender inequity] dot the tax code, regulation of sexual conduct, and the social security laws. Equal liberty, if taken seriously, would change much of this society's gender policy" (Kirp, Yudof, & Franks, 1986, p. 204). Although educators are loathe to consider it, they have had a crucial role, since the founding of the common schools, in educating girls and boys to adapt to gender inequity. Women as well as men have participated in this enterprise.

The barriers to overcoming inequities are institutional as well as ideological. Even feminist teachers critical of sexist practices are often "unclear how to fight them except by engaging in their own best practices" (Biklen, forthcoming, ch. 8). Educators have created their own inequitable hierarchies within schools, colleges, universities, teachers' unions, and professional organizations. "We must recognize the degree to which women who teach are complicit in this distribution of power between the sexes in the education establishment" (Grumet, 1988, p. 85). Shakeshaft (1986) claimed that any discussions of excellence in schooling can succeed only if equity is placed as the central focus. Though gender equity is the subject of this chapter, it is only one aspect of a broader concept of equity. Discussions of that broader concept have to include the other equity issues that impact the education of girls and boys, such as race, ethnicity, socioeconomic status, age, and ability.

GENDER IN THE CONSTRUCTION OF WHAT IT MEANS TO BE A PROFESSIONAL

Gender becomes an important category of analysis when we consider that the traditional definition of a professional has been based on the life experiences of men and that the majority of those with ultimate authority in schools and universities are men. Women's life experiences are significantly different from men's. According to feminist theorists, women place a greater emphasis on social interaction and personal relationships than men do. Women's lives often do not fit the linear structure proposed by accepted developmental theories, which were formulated by studying only the lives of men (Gilligan, 1982; Belenky et al., 1986). New ways of envisioning the adult lifespan include the interweaving of individual, family, and work as continuous threads, with different ones becoming salient for a person at various moments in time (Hughes & Graham, 1990; Juhasz, 1989; Merriam & Clark, 1991). Women's practice of improvisation has been suggested as a model worthy of adoption by men as well as women in the twenty-first century (Bateson, 1990) and has been documented in several longitudinal studies (Hulbert & Schuster, 1993).

None of these areas of research has impacted the reform literature on schooling or the discussions of professional development schools. Plans to increase the length of time between the end of formal course work in college and final qualification to teach in a classroom have been introduced with scant consideration of the differences between men's and women's life tasks or of possible different financial needs of men and women in their twenties. Bateson's arguments would lead one to take this issue further, since not only gender, but race, class and other variables, make it desirable that opportunities for a person's progress in any occupation be flexible rather than rigid throughout their lifetime.

Although our society prides itself on moving toward gender equity, the environment affects women differently from men. Success or failure at school and university, the demands of home and family, the demands of the workplace, each has been identified as affecting men and women differently. If men and women are to have equal access to professional careers, the demands placed upon professionals need to become more flexible, particularly at the start of their careers, a time that often coincides with family formation.

There is evidence, also, that women and men fare differently as they progress along the career path of educator. The plans, put forward in the mid-1980s by the Holmes Group and the Carnegie Commission, to provide advanced positions for teachers with leadership skills, indicate that gender has already influenced the discussions about the professional development of teachers. Women teachers have often said that they would prefer to remain teaching rather than take on administrative tasks. Thus, the move to increase the number of career development opportunities for teachers could be seen as addressing the needs of women teachers in particular, not only because women have voiced their preference but also because the number of administrative positions is limited. Men are more likely than women to obtain such positions. More teachers than ever before in the nation's schools have reached their forties and fifties and are therefore eligible for senior positions. In the past, the only way to "progress" up a career ladder in education was to move from teaching to administration. The reform plans make it possible to remain a teacher and still participate in professional development through additional responsibilities for mentoring young teachers and developing leadership in curriculum development. Such activities may take a teacher out of the classroom for some of his or her time but not for the majority of it.

Although a career ladder within teaching may meet women teachers' desire to remain primarily in the classroom, the very metaphor of a ladder creates a problem: classroom teachers are on the bottom rung. Those teachers who want to teach throughout their careers, without moving into curriculum development or supervision of junior colleagues, will come to be considered losers. What will result from assigning supervisory authority to "career" or "lead" teachers? Collegial relations among teachers will be destroyed. We need to ask: why has this new hierarchical structure been suggested for teaching now, at a moment when businesses are abandoning their hierarchies because new information technology can best be exploited through collaboration among equals (Zuboff, 1988). Where did the plan for developing career stages among teachers originate? Did it come from the university faculty among the reform groups? Was it their idea to superimpose upon schoolteachers the tripartite model of the university professoriate? Or did teachers urge the changes in order to provide themselves with new opportunities for professional growth? Wherever the plan originated, it runs counter to the egalitarian mode of operating favored by women teachers in the past and counter to new trends in business and industry. Before proceeding, we need to examine how it will change the culture of teaching, whether it will further a climate of care and equity among teachers themselves and among the students they teach.

We also need to step back and examine what it means to be a professional. For while professional development schools promise renewed empha-

sis on the professionalism of teachers, they do so at a moment when the traditional meaning of professionalism has been challenged. The original Holmes
Report, *Tomorrow's Teachers* (1986) treated the terms "professional" and
"professionalism" as unproblematic. One critic called the Group to task,
claiming

> the considerable literature on professions and professionalization suggests we
> are dealing with notions of importance; the terms are contested, the concepts
> are contested, with little agreement to be found. . . . To define professionaliza-
> tion is to make statements about the distribution of knowledge, power, and
> resources in society. (Soder, 1986, p. 5)

The literature on professional development schools refers to traditional
models of professionalism, citing, for example, the training for its members
provided by the medical profession. Yet, today, the medical model and the
whole edifice of technical rationality on which it is based have come under
attack. Roger Soder sees teachers' obsession with the medical model as blind-
ing them to future opportunities: "once teachers (and their leaders) cease
attempts to define themselves as 'professionals' in terms of the ideal of the
medical model, they will begin to free themselves from the tyranny of their
own dreams" (Soder, 1990, p. 72).

The challenges to the medical model of professionalism for schoolteachers come from parent advocates, usually mothers, and from paraprofessionals,
usually women. Both demand full partnership in the teaching-learning
process. Curiously, then, while women stand to benefit most from an increase
in teachers' professional status because women make up a majority of teachers, it is women, also, who make up the vanguard of the challenge to teachers.

The literature on professional development schools mentions little
about the contested nature of the term "professional," or the role of gender in
the construction of the term, or the challenges to that construction today.
These challenges suggest that the very distinctions between professional and
nonprofessional, and between professional and semiprofessional, need to be
reconsidered. Parent advocates of children with disabilities, for example,
(who most often are the mothers, not the fathers, of the children) usually
know their own child better than any teacher. They locate their child's learning within a broader context than the school.

However, their ability to communicate with their child's teacher is often
limited. To transpose Donald Schon's words, parents and teachers rarely share
the same appreciative system; the language they use, the repertoire of skills
they have, and the media they use for their work with children rarely corre-
spond (Schon, 1983).

Professional development schools certainly need to prepare new teacher
practitioners to reflect on their practice. Only when professionals understand
their own appreciative system, can they "construct virtual worlds in which to

carry out imaginative rehearsals of action" (Schon, 1983, p. 271). However, professional development schools must go further. Teachers also need to learn how to challenge the traditional appreciative system of teaching in order to expand their ability to define problems.

I think Schon underestimates the changes that must take place in the self-concept and practice of professionals once they accept the need to include clients and assistants, not previously thought capable of such action, in defining and resolving problems. Schon claims that professionals trained traditionally are well-equipped to solve problems but not to define problems for themselves. His solution is for professional education to include activities that call upon students to define problems as well as to solve them. However, I believe professional development schools must find another model. Rather than prepare teachers to define problems for themselves, or even prepare teachers to work merely with teams of other professionals to define problems, professional development schools have to experiment with ways to involve parents and so-called paraprofessionals also as full members of educational teams. Such teams have to be concerned with both defining and solving educational problems. To collaborate in those teams, teachers (as well as parents and paraprofessionals) may have to traverse boundaries of gender, race, and class prejudices as well as boundaries of traditional professional practice. This may call for courage because as Michelle Fine commented: "In low-income public schools organized around control through silence, the student, parent, teacher, or paraprofessional who talks, tells, or wants to speak transforms rapidly into the subversive, the troublemaker" (Fine, 1992, p. 132). Teachers have to learn not to transform some people into "the subversive, the troublemaker."

Professional development schools can play an important role in bringing this change about through substantively changing the education of teachers. Research into a new practice of collaboration among all the adults helping the development of each child will not only enlighten teaching but also will yield new theory concerning professionalism.

PROFESSIONAL DEVELOPMENT SCHOOLS:
WHERE TWO CULTURES MEET

If "discourses shape how people understand the world and therefore how they act in it" (Biklen, forthcoming, ch. 8), forging links among discourses must enable a person to expand his or her understanding of the world. Currently, the discourses among educators on equity and on professional development schools rarely intersect. While those writing about professional development schools rarely discuss gender equity, they do often contrast the culture of the school and the culture of the university. I examine what they say about these two cultures in the light of gender equity.

Many aims of professional development schools are similar to those of earlier university-school partnerships, such as laboratory schools. Most laboratory schools intended to prepare teachers and carry out empirical research conducted jointly by faculty and teachers. According to Stallings and Kowalski (1990) "No aspect of the laboratory school produced higher expectations and more disappointments than the area of research" (pp. 251–252). Similar expectations for teacher preparation and joint research are held for professional development schools. Despite its caveats against expecting such schools to deal with the whole spectrum of educational problems, the Holmes Group, for example, expects professional development schools to "be laboratories where astute people from universities and schools form alliances with the broader community to anticipate solutions to emerging social, economic, and political concerns" (Holmes Group, 1990, p. 4). While professional development schools should be places "where students and teachers work at the outer edges of their expertise, so too should they be places where educators and community leaders work at the outer edges of the educational and social problems facing children." This is a grandiose goal for university-school-community collaboration.

Most professional development schools have been started with more modest intentions but with high aspirations nonetheless. For example, a summer institute for Michigan State University faculty and schoolteachers working in six professional development schools was organized "to develop shared understandings about the new kinds of teaching, learning, and school organization and management that are needed and possible for the future" (Rosaen & Hoekwater, 1990, p. 145). After accepting as their purposes: "(a) teaching and learning for K-12 students; (b) pre-service and continuing professional development; and (c) the organization and management of schools" (p. 148), the university faculty and school teachers of the Elliott-MSU professional development school decided on three specific projects: Learning Community and Restructuring, Math Study Group, and Literacy in Science and Social Studies (p. 146). Rosaen and Hoekwater commented that "working together, collaborating, for these broad purposes and eventual benefits was an appealing idea that was very difficult to do" (p. 148). Several authors in the section of this book describing the professional development school in practice provide more detail about the difficulties collaborators encounter, particularly when they try to blend the separate cultures of schools and universities.

A significant difference in culture between schoolteachers and university faculty, identified by Case, Norlander, and Reagan (1993) is the different discourses each engage in. Discourse reveals both the power relationships among the participants and the social structure of their respective environments. The rules of discourse prescribe who may speak, whose experience will be valued, and what may be spoken about.

Established patterns of discourse tend to silence teachers in the presence of university faculty. When considering collaboration for teacher preparation and research, as when considering collaboration to articulate programs between schools and colleges, "the greatest stumbling blocks are not physical, but intellectual and social. . . . The details have to be worked out through a process of give and take [between equals]. . . . University professors, however, do not perceive schoolteachers to be their equals; professors feel they have a higher social status; intellectually they are closer to the frontiers of knowledge than are schoolteachers" (Burstyn, 1986, p. 186). Case, et al. suggested that a new culture of inquiry has to be generated among all members of a professional development school in order to overcome status differences, obliterate established patterns of discourse, and ensure the success of long-term collaborative efforts.

Despite Case, et al.'s optimism, I think such a culture of joint inquiry will be successful only if those devising it adopt a policy of gender equity, because gender is another source of status difference in the discourse between university faculty and schoolteachers. Despite recent attempts to foster equality between men and women, our society still assigns differential status to individuals according to their gender, assigning higher status to men than to women and to work performed by men than to work performed by women. Among the reasons for society assigning university teachers a higher status than schoolteachers is that the majority of university teachers are men while the majority of schoolteachers are women. A new culture of inquiry would overcome traditional roles of dominance and subordination between men and women and substitute egalitarian discourse between them only if members of the group agreed that these roles should be overcome and if there were open discussion about the ways they are, wittingly or unwittingly, played out.

Subcultures flourish, even within the university itself. Stoddart (1993) noted that within schools of education the faculty is divided between those who are teacher educators and work with the schools and those who concentrate on foundational subjects within the university. Stoddart draws attention to the fact that teacher educators are "often the most overworked and politically weakest group;" an increasing number are nontenured women. Stoddart claims here that a new source of gender discrimination is in creation at this very moment. Given the difficulties of designing collaborative research, the time needed to decide its form, to carry it out, and to write about it in a manner acceptable to all participants, many teacher educators, increasingly women, may find their chance for tenure dashed because they are less productive than their predominantly male peers who do not attempt to collaborate with practitioners in the field.

Only if school and university administrators provide care and equity for the schoolteachers and the faculty who work in professional development schools will those schools be capable of fostering the values of care and equity in their students.

GENDER EQUITY AND CAREER DEVELOPMENT FOR TEACHERS

As well as for the education of new teachers, professional development schools provide for the career development of experienced teachers. Are the values of care and equity central to the activities planned for career development? As Shakeshaft (1987) and others pointed out, the effective schools research emphasizes the importance of administrators' exhibiting caring and consideration while at the same time holding both faculty and students to high standards. These attributes characterize a style of administrative behavior often exhibited by women. Ortiz and Marshall (1988) reported that women administrators contribute to high standards by being actively engaged in instructional leadership. Insofar as professional development schools plan to further the development of a professional ladder for classroom teachers, they will add to the numbers of schoolteachers with advanced skills in instruction and curriculum development.

However, while women's expertise and interest in issues of instruction and curriculum may serve them well in some administrative positions, it may not be sufficient preparation for others. A study of women superintendents who had left the superintendency by Tallerico, et al. (1993) suggested that women aspirants to the superintendency may be less well prepared than men for the political give-and-take of the job and for the supervision of nonacademic operations such as building maintenance and transportation. As one of the respondents in the study said: "Technically I was able to run the school district very well. It was the politics of it that were very, very, very difficult" (Tallerico, et al., 1994, p. 443). I suggest that professional development schools are places where innovative internships for women and men might be devised that expand their knowledge of ways to interact with local politicians, parents, and other concerned citizens. This project would be another context for exploring the redefinition of professionalism described above.

GENDER EQUITY IN THE RESEARCH AGENDAS OF
PROFESSIONAL DEVELOPMENT SCHOOLS

Is gender equity central to the research activities of professional development schools? Not yet. Gender equity, either as subject or process, has not taken center stage. Research projects often focus on the teaching and learning of traditional school subjects. These are rarely problematized by the researchers as being possibly gender-specific, racist, or classist.

Issues of care and equity are not ignored in the public schools, however. For example, in several middle and junior high schools, the New York State Occupational Education Equity Center promotes gender equity in conjunction with the National Career Development Guidelines. The aim is to help girls as well as boys understand that the choices they make in middle and high school regarding mathematics and science courses will shape their future career. The project also impresses upon their teachers and counselors that certain jobs—among them those that are highly rewarded—will be closed to students steered away from or unsuccessful in advanced math and science courses. Data on achievement in the United States show that girls score lower on mathematics tests than boys. Girls also feel less confident of their abilities in mathematics, they are unlikely to connect those abilities with their career plans, and they play down their mathematical abilities in front of their peers (Kramer & Lehman, 1990). These behaviors have important consequences for girls in later life because many well-paid jobs demand advanced mathematical skills and our society may already have begun a "long-term process whereby highly-educated women make strides toward greater parity with men, while less-educated women remain trapped in female job ghettoes" (Wrigley, 1992, p. 19).

Minority women are likely to suffer more than white women from such a process because a larger proportion of them are among the less-educated. As I have written with regard to gender and technology: "Gender segregation should be a source of great concern to all citizens, but especially to educators. It indicates that, while we may claim to be a society committed to equal opportunity and to eliminating gender (as well as racial and other) inequities, we hold to an ideology that runs counter to this claim" (Burstyn, 1993, p.113).

Although the data indicate that biases against equity still exist in society, some girls and women, as some boys and men, resist societal norms. They break through barriers not only to advance personally but also to make and maintain relationships (Bateson, 1990). Professional development schools need to innovate ways to foster such resistance. They need to encourage caring and equity in the curriculum and in methods of teaching, assess the results of such innovations, and publicize them as widely as possible.

CONCLUSION

Teachers and university faculty have high expectations for professional development schools. The rhetoric has been exuberant, the reality less dramatic. As mentioned at the beginning of this chapter, professional development schools are expected to become "places where educators and community leaders work at the outer edges of the educational and social problems facing children" (Holmes Group, 1990, p. 4). However, in this chapter I have argued that such expectations cannot be met so long as those running professional development schools evade the problematic nature of assumptions that underlie their enterprise.

I have suggested that the values of gender equity and care should be at the heart of the work of professional development schools. In the light of these values, the very definition of professionalism adopted in the literature on professional development schools becomes subject to contestation. Any questioning of that definition will, inevitably, involve both schoolteachers and university faculty in a reconsideration of the roles and the reward systems of their own institutions. If professional development schools are to flourish in the long-term, they will inevitably have to forge new roles and new rewards for those working in them. I have argued, also, that by critiquing the term professional from the perspective of gender equity and care, those in professional schools may challenge the stages of career development for teachers put forward by reform groups in the 1980s.

Lastly, I have proposed that by focusing on the values of gender equity and care, researchers will be able to change the attitudes and behaviors of those students who currently are disadvantaged in our educational system. I have concentrated on gender inequity, but I know that it intersects with other inequities such as those relating to race, class, and disability. Each has to be addressed. In the new professional development schools, schoolteachers and university faculty, as members of teams investigating practice, have the opportunity to try out and assess innovations to bring about a caring and equitable society. We must not let this opportunity slip by us. We must place issues of care and equity at the heart of our work.

NOTE

1. I should like to thank Miu-yin Mak for her assistance in preparing materials for this chapter.

REFERENCES

American Association of University Women. (1992). *How schools short-change girls. A study of major findings on girls and education.* Researched by the Wellesley College Center for Research on Women. Washington, D.C.

Bateson, M. C. (1990). *Composing a life.* New York: Penguin Books.

Belenky, M. F., Clinchy, B. M., Goldberger, N. R., & Tarule, J. M. (1986). *Women's ways of knowing: The development of self, voice, and mind.* New York: Basic Books.

Biklen, S. K. (1995). *School work: Gender and the cultural construction of teaching.* New York: Teachers College Press.

Burstyn. J. N. (1986). The challenge to education of new technology. In J. N. Burstyn (Ed.), *Preparation for life? The paradox of education in the late twentieth century* (pp. 178–195). Philadelphia: Falmer Press.

Burstyn, J. N. (1993). Who benefits and who suffers: Gender and education at the dawn of the age of information technology. In S. K. Biklen and D. Pollard (Eds.), *Gender and education* (pp. 107–125). Chicago: National Society for the Study of Education.

Case, C. W., Norlander, K. A., & Reagan, T. G. (1993). Cultural transformation in an urban professional development center: Policy implications for school-university collaboration. *Educational Policy, 7*(1), 40–60.

Cheatham, A. (1989). *Annotated bibliography for teaching conflict resolution in schools.* 2nd. ed. Amherst, MA: National Association for Mediation in Education.

de Bono, E. (1985). *Conflicts: A better way to resolve them.* Harmondsworth: Penguin Books.

Fine, M. (1992). *Disruptive voices: The possibilities of feminist research.* Ann Arbor: University of Michigan Press.

Fisher, R., & Ury, W. (1981, 1986). *Getting to yes: Negotiating agreement without giving in.* Harmondsworth, Penguin Books.

Gilligan, C. (1982). *In a different voice: Psychological theory and women's development.* Cambridge, MA: Harvard University Press.

Goldin, C. (1990). *Understanding the gender gap: An economic history of American women.* New York: Oxford University Press.

Grumet, M. R. (1988). *Bitter milk: Women and teaching.* Amherst: University of Massachusetts Press.

Holmes Group. (1986). *Tomorrow's teachers.* East Lansing, MI: Author.

Holmes Group. (1990). *Tomorrow's schools: Principles for the design of professional development schools.* East Lansing, MI: Author.

Hughes, J., & Graham. S. (1990, Spring). Adult life roles. *Journal of Continuing Higher Education 38*(2), 2–8.

Hulbert, K. D. & Schuster, D. T. (1993). *Women's lives through time: Educated American women of the 20th century.* San Francisco: Jossey Bass.

Juhasz, A. M. (1989). A role-based approach to adult development: The triple helix model. *International Journal of Aging and Human Development, 29*(4), 301–315.

Keltner, J. W. (1987). *Mediation: Toward a civilized system of dispute resolution.* Urbana, IL: ERIC Clearinghouse on Reading and Communication Skills, and Annandale, VA: Speech Communication Association.

Kirp, D. L., Yudof, M. G., & Franks, M. S. (1986). *Gender justice.* Chicago: University of Chicago Press.

Kramer, P. E., & Lehman, S. (1990, Autumn). Mismeasuring women: A critique of research on computer ability and avoidance. *Signs: Journal of Women in Culture and Society, 16*(1), 158–172.

Kreidler, W. J. (1984). *Creative conflict resolution: More than 200 activities for keeping peace in the classroom K–6.* Glenview, IL: Scott, Foresman & Company.

Merriam, S. B., & Clark, M. C. (1991). *Lifelines: Patterns of work, love, and learning in adulthood.* San Francisco: Jossey-Bass.

Noddings, N. (1984). *Caring: A feminine approach to ethics and moral education.* Berkeley: University of California Press.

Noddings, N. (1993). *The challenge to care in schools.* New York: Teachers College Press.

Ortiz, F. L. & Marshall, C. (1988). Women in educational administration. In N. J. Boyan (Ed.), *Handbook of research on educational administration.* White Plains, NY: Longman.

Prutzman, P., Burger, M. L., Bodenhamer, G., & Stern, L. (1988). *The friendly classroom for a small planet: A handbook on creative approaches to living and problem solving for children.* Wayne, NJ: Avery Publishing Group.

Riley, M. Dissertation in process on the promotion of gender equity in middle and junior high schools in New York State, Syracuse University.

Rosaen, C. L., & Hoekwater, E. (1990, Spring). Collaboration: Empowering educators to take charge. *Contemporary Education, 61*(3): 144–51.

Schon, D. A. (1983). *The reflective practitioner: How professionals think in action.* New York: Basic Books.

Shakeshaft, C. (1986, March). A gender at risk. *Phi Delta Kappan:* 499–503.

Shakeshaft, C. (1987). *Women in educational administration.* Newbury Park, CA: Sage.

Soder, R. (1986, November/December). Tomorrow's teachers for whom and for what? Missing propositions in the Holmes Group report. *Journal of Teacher Education, 37*(6) 2–5.

Soder, R. (1990). The rhetoric of teacher professionalization. In J. I. Goodlad, R. Soder, & K. A. Sirotnik, (Eds.), *The moral dimensions of teaching.* San Francisco: Jossey-Bass.

Stallings, J. A., & Kowalski, T. (1990). Research on professional development schools. In W. R. Houston, M. Haberman, and J. Sikula. (Eds.), *Handbook of research on teacher education* (pp. 251–263). New York: Macmillan.

Stoddard, T. (1993). The professional development school: Building bridges between cultures. *Educational Policy, 7*(1), 5–23.

Tallerico, M., Burstyn, J. N., & Poole. W. (1993). Gender and politics at work: Why women exit the superintendency. (Research Monograph). Fairfax, VA: National Policy Board for Educational Administration.

Tallerico, M., Poole, W., & Burstyn, J. N. (1994, January). Exits from urban superintendencies: The intersection of politics, race, and gender. *Urban Education, 28*(4): 439–54.

Wrigley, J. (Ed.) (1992). *Education and gender equality.* London: Falmer Press.

Zuboff, S. (1988). *In the age of the smart machine.* New York: Basic Books.

Part VI

A New Paradigm for Practical Research

A number of threads have been running throughout the foregoing chapters—culture clashes and changes; issues of professionalism, partnership, and power; traditional roles of teachers in both schools and colleges and universities; and the nature of research and inquiry in professional development schools. The reigning conception of educational research as applied social science aimed at discovering laws of teaching and learning provides a kind of rationale for the traditional separation of roles between school and higher education faculty. Higher education discovers the laws of teaching and learning and then transmits them to the schools where they are faithfully implemented to improve education. Unfortunately, long before the rise in popularity of professional development schools, there were precious few examples of how such putative research actually made a difference in the practical business of schooling.

As school and higher education faculty begin to interact more and more with each other in professional development settings, the nature of the appropriate kind of inquiry for such settings comes more and more into question. The concrete, particularistic, situated nature of inquiry in the schools seems much different from laboratory investigations into general laws of teaching and learning. More and more thinkers are beginning to question just how helpful traditional applied social science research can be in the context of professional development schools.

In this concluding section, I examine some of the reasons why traditional research may have been of such little help to the practical business of education. I then outline an emerging view of human action that seems much more compatible with the kinds of inquiry arising from professional development schools than the more traditional forms of educational research.

Chapter Seventeen

A New Paradigm for Practical Research

Why has nearly a century or more of educational research been of so little help in actually improving teaching and learning? Why is educational research preoccupied with "method" and methodological disputes to a much higher degree than "real" science? With the increased attention during the last several years to inquiry in authentic educational settings, such as professional development schools, what kind of educational research is likely to make a difference? How will we know?

There are doubtless any number of answers to these questions, but in this chapter, I want to explore one possible line of thought that can both account for the paucity of serious research results in teaching and learning as well as suggest why certain kinds of situated and context-dependent inquiry in professional development schools hold much more promise of actually making a difference.

It is important that I say what I am not going to do. I am not going to consider the vast quantity of philosophical, historical, political, and sociological analyses of various aspects of education. Much of this work has been of significant importance in increasing our understanding of education and may well escape the critique I will offer. Nor am I going to conduct an exhaustive review of the literature to cover all of the claims and counterclaims and methodological disputes and controversies surrounding educational research.

Rather, I want to concentrate on the core psychological and social psychological research that has long been taken by many to be the key to understanding teaching and learning and how to make them better. I will examine in some depth four representative analyses of research into teaching and learning over the past several decades and consider why these penetrating critiques have not, at least up until now, had much effect on our conduct of educational research into teaching and learning.

What I will suggest is that the theories of learning and behavior of the past 100 years or so, from behaviorism to constructivism, have relied on a flawed conception of human nature. However, as Kuhn (1970) clearly showed, until a more reasonable conception comes along, all of the problems in a research paradigm will be "solved" by adding complications to the existing theory or by that most ubiquitous of journal article endings, "more research is needed!" Just as the Ptolemaicists added epicycle upon epicycle to save their earth-centered theory of the universe from constant anomalies, so also do traditional psychologists protect their core beliefs by adding ad hoc assumption after ad hoc assumption. Indeed, the psychologists are even worse. To compensate for an inadequate fundamental conception of human nature, they have utilized the sophisticated mathematical discipline of statistics to explain away what would otherwise be plain to everyone as wholly inadequate accounts of human behavior.

THE IMPOTENCE OF CRITIQUE

Upon the occasion of his receiving the Distinguished Scientist Award of Division 12, Section 3 of the American Psychological Association, Paul Meehl delivered a lecture later published (1978) with the revealing title, "Theoretical Risks and Tabular Asterisks: Sir Karl, Sir Ronald, and the Slow Progress of Soft Psychology." In this article, Meehl argued forcefully that one of psychology's major mistakes has been in trusting too much in Sir Ronald (Fisher) and his notions of significance testing and too little in Sir Karl (Popper) and his theory of falsification.

The point is well known in philosophy of science. If one is trying to test a scientific hypothesis (H), in conditions (C), using auxiliary apparatus and methods (A), then typically one tries to predict from the conjunction of these situations some observation (O), that one believes one can make. That is, if H and C and A, then O. The problem is that if one actually does observe what is predicted, there is nothing, logically, that can be concluded, for the observation might well have been an accident. To conclude that H is, in fact, true, would be to commit the logical fallacy of affirming the consequent. This is the well-known "paradox of confirmation" (Carnap, 1950).

On the other hand, as Popper (1959, 1962, 1972) has pointed out, if the predicted observation does not occur, that is, if not-O, then a very strong conclusion can be reached via the logical inference of modus tollens. Either the hypothesis is not true or the conditions did not hold, or the auxiliary apparatus and methods are wrong. In the hard sciences (perhaps this is why they are hard), there is seldom any doubt that the conditions did hold and the apparatus, for example, measuring devices, are based on well-established theories. Consequently, one can usually conclude that the hypothesis is false. From these facts, Popper develops his notion of falsification. The important thing for a science to do is to expose its hypotheses to strong tests that would tend to falsify them. Platt (1973) elaborated this into the notion of "strong inference" which suggests that sciences that are really on the right track seldom, if ever, engage in significance testing. Rather they elaborate alternatives to account for the phenomena and quickly proceed, through exposing them to strong possibilities of falsification, to eliminate them. The ones that withstand this process of falsification have some real claim to validity and are embedded into the well-tested core of the science.

Not so with the soft sciences of psychology. Instead, as Meehl (1978) so aptly pointed out, hypotheses in psychology "suffer the fate that General MacArthur ascribed to old generals—they never die, they just slowly fade away" (p. 807). Meehl listed some 20 intrinsic difficulties in making psychology into a real science. I shall return to one of them—the problem of intentionality—below, but his major target is the poor way of doing science represented by the overwhelming reliance on significance testing instead of falsification. He said:

> I believe that the almost universal reliance on merely refuting the null hypothesis as the standard method for corroborating substantive theories in the soft areas is a terrible mistake, is basically unsound, poor scientific strategy, and one of the worst things that ever happened in the history of psychology (p. 817).

Essentially, Meehl's argument is that because of the extremely complex nature of human behavior, it will never be possible to make certain that all of the potentially contributing factors to any result are either equal or properly counterbalanced. For example, test scores of students taught by whole language versus phonics may be due to the treatment *or* to one or another of the complexities of the conditions affecting individual students. Consequently, with any reasonable set of measures the null hypothesis will *always* be falsified, but we will never know whether or not it is because the substantive hypothesis is actually true or because of one or more of the complexities in the antecedent conditions. Consequently, the *inevitable* result in psychological theorizing with significance testing will be that we will have mixed results.

Why then, in the face of this powerful methodological critique, do we still find journal articles and graduate methodology courses religiously using significance testing? Even worse, why do we eyeball the tables of results and count up the places in which there is a significant difference and those in which there is not and somehow conclude something substantive about what has occurred? Meehl's answer is that the hard scientist

> has a sufficiently powerful invisible hand theory that enables him to generate an expected curve for his experimental results. He plots the observed points, looks at the agreement, and comments that 'the results are in reasonably good accord with theory.' Moral: *It is always more valuable to show approximate agreement of observations with a theoretically predicted numerical point value, rank order, or function form, than it is to compute a 'precise probability' that something merely differs from something else* (1978, p. 825).

What does Meehl mean by an "invisible hand theory?" I suggest that he is referring to an underlying model, which, if it operates as hypothesized, would yield the predictions. This would be like the kinetic theory of gases, or electromagnetism, or chemical bonding. These models in the hard sciences allow us to make precise predictions of observed features of temperatures, meter readings, and chemical reactions. We have historically had nothing remotely resembling such a model in the soft science of psychology, and the bare bones empiricism of speaking of stimuli and responses or independent and dependent variables succeeds at best in redescribing the phenomena rather than providing an explanatory theory. Consequently, despite the power of Meehl's critique of significance testing, in the absence of any notion of a powerful generative model, psychologists continue to rely on statistical significance testing.

Three years before Meehl's 1978 article, Lee Cronbach (1975) published, "Beyond the Two Disciplines of Scientific Psychology" based on his Distinguished Scientific Contribution Award from the American Psychological Association. In critiquing the paucity of results from aptitude-treatment interaction (ATI) research that he himself had strongly advocated nearly twenty years earlier, Cronbach asked, "Should social science aspire to reduce behavior to laws?" (p. 116).

Cronbach, too, accepts the basic formulation of the problem facing psychology to be that of predicting observed behavior from the conjunction of hypothesized laws, initial conditions, and experimental apparatus. If H and C and A, then O. The aptitude-treatment interaction line of research is essentially an attempt to specify the various conditions, C, under which different observations might be predicted. For example, if one's instructional hypothesis, H, is that students learn better if they are challenged by the instructor, ATI research suggests that this tends to be true under conditions, C_1, where the student has the personality type to seek challenges and accept responsibility, but not so under conditions, C_2, where the student is more defensive.

But, as Cronbach (1975), pointed out, the potential number of conditions that might need to be considered is limitless.

If Aptitude × Treatment × Sex interact, for example, then the Aptitude × Treatment effect does not tell the story. Once we attend to interactions, we enter a hall of mirrors that extends to infinity. However far we carry our analysis, to third order or fifth order or any other, untested interactions of a still higher order can be envisioned (p. 119).

The complexity of seemingly limitless potential interactions was not all that troubled Cronbach. He also suggested that generalizations decay over time and psychological generalizations decay more rapidly than do generalizations in the physical sciences. This is due to a number of factors, chief among which is the changeable nature of the social and psychological world that render any hypotheses we might suggest valid for only a very short period of time.

Our troubles do not arise because human events are in principle unlawful; man and his creations are part of the natural world. The trouble, as I see it, is that we cannot store up generalizations and constructs for ultimate assembly into a network. . . . If the effect of a treatment changes over a few decades, that inconsistency is an effect, a Treatment × Decade interaction that must itself be regulated by whatever laws there be (p. 123).

There are regularities of the "if H and C and A, then O" variety in psychology according to Cronbach, but they change so rapidly that we can never assemble them into a theory. So what did he suggest?

Instead of making generalization the ruling consideration in our research, I suggest that we reverse our priorities. An observer collecting data in one particular situation is in a position to appraise a practice or proposition in that setting, observing effects in context. In trying to describe and account for what happened, he will give attention to whatever variables were controlled, but he will give equally careful attention to uncontrolled conditions, to personal characteristics, and to events that occurred during treatment and measurement. As he goes from situation to situation, his first task is to describe and interpret the effect anew in each locale, perhaps taking into account factors unique to that locale or series of events. . . . (pp. 124–125)

So *context* and the interpretation of events in context become important to the psychologist. We must pay particular attention to the variability of human action in even one actor, let alone across different individuals and how (presumably) the *same* effect can occur anew in differing and unique locales. Yet, despite the trenchant critique of seeking if-then lawlike generalizations, Cronbach continues to hold to the position that there are such laws; we just cannot discover them quickly enough. Consequently, those who would take an anthropological approach to interpreting human behavior are still not quite fully scientific. They are just doing the best that they can.

Going back even farther, I investigated another reason for the paucity of educational results emanating from psychology in my paper, "Why Has Learning Theory Failed to Teach Us How to Learn," (Petrie, 1968). The major burden of the argument was that classical stimulus-response theory, along with most then-extant variants, was simply inadequate to account for human intentionality. Furthermore, educational practice is shot through and through with presumptions that human behavior is fundamentally intentional in character. That is, teachers, students, administrators, parents, policy makers, indeed, all of us, do things on purpose, in order to pursue certain goals, not because of the operation of some "if-then law," no matter how complex or short its half-life might be.

Thus, learning theory had failed to teach us how to learn, I argued, because it was, in an essential way, talking about something quite different from what educators were talking about. The solution I proposed at that time was either to recast education into stimulus-response terms (something I felt had little chance of success) or find a way in which our psychological theorizing could take account of human intentionality. In the language of the time, the problem was to show how reasons could be conceived of as causes, not simply "if-then" causes, but rather "in order that" causes.

I would now slightly rephrase the point that learning theorists and educators are essentially talking about different things. The fundamental interest of the educator is in the individual student. What can I do to help Suzy or Johnny learn about diverse cultures? How can I do this when I know that Suzy comes from a bigoted family and Johnny is the son of a biracial couple? The fundamental interest of the learning theorist is in the laws of learning as they apply to all students. In principle, these interests of the educator and the learning theorist could overlap considerably. It is logically possible that the laws of learning apply to all individuals, just as the laws of mechanics apply to all point masses.

However, it is clear by now that this logical possibility has not been realized in practice. We have no degree of real assurance that any laws of learning apply to individuals. Any given person may or may not react as predicted. This could be due to a variety of reasons. It might be that human behavior is simply so complex that, although the laws of learning do apply, the complexities of the situation preclude our being able to use them with any reliability. To continue the mechanics analogy, it would be like trying to predict when a given leaf from a tree would fall in the autumn and what path it would take in reaching the ground. All of those phenomena are clearly governed by the laws of mechanics, but the situation is too complex to allow for any meaningful prediction.

My suspicion is that most learning theorists implicitly assume this tack. This approach maintains the hegemony of traditional psychology and learning theory in educational research, while explaining away the lack of any more useful guidance than has been forthcoming. Furthermore, there are just enough semiuseful statistical generalizations to allow teachers to "apply" learning theory in their classrooms and reach some kind of success with at least a portion of their students. They are, however, completely befuddled by why they are unsuccessful with the rest. The learning theorists, on the other hand, as we have seen with Cronbach, paint a picture of very complex laws, highly dependent on individual differences, which might, nonetheless, ultimately yield to more sophisticated investigations.

An alternative explanation of the difference between learning theorists and educators is that educators, in their emphasis on the individual, intuitively know that not only do different individuals behave differently, but that the same individual will vary his or her behavior in varying circumstances in order to reach consistent ends. In short, educators recognize what conventional learning theorists typically do not, that individual behavior is fundamentally purposive and intentional. The question then becomes not one of increasing the complexity of traditional learning theory accounts but of giving a persuasive account of how intentional action on the part of students and teachers is possible.

To put the problem in terms of the preceding discussion, we need to come up with a generative model of human behavior, an invisible hand theory in Meehl's terms, that can account for the seemingly indefinite number of ways in which human beings can pursue their goals in the face of the kind of constantly changing circumstances noted by Cronbach. Furthermore, if at all possible, the model should not be that of infinitely complex "if-then laws" that would cover all of the possible interactions.

In many respects, the current so-called constructivist theories of behavior (e.g., Brown, Collins, & Duguid, 1989) have taken seriously the challenge to account for human intentionality. We construct meaning out of our individual experience on the basis of our wants, desires, needs, and the limitations imposed by the physical and social environments.

However, it is not clear that the recent spate of constructivist theories has yet broken free of the linear causation implied by the "if-then" form of causal laws. The constructivists still tend to phrase their speculations in the form of, "If I *intend* to get to students to learn to read and I *believe* in the efficacy of phonics instruction, then I will drill students on the various sound combinations." This is, of course, tremendously oversimplified, but it illustrates the kind of linear causation from intention and belief to behavior.

But what has not happened, for the most part, is the creation of invisible hand or generative models of behavior that would allow the specific, "point predictions" spoken of by Meehl. There is one promising exception that I will note later, but in general we are still at a very primitive level in our psychological theorizing. In fact, most of the "theorizing" is probably not much more than a kind of "explanation by redescription." That is, our theories are seldom much more than describing consistent phenomena with pretentious language and claiming that we have constructed a theory. "Why isn't Johnny paying attention?" "Oh, he has attention deficit disorder." "What is that?" "Attention Deficit Disorder is the tendency not to pay attention."

Faced with this kind of impasse in traditional approaches to psychological theorizing, it is no wonder that some educational researchers simply throw up their hands at any possibility of finding an underlying theory of human behavior and turn to exploring what they call alternative forms of understanding. In his 1993 AERA Presidential Address, "Forms of Understanding and the Future of Educational Research," Elliot Eisner explored just these notions. He built upon his deep experience with the arts to argue for multiple conceptions of ways of knowing related to multiple forms of representation that different people bring to experience.

Eisner (1993) paid particular attention to how we learn to experience the world. He argued persuasively that perception or experience is not some neutral given upon which we impose interpretations; rather the very substance of what we experience is the result of an interaction of mind and sense. "I came to believe that humans do not simply have experience; they have a hand in its creation, and the quality of their creation depends upon the ways they employ their minds" (p. 5).

It is important to note, as Eisner (1993) said,

> In talking about experience and its relationship to the forms of representation that we employ, I am not talking about poetry and pictures, literature and dance, mathematics and literal statement simply as alternative *means* for displaying what we know. I am talking about the forms of understanding, the *unique* forms of understanding that poetry and pictures, literature and dance, mathematics and literal language make possible (Emphasis added, p. 8).

In short, Eisner is suggesting that traditional psychology, with its impoverished conceptual schemes, simply cannot account for the multiple experiences that we have. Consequently, we need to simply cordon off these multiple modes of experience and grant them their own autonomy as ways of knowing.

To this end, Eisner suggests a number of changes that might take place in educational research. We would probably see an expansion of research methods, for example, an increasing use of narrative and poetic forms of research. Furthermore, such an expansion would likely have an effect on the ways in which we teach various subjects. We would be more likely, for example, in teaching history to make use of music, architecture, film, stories, and the like, not only as parts of traditional lectures but as unique ways in which they can shed light on the history in question. Student demonstrations of competence would also differ. We might see some preparing a video, others writing a poem, still others engaging in some action project, and some continuing to demonstrate their competence through multiple choice exams and traditional dissertations.

Carrying the speculation even further, Eisner asks what might the presentation of educational research look like? Would novels count? A multimedia presentation? An MTV video? How might all of this be judged?

Yet, there are difficulties that this kind of "multiple forms of understanding" approach raises. How, for example, is it even possible for us to understand what Eisner is proposing, unless we have some overarching form of understanding in terms of which we can see and appreciate the possibility that poems might complement or supplement what we can learn from descriptions and numbers? In other words, if these different forms of understanding are *completely* different, how will we ever be able to integrate the understandings that each provides into some sort of human whole? Will we each be segregated into a literal self, a numerical self, a poetic self, an artistic self? As Eisner (1993) himself asked, "Can we translate what is specific and unique to forms other than those in which such understanding is revealed?" (p. 10)

So, despite the allure of the concept of multiple forms of understanding, we seem to be driven back toward some general notion of human understanding and behavior that could account for our ability to engage in and understand these different forms. We need, apparently, to be able to see these multiple activities and understandings in a unified way *both* as something human beings do *and* as diverse activities within that understanding. Once again the critique of traditional psychological theorizing can be seen as important but not quite powerful enough to turn the tide.

A POSSIBLE SYNTHESIS

What, then, are the major challenges facing psychological educational research? From Meehl we get a powerful critique of traditional significance testing as a way of deciding among hypotheses. He also suggests that we need a generative model (invisible hand theory) that can underlie and account for the surface predictions we do make. From Cronbach we see the indefinite complexity that appears to attend the attempts to get traditional if-then laws to account for individual human behavior. He suggests that we must always take context into account. I have argued that human purposefulness and intentionality must be the central feature for which any theory of behavior must account. Eisner reminds us of the incredible variety of ways of dealing with our world we human beings employ and of just how central is the function of how we perceive or experience that world.

Interestingly, over the past 20 years or so, there has begun to emerge a small, still highly controversial, body of work that promises to meet all of the challenges to psychological educational research enumerated above. This conception of human behavior was given its most powerful formulation by W. T.

Powers (1973) in his book, *Behavior: the Control of Perception*. Most recently in education, it has been the subject of a spirited debate in the pages of *Educational Researcher* (Cziko, 1992a, 1992b; Amundson, Serlin, & Lehrer, 1992). There are also a number of other researchers from a variety of disciplines contributing to this body of research in psychology (Powers, 1989; Robertson and Powers, 1990), experimental psychology (Bourbon, 1990; Hershberger, 1988; Marken, 1986, 1989, 1990, 1992), clinical psychology (Ford, 1993, 1994; Goldstein, 1990), education (Bohannon, Powers, & Schoepfle, 1974; Petrie, 1974, 1979, 1981), management (Forssell, 1993), sociology (McClelland, 1994; McPhail, 1991; McPhail, Powers, & Tucker, 1992), ethology (Plooij & van deRijt-Plooij, 1990), law (Gibbons, 1990), and economics (Williams, 1989, 1990).

This new conception of human nature is called perceptual control theory and, as the title of Powers' book implies, it fundamentally turns our conceptions of human nature on their heads. Instead of viewing behavior as the outcome of stimuli or perceptions (as modified by cognition, emotions, or planning), perceptual control theory views behavior as the means by which a perceived state of affairs is brought to and maintained at a (frequently varying) reference or goal state. Perceptual control theory escapes the problem of modeling behavior as planned and computed output, an approach that requires levels of precise calculation that are unrealistic in a physical system and impossible in a real environment that is changing from one moment to the next. Instead, perceptual control theory provides a physically plausible explanation both for the consistency of outcomes of human action and the variability of means utilized to achieve those outcomes in a constantly changing environment.

Perceptual control theory makes use of the "circular causation" found in engineering control and servo-mechanism theory. Thermostats and cruise control systems are everyday examples of mechanical control systems that keep the perception of temperature or speed near the reference levels set for them. Many people, when hearing of these engineering control systems as examples, are immediately put off by perceptual control theory, thinking that it must be a highly mechanistic theory. Nothing could be further from the truth. Engineering control systems arose precisely from the problem of wanting to create mechanical systems that behaved like human beings as we might go about the tasks of governing temperature, maintaining speed, tracking targets and so on.

Paradoxical as it may seem, traditional psychology with its emphasis on if-then, stimulus-response, input-output, independent-dependent variable kinds of laws and its efforts to model itself on physics adopted the truly mechanistic view of behavior. On the other hand, engineers, unencumbered by worries about psychology and interested only in obtaining performances from mechanical systems analogous to what real people can do, were able to create a theory that is much more amenable to modeling actual human behavior than those created by the psychologists.

It is not possible in this short chapter to give a complete introduction to perceptual control theory. Cziko (1992a) gives a brief introduction and the classic is still Powers' (1973) wide-ranging and very readable presentation. What I will do here is provide a very brief sketch of how perceptual control theory begins to answer the major challenges to traditional psychology outlined previously.

Meehl's critique of significance testing and call for appropriate "invisible hand" models are met head-on. In the areas in which they have been tested, generative models based on perceptual control theory have been developed that correlate with the actual point by point behavior of individual subjects at values between .97 and .99 (e.g., Bourbon, 1990; Marken, 1986, 1989, 1992). These are, furthermore, real "invisible hand" models, in that, once built, they predict entirely novel behavior in situations not before encountered.

This capacity of the theory relates to Cronbach's concerns with the seemingly indefinite number of variables that might enter into any of the more traditional laws of learning. Consider the mechanical cruise control system. There are an indefinite number of factors that might keep a car from maintaining a certain speed—headwinds, crosswinds, hills, curves, poor quality gasoline—the list is endless. If we tried to build a mechanical system that would be able to determine when any of these features might interfere with the desired speed (which desired speed itself might change from time to time during a trip), and also include the capacity for calculating just how much gas to deliver to the engine to overcome any of these disturbances, we might well conclude that the "individual differences" in the mechanical case were every bit as daunting as Cronbach concluded they were in the human case.

But that is not what the engineers did. Rather, they built a mechanism that sensed the speed of the car, compared that speed to the desired one, and if it was too slow, fed more gas to the engine and if too fast, decreased the gas. The cruise control *does not know and does not care* what causes the speed to depart from its desired level, it just compensates for it when it does. In short, it controls the perception of the speed of the car, keeping it very close to the desired level, and it does this in a "circular causation" kind of way in which the output affects the input at the same time as the input is being compared to the reference speed and the difference between the two is actuating the output.

Note, too, that this is just how the human driver without cruise control behaves. We do not check headwinds or hills, especially if they are slight, and compute how much to depress or let up on the accelerator. Rather, we monitor the speedometer and no matter what the cause of a change in the speed we want to maintain, we depress or let up on the accelerator accordingly.

Similarly with learning. The expert teacher (e.g., Berliner, 1989) does not calculate what to do to counteract each disturbance to a child's learning. Rather, the expert senses the difficulties the child is having and in a flowing way adjusts to the situation. Indeed, such an ability to sense the teaching act at this more abstract level is precisely what distinguishes the more expert teacher from the novice who mostly relies on mechanical step-by-step recipes. In short, the expert teacher has a reference level for students learning a particular concept or fact and is constantly comparing the perception of the students' performance with that level and varying outputs to bring the teacher's perception into congruence with the reference level for learning. The expert teacher no more needs to know the detailed "laws of learning" than does the cruise control system need to know the physics of how an incline will slow down the momentum of the car.

Context is, indeed, all important, but a control system does not, in most cases, need to sense the context in order to take it into account. Context is simply another name for the myriad differences in a constantly changing environment. These changes act as disturbances to the perceived variable (e.g., the speed of the car or the learning of the student) that is being controlled. Unless the disturbances are overwhelming, good control systems sense the difference between what they desire to perceive and what they are perceiving and automatically behave in ways tending to counteract the disturbance.

A central function of perceptual control theory is to account for intentionality and purpose. Control systems are precisely organized to allow a consistent end to be reached with varying means in a constantly changing environment. If, on my trip to the office, I find a street blocked off, I find another way, even if I have never gone that way before. I usually do not even need a "detour" sign to tell me what to do. I can simply vary my behavior appropriately in these changed circumstances to achieve my goal. I can also vary my proximal goal of getting to the office in light of the higher order goal of stopping to help an accident victim.

Similarly with the expert teacher. If the books for the students have not arrived, adjustments can be made. In order to achieve the overall goal of understanding the United States constitution, the teacher can throw out the original lesson plan and adapt the discussion to take advantage of newspaper accounts of Russia changing its constitution. If an earthquake requires attention to immediate student fears, the teacher readjusts the lessons accordingly in view of the higher order goal of caring for the students in a crisis.

Furthermore, the conception of behavior as the control of perception gives a transparent account of why, as Eisner reminds us, our perceptions of the world are so important. What human beings *do* in the world is control their perceptions. Coming to understand or be competent in a "way of knowing" is, on this account, coming to be able to recognize and control those kinds of perceptions. The .300 hitter in baseball can *see* the ball better than others. The chess grandmaster *perceives* strength in the middle. The astute social commentator *senses* the breakdown of family life. The "with it" teacher has *eyes* in the back of her head. The artist *observes* the world with more clarity than do the rest of us.

The vast range of ways we humans have of dealing with the world is, indeed, remarkable. From the standpoint of perceptual control theory, however, what is truly remarkable is that this diversity of means in the face of a constantly changing environment is usually for the sake of achieving the same consistent ends. Perceptual control theory shows us how we make the one out of the many, how we find the *unum* in the pluribus.

Finally, perceptual control theory is fundamentally a theory of how individuals behave. In this respect, it is precisely the kind of theory that teachers need. They need to know about individual students who face them in their classrooms, not about what kids learn or do "on the average." The problem with the average is that it often washes out the interesting stuff. Because of both individual differences in children and differences in the means employed by a single child across time to achieve consistent ends, it becomes obvious that it is not a question of either praise or blame for a student's behavior, but rather a question of when to use what for which child.

PROFESSIONAL DEVELOPMENT SCHOOLS

If perceptual control theory does supply a superior model for understanding human behavior, then it does so in the laboratory and the classroom as well as in the professional development school. Nevertheless, the professional development school notion seems particularly congenial to practical research conducted from the standpoint of perceptual control theory.

The professional development school is a place in which best practice is to be modeled, learned, and evaluated. It is a profoundly practical site, a place where teachers, students, administrators, other educators, and professors come together to try to figure out what to do when faced with specific goals and challenges in a specific environment. It is a place where "theory is put into practice."

Yet, the insight of perceptual control theory is that there are no overall theoretical laws of human behavior governing what people always do in given circumstances. Such laws would only be possible in an extremely stable universe, which is certainly not the one in which we live. The very concept of putting theory, perhaps generated in an orderly laboratory, into practice in a disorderly world is wholly inappropriate. Indeed, we can see that theory, at least as traditionally conceived, could not possibly work in practice. The only possibly correct theory would have to take into account the fundamental fact that human beings are able to achieve consistent ends in indefinitely varying circumstances. The "laboratory" *must* be the real world because human nature is such as to be able to pursue our goals in the real, constantly changing world.

There is also a very immediate reason why a professional development school would be a natural place for research on teaching and learning. Under perceptual control theory what people learn to do is to control their perceptions, not necessarily to perform certain routinized actions. Thus, the most effective teaching is likely to be providing students with exemplary perceptions of what it is they are trying to learn, not detailed instructions on how to get there (Petrie, 1974, 1986; Petrie & Oshlag, 1993). We should, for the most part, show students what the finished product should look like, rather than give them recipes to follow. It is usually much easier to show aspiring teachers, for example, what good teaching looks like in a real school rather than to describe it in the university classroom.

One way of interpreting the common wisdom regarding quantitative and qualitative research is that individual qualitative research might suggest hypotheses that must then be seriously confirmed quantitatively through large samples. Perceptual control theory turns this common wisdom on its head. At best, quantitative research on large groups of people might suggest general tendencies that may hold true in limited circumstances. But those suggestions would have to be confirmed with individual teachers and students living in an ever-changing world. Traditional psychological research may provide a few hints about how to start real research on teaching and learning in real contexts.

The professional development school, then, is the real laboratory. The aspiring teachers and administrators and counselors and psychologists and social workers need to be provided with examples of the perceptions of learning, classroom order, cooperation, and the like, that they are learning to control. They need to learn how to determine their own goals and those of their co-workers as well as those of students and parents. They need to practice the skills of situational analysis and consensus building so that all can control successfully as much of their perceptual worlds as possible. They need to come to respect others as persons. What this means is recognizing that others, like oneself, are control systems who will try to resist disturbances to the perceptions they are trying to control. It means understanding that the only way actually to control others is through overwhelming physical force and then only until they find a way of evading the force. It means searching for ways of looking at and dealing with the world that can allow for a maximum of mutual satisfaction.

In an extremely important way, human beings are even more predictable than are physical events. Human beings are organized to attain consistent goals *despite* varying circumstances. An automobile mechanically programmed to drive around a given track will be less predictable in its path in the face of significant crosswinds than will the path of that same automobile in the hands of a human driver wanting to drive around the track.

When we know what people want, we know that they will do what they have to do to attain what they want. That is what control systems do. We do not know just *how* they will get to their goal, but we do know that they will likely achieve it, assuming it is within normal ranges of possibility. If I want a drink, we can predict I will get it, even if we cannot predict whether I will use a cup, a glass, my hands, or just stick my head under the spigot.

Of course, we also know that people's wants and desires are complicated and interrelated. Some things that we desire are desired in order to attain higher-order goals. I want to go to the office in order to work in order to do something I enjoy and find worthwhile that is consistent with my view of the kind of person I want to be. Some things that I want at one time, I do not want at another time, or I want less of them. As much as I like chocolate, I do not want only it nor do I want it all the time, probably because I also want to live a reasonably healthy life.

There are, of course, many, many issues to be explored regarding how our wants and desires fit together or fail to fit together. What roles do memory and imagination and hallucination play? How do independent control systems interact with each other in social arrangements? How do we learn or change our control systems when we persistently fail to be able to control our perceptions? How do we find out what other people want so that we can begin to understand how to interact with them? These and a host of other questions suggest themselves.

What is critical for this discussion, however, is that perceptual control theory gives us a very different perspective on the kind of practical knowledge educators need. Traditional psychology with its presumptions of if-then laws of behavior can maintain its hegemony over practical research as long as there is the hope of actually finding such laws. No matter how complicated such laws may be, if human beings really are subject to them, the professional development school and its kin will be seen as the place in which these laws are applied, not discovered. If, on the other hand, we have an alternative conception of human action as controlling perception rather than being controlled by it, as being purposeful and able to attain consistent goals by varying means in a constantly changing environment, then we will recognize that these achievements can only be explained by the operation of a control system. In that event the professional development school will be seen as the very place in which individuals as autonomous control systems learn about each other and how they can coexist and mutually satisfy their needs and wants.

There are no "laws of learning," at least as that phrase is ordinarily understood. There are only the laws governing the way in which human beings are organized and how they can come to be reorganized, and those laws predict exactly the autonomous goal-seeking, yet variable behavior we see. For those of us who would educate educators, professional development schools are where those laws of human organization and reorganization are most fully on display.

REFERENCES

Amundson, R., Serlin, R. C., & Lehrer, R. (1992). On the threats that do not face educational research. *Educational Researcher, 21*(9), 19–24.

Berliner, D. (1989). Implications of studies and expertise in pedagogy for teacher education and evaluation. *New directions for teacher assessment: Proceedings of the 1988 ETS international conference*, 39–78.

Bohannon, P., Powers, W. T., & Schoepfle, M. (1974). Systems conflict in the learning alliance. In L. J. Stiles (Ed.), *Theories for teaching* (pp. 76–96). New York: Praeger.

Bourbon, W. T. (1990). Invitation to the dance: Explaining the variance when control systems interact. *American Behavioral Scientist, 34*(1) 95–105.

Brown, J., Collins, D., & Duguid, P. (1989). Situated cognition and the culture of learning. *Educational Researcher, 18*(1), 32–42.

Carnap, R. (1950). *Logical foundations of probability*. Chicago: University of Chicago Press.

Cronbach, L. J. (1975). Beyond the two disciplines of scientific psychology. *American Psychologist, 30*, 116–126.

Cziko, G. A. (1992a). Purposeful behavior as the control of perception: Implications for educational research. *Educational Researcher, 21*(9), 25–27.

Cziko, G. A. (1992b). Perceptual control theory: One threat to educational research not (yet?) faced by Amundson, Serlin, and Lehrer. *Educational Researcher, 22*(7), 5–11.

Eisner, E. (1993). Forms of understanding and the future of educational research. *Educational Researcher, 22*(7), 5–11.

Ford, E. E. (1993). *Freedom from stress*. Scottsdale, AZ: Brandt Publishing.

Ford, E. E. (1994). *Discipline for home and school*. Scottsdale, AZ: Brandt Publishing.

Forssell, D. C. (1993). Perceptual control: A new management insight. *Engineering Management Journal, 5*(4), 1–7.

Gibbons, H. (1990). *The death of Jeffrey Stapleton: Exploring the way lawyers think*. Concord, NH: Franklin Pierce Law Center.

Goldstein, D. M. (1990). Clinical applications of control theory. *American Behavioral Scientist, 34*(1), 110–116.

Hershberger, W. A. (Ed.). (1988). *Volitional action: Conation and control.* Amsterdam: Elsevier.

Kuhn, T. S. (1970). *The structure of scientific revolutions* (2nd ed.). Chicago: University of Chicago Press.

Marken, R. S. (1986). Perceptual organization of behavior: A hierarchical control model of coordinated action. *Journal of Experimental Psychology: Human Perception and Performance, 12*, 267–276.

Marken, R. S. (1989). Behavior in the first degree. In W. A. Hershberger (Ed.), *Volitional action: Conation and control.* Amsterdam: Elsevier.

Marken, R. S. (1992). *Mindreadings: Experimental studies of purpose.* Gravel Switch, KY: CSG Books.

McClelland, K. (Winter, 1994). Perceptual control and social power. *Sociological Perspectives, 37*, 461–496.

McPhail, C. (1991). *The myth of the madding crowd.* New York: Aldine DeGruyter.

McPhail, C., Powers, W. T., & Tucker, C. W. (1992). Simulated individual and collective action in temporary gatherings. *Social Science Computer Review, 10*(1), 1–28.

Meehl, P. (1978). Theoretical risks and tabular asterisks: Sir Karl, Sir Ronald, and the slow progress of soft psychology. *Journal of Consulting and Clinical Psychology, 46*(4), 806–834.

Petrie, H. G. (1968). Why has learning theory failed to teach us how to learn. In G. Newsome (Ed.), *Philosophy of Education 1968* (pp. 163–170). Lawrence: University of Kansas Press.

Petrie, H. G. (1974). Action, perception, and education. *Educational Theory, 24*, 33–45.

Petrie, H. G. (1979). Against 'objective' tests: A note on the epistemology underlying current testing dogma. In M. N. Ozer (Ed.), *A cybernetic approach to the assessment of children: Toward a more humane use of human beings* (pp. 117–150). Boulder, CO: Westview Press.

Petrie, H. G. (1981). *The dilemma of enquiry and learning.* Chicago: University of Chicago Press.

Petrie, H. G. (1986). Testing for critical thinking. Presidential address, *Proceedings of the philosophy of education society*, 3–20.

Petrie, H. G., & Oshlag, R. S. (1993). Metaphor and learning. In A. Ortony (Ed.), *Metaphor and thought* (2nd ed.). Cambridge: Cambridge University Press, 579–609.

Platt, J. (1973). Strong inference. In H. S. Brody, R. H. Ennis, & L. I. Krimerman, (Eds.), *Philosophy of Educational Research* (pp. 203–217). New York: Wiley.

Plooij, F. X, van deRijt-Plooij (1990). Developmental transitions as successive reorganizations of a control hierarchy. *American Behavioral Scientist, 34*(1), 67–80.

Popper, K. (1959). *The logic of scientific discovery.* New York: Basic Books.

Popper, K. (1962). *Conjectures and refutations: The growth of scientific knowledge.* London: Routledge and Kegan Paul.

Popper, K, (1972). *Objective knowledge: An evolutionary approach.* Oxford: Clarendon Press.

Powers, W. T. (1973). *Behavior: The control of perception.* Chicago: Aldine.

Powers, W. T. (1989). *Living control systems: Selected papers.* Gravel Switch, KY: CSG Books.

Robertson, R. J. & Powers, W. T. (Eds.). (1990). *Introduction to modern psychology: The control theory view.* Gravel Switch, KY: CSG Books.

Williams, W. D. (1989). Making it clearer. *Continuing the conversation: A newsletter of ideas in cybernetics,* 9–10.

Williams, W. D. (1990). The Giffen effect: A note on economic purposes. *American Behavioral Scientist, 34*(1), 106–109.

Contributors

Cheryl M. Albers was a research associate at the Buffalo Research Institute on Education for Teaching at the State University of New York at Buffalo. She is currently pursuing graduate work at the State University of New York at Buffalo.

Joan N. Burstyn is a professor of cultural foundations of education and curriculum at Syracuse University. She is the editor of *Preparation for life? The paradox of education in the late twentieth century*, published by Falmer Press.

Charles W. Case is the dean of the School of Education and a professor of educational administration at the University of Connecticut. He has published extensively in *Educational Policy, Journal of Teacher Education, Planning and Changing,* and *Journal of Educational Administration,* and has written books and chapters for SUNY Press, McCutchan, and Praeger, among others. His areas of interest include urban education, leadership, teacher education, planning, and desegregation.

Michelle Collay is director of graduate education programs at Hamline University in St. Paul, Minnesota. She taught music and mathematics in grades kindergarten though nine in California and Oregon and completed her graduate work at the University of Oregon. Collay's interest in new teacher socialization and school culture began with her experiences in California and continued through research projects in rural schools in Oregon and North Dakota. She is currently working to link school-based professional development with graduate teacher education.

James L. Collins is an associate professor of English Education in the Graduate School of Education at the State University of New York at Buffalo. He edited *Teaching all the children to write* for the New York State English Council and the *Vital signs* series for Heinemann. The three volumes in that series are *Bringing together reading and writing, Teaching and learning language collaboratively,* and *Restructuring the English classroom.* He also coedited *Writing on-line: Using computers in the teaching of writing* with Elizabeth A. Sommers for Boynton/Cook. His current research and writing focuses on literacy learning in urban schools.

Roy J. Creek is the director of the Falk Laboratory School at the University of Pittsburgh. The author of many articles on inquiry teaching, locus of control, and the acquisition of teaching competencies, he serves on the editorial board of the *National Association of Laboratory Schools Journal*. Dr. Creek is an advocate of transformational leadership, which emphasizes teacher empowerment, shared decision making, and constructed incentives.

Joseph P. Ducette is associate dean for academic affairs and graduate studies in the College of Education at Temple University, and is a professor in the Department of Psychological Studies. He received his Ph.D. in experimental and educational psychology from Cornell University.

Jeanne Ellsworth is an assistant professor of education at the State University of New York College at Plattsburgh. Prior to her appointment at Plattsburgh, she was a research associate at the Buffalo Research Institute on Education for Teaching. She recently published an award-winning article, coauthored with Catherine Cornbleth, on clinical faculty in *American Educational Research Journal*.

John I. Goodlad is a professor and director of the Center for Educational Renewal at the University of Washington, where together with colleagues he produced in 1990 a trilogy of books based on a comprehensive, five-year study of the conduct of teacher education in the United States. Currently, the center coordinates the National Network for Educational Renewal, which is composed of educational settings in 15 states where school and university personnel are engaged in the simultaneous renewal of schooling and the education of educators.

Richard D. Hawthorne is a professor of education at West Virginia University. His publications focus on the connections between curriculum, teacher education, and school reform.

James G. Henderson is an associate professor of curriculum and instruction in the College and Graduate School of Education at Kent State University. His work focuses on the relationships between curriculum studies, teacher education, and school reform.

Stephanie L. Knight is an associate professor of educational psychology in the College of Education at Texas A&M University. Her research interests include the study of classroom processes and learning environments.

David F. Labaree is an associate professor in the Department of Teacher Education at Michigan State University. He is the author of *The mak-

ing of an American high school (Yale University Press, 1988). More recently, he has been writing about issues related to teacher professionalization and the history of teacher education.

Frank B. Murray is the H. Rodney Sharp Professor in the Departments of Educational Studies and Psychology at the University of Delaware, where he has served as dean since 1980. He chairs the national board of the Holmes Group. He is a member of the editorial boards of several journals in educational and developmental psychology. He serves on the teacher program of the Educational Testing Service.

Kay A. Norlander is an assistant professor of special education in the Department of Educational Psychology at the University of Connecticut. Her work has been published in *Learning Disabilities Focus* and the *Journal of Learning Disabilities*. In addition to her interest in special school populations, she is involved in teacher preparation and urban education.

Hugh G. Petrie is a professor of education and dean of the Graduate School of Education at the State University of New York at Buffalo. Among his research interests is the reform of teacher education. He is a founding member of the Holmes Group and serves on its board of directors. He is an editor of *Educational Policy* and served as a member of the New York State Special Commission on Educational Structures, Policies, and Practices.

Timothy G. Reagan is an assistant professor of educational studies in the Department of Educational Leadership at the University of Connecticut. He has published in *Harvard Educational Review, Educational Theory*, and the *Journal of Research and Development in Education*. He is the coauthor, with John Burbacher and Charles Case, of *Becoming a reflective practitioner*. His interests include the education of cultural and linguistic minorities, issues of language policy, and urban education.

Jayminn S. Sanford is an assistant professor of education at Temple University and coordinator of the professional development schools program and the undergraduate five-year teacher education program.

Trevor E. Sewell is dean of the College of Education at Temple University and a professor in the Department of Psychological Studies in Education.

Joan P. Shapiro is associate dean in the College of Education at Temple University and an associate professor in the Department of Educational Leadership and Policy Studies.

Jane A. Stallings is dean of the School of Education and a professor of educational curriculum and instruction at Texas A&M University. She is past president of the American Educational Research Association and member-at-large of the American Association of Colleges of Teacher Education. Her long-term commitment to bridging the gap between research on teaching and the practice of teaching led in the development of the ATE national award-winning teacher education program, *Learning to teach in inner city schools*. Dr. Stallings is committed to the restructuring of colleges of education so that they become clearly responsible to societal needs.

Robert B. Stevenson is an associate professor of educational administration in the Graduate School of Education at the State University of New York at Buffalo. He recently coedited a book on action research with Susan Noffke that has been published by Teachers College Press. His research interests include practitioners' critical inquiries into their own practices, the influence of the structure and culture of secondary schools on curriculum and teaching, and student perspectives on schooling.

Trish Stoddart is an associate professor of education at the University of California at Santa Cruz. She is a cognitive and development psychologist who conducts research on teacher learning and development and school restructuring. She was previously a member of the education faculty and co-director of the Center for Integrated Science Education at the University of Utah.

Lee Teitel is an assistant professor of education in the Graduate School of Education at the University of Massachusetts Boston. His research has focused on professional development school partnership formation and the influence of that involvement on teacher preparation institutions. His other professional interests include mentoring and peer coaching, as well as research on changes in the dynamics of graduate teacher education and their possible effect upon risk-taking and reflection.

Margaret A. Wilder recently completed her doctoral studies in social foundations of education at the State University of New York at Buffalo. She is an assistant professor of social foundations of education in the Department of Social Science Education at the University of Georgia. Her research interests include African-American students' perceptions of their schools, teachers and learning, and the factors associated with the underrepresentation of African-American teachers. She is a Holmes Scholar.

Donna L. Wiseman is associate dean and interim chairperson for the Department of Teacher Education in the College of Education at Texas A&M University. Her research interests include the impact of school renewal on colleges of education and the identification and analysis of processes evident in school-university partnerships. She is an associate with John Goodlad's Institute for Educational Renewal.

Index